GETTING THE THIRD DEGREE:
FRATERNALISM, FREEMASONRY AND HISTORY

GETTING THE THIRD DEGREE

FRATERNALISM, FREEMASONRY AND HISTORY

GUILLERMO DE LOS REYES
& PAUL RICH, EDITORS

Westphalia Press
An Imprint of the Policy Studies Organization
Washington, DC
2016

GETTING THE THIRD DEGREE: FRATERNALISM, FREEMASONRY AND HISTORY
All Rights Reserved © 2016 by Policy Studies Organization

Westphalia Press
An imprint of Policy Studies Organization
1527 New Hampshire Ave., NW
Washington, D.C. 20036
info@ipsonet.org

ISBN-10: 1-63391-368-6
ISBN-13: 978-1-63391-368-4

Cover and interior design by Jeffrey Barnes
jbarnesbook.design

Daniel Gutierrez-Sandoval, Executive Director
PSO and Westphalia Press

Updated material and comments on this edition
can be found at the Westphalia Press website:
www.westphaliapress.org

I

FRATERNALISM IN TIMES OF WAR: A HUNDRED YEARS SINCE THE EMBLEMATIC CASE OF THE LODGE EUPHRATES NO. 1078

JUAN AUGUSTO ABADJIAN

I

II

A CONTEMPORARY LOOK AT THE VARIOUS FORMS OF FREEMASONRY AMONG AFRICAN-AMERICANS IN THE UNITED STATES

DR. ELQUEMEDO OSCAR ALLEYNE

27

III

THE CITY OF LONDON AND ITS MEDIEVAL GUILDS AND ITS INFLUENCE ON THE STRUCTURE FREEMASONRY

YASHA BERESINER

49

IV

FREEMASONRY—THE MISSING LINK BETWEEN JACOBITISM AND THE AMERICAN REVOLUTION?

SAMUEL BIAGETTI

55

V

RESHAPING VIRTUE: THE CASE OF EIGHTEENTH-CENTURY FRENCH AND ITALIAN MASONIC POETRY

GIULIA DELOGU, PH.D

65

VI
REMBRANDT'S SECRET
ZHENYA GERSHMAN

77

VII
FLAME OF ENLIGHTENMENT:
FREEMASONRY AND THE FEAR OF METAPHOR
KLAUS-JÜRGEN GRÜN

97

VIII
THE MASONIC TEMPLE
BETWEEN UNIVERSAL MODEL AND CULTURAL TROPISMS
FRANÇOIS GRUSON

105

IX
EVOLUTION OF CO-MASONIC ENGLISH-LANGUAGE BLUE LODGE
FREEMASONIC RITUAL
KAREN KIDD

111

X
FRANCIS PULSZKY'S MASONIC PERIODS
LÁSZLÓ VÁRI

137

XI

REPORT ON THE SPECIAL COMMITTEE ON THE FRANCKEN DOCUMENTS

BRENT MORRIS

147

XII

UNVEILING THE COPIALE-MANUSCRIPT: LAYERS OF FRATERNALISM, RITUAL AND POLITICS IN EIGHTEENTH CENTURY GERMANY

ANDREAS ÖNNERFORS

155

XIII

PRAIRIE CHARITY: MASONIC BENEVOLENCE IN LATE NINETEENTH CENTURY MANITOBA

BRIAN ROUNTREE

173

XIV

SANTA ANNA, THE MASON

CASEY D. STANISLAW, M.A.

189

XV

A MASONIC PRETENDER TO THE HUNGARIAN THRONE: FRANÇOIS CLAUDE AUGUSTE DE CROUY-CHANEL

DEMETRIO XOCCATO

215

GETTING THE THIRD DEGREE: FRATERNALISM, FREEMASONRY AND HISTORY

GUILLERMO DE LOS REYES AND PAUL RICH, EDITORS

These papers, augmented and revised as a result of discussions at the first World Conference on Fraternalism, Freemasonry and History hosted at the Bibliothèque nationale de France in Paris in May 2015, reflect growing interest in the contributions of secret and ritualistic societies to society. If the subject has been neglected, that may be partly because of notions that it sometimes has sinister and esoteric aspects. After all, giving someone the third degree gets its meaning from Freemasonry. Putting aside such suspicions, the topic of fraternalism embraces not just Masonry but organizations like the Orange, Grange, Odd Fellows, Eastern Star, and an infinite number of groups named for animals such as the Elks, Moose, Eagles, and Owls.

Whether with the Enlightenment and the Masons, Ireland's troubles and the Orangemen, or racism and the Klan, clearly there has been and continues to be an impact, and we need to understand much better than we do just why and how. It is proposed to hold the conference alternatively in Paris and Washington. The next Paris conference will be May 26–27, 2017 at the Bibliothèque nationale de France, and the Washington conference will be at the Whittemore House on June 1 and 2, 2018. The conference sponsors the journal Ritual, Secrecy and Civil Society as well as numerous books published by Westphalia Press. Full information can be found on the Policy Studies Organization website, ipsonet.org

Everyone is welcome to these activities. Some are members of lodges and bring unique knowledge of inner workings. Others come from academic disciplines such as sociology, political science, anthropology, architecture, popular culture. Some are art and music historians. Some are simply curious. All are welcome.

GUILLERMO DE LOS REYES
PAUL RICH
WCFFH

I

FRATERNALISM IN TIMES OF WAR:
A HUNDRED YEARS SINCE THE EMBLEMATIC CASE OF THE
LODGE EUPHRATES NO. 1078

JUAN AUGUSTO ABADJIAN

Assistant Grand Master and Grand Inspector for South America and the Inter-American Masonic Confederation (CMI) for the Grand Lodge of Armenia; Honorary Member and Worshipful Master AD VITAM of the Lodge Urartu No. 442 under the Jurisdiction of the Grand Lodge of Argentina; Member of the Lodge Massis No. 1 under the Jurisdiction of the Grand Lodge of Armenia; Attorney at Law, University of Buenos Aires.

I. INTRODUCTION: THE FREEMASONRY OF ARMENIAN ORIGIN.
SUMMARY FROM ANCIENT TIMES TO THE OTTOMAN ERA.

Armenians have been one of those nations who maintained their culture and traditions almost intact from antiquity to the present day. Through centuries they've adapted to dozens of different currents of thought and suffered persecutions of all kinds because of religion and geographic position. From an ancient Indo-European origin, they have forged their own language and coined a vast pagan history until they became the first nation that accepted Christianity as the Official State Religion. (c.301).

From ancient times, in the Armenian Plateau, in the Caucasus and in the whole of Anatolia, many brotherhoods and initiation orders have developed. These "brotherhoods", whether of a religious, political or social character, created dominant cultures and emerging subcultures for hundreds of year in Asia Minor. The Tondrakian and the Paulician[1] movements that followed Christian teachings very close to Manichaeism; the Knights Templars; Hospitallers and Teutonic Knights, important actors during the Armenian Kingdom of Cilicia[2]; the Children of the Sun *(Arevortik)*[3], an Armenian neo-pagan heresy of the 13th century; as well as the polemic Hashashin. All of them have developed in the territory of Historical Ar-

1

menia. Also in historic Armenia, the "Operative Freemasonry," that is to say, the pure architectural masonry, has created master craftsmen, superb stonecutters and cathedral builders who reached their peak during the Middle Ages. Important historic characters such as Trdat, Momik, Sarkis and Manvel, among others, left their trace through signatures, signs and secret symbols spread in the hundreds of monuments, churches and stone crosses *(Khachkars)* still decorating the Armenian Republic and its neighboring countries[4]. Some of these builders were traveling masons who have left their mark in numerous churches throughout Europe and Asia.

The History of the Armenian Freemasons begins under the auspices of the United Grand Lodge of England. The English "East India Company" introduced freemasonry of English origin in Madras (now Chennai) in 1730. Many Armenian merchants who were already established tradesmen in India and Southeast Asia also played an important role in the East India Company.[5] They followed the English rules of conduct and often traveled throughout Europe and, at the same time, had ascended in the Indian social strata.

As the first instance of an active member of Armenian origin in one of the Informative Bulletins of the Cannongate Lodge in Edinburgh, (1762) it is stated that "... four Worshipful Masters would represent the United Grand Lodge of England in the territories of the Middle East, Aleppo and Iran ..." (Berberian, 128) Among those four persons, it was the name of the Armenian Dr. Manasse[6] who was appointed as Provincial Grand Master for "Armenia" by order of the Grand Master of the Premier Grand Lodge of England, Earl Ferrers, from 1762 to 1764. Until 1805, when the name of Manasse officially disappeared, the group of four lodges headed by these Worshipful Masters was called "All Armenia in the East Indies"[7] —remarkable for this period, the foundation of the First Lodge composed of members of Armenian origin.

On October 6th 1837, in the city of Madras, Colonial India, the Lodge "Armenia" No. 685 was consecrated under the auspices of the United Grand Lodge of England. This lodge had a brief life (1865) as a result of ups and downs in its activities. It was linked to prestigious families of established Armenian merchants in that city.[8] The Lodge "Armenia" No. 685 worked in the "Armenia Street" of Madras.[9]

The last Masonic link of Armenian origin, and of relevant importance in Victorian India, was Sir Paul Chater[10] (Khachik Pogos Astvatsatoor). Born in Calcutta in 1846, he was a prestigious and successful man who developed all his potential in imperial Hong Kong. He has been Worshipful Master of the Lodge "Perseverance" No. 1165, Grand Master of the Hong Kong District and the South of China for the United Grand Lodge of England (1881-1909), one of the first Armenian masons in having the Masonic High Degree 33° and, even today, the District of the United Grand Lodge of England for Hong Kong and the Far East auspices a lodge called "Paul Chater Lodge of Installed Masters" No. 5391. Undoubtedly, he was one of the masons of Armenian origin who had reached one of the highest points on the scale of Regular Freemasonry.

Closer to Historic Armenia and after the last independent Armenian Kingdom of Cilicia (Leo V in Cilicia (1373), the Armenians continued to develop their culture within the lands inhabited by them for thousands of years, now being part of what would be called after the fall of Constantinople (1453), the Ottoman Empire.[11] For hundreds of years Armenians have witnessed the formation and rise of the Ottomans and they still have suffered as no other nation, its fall and dismemberment.

During the mid-nineteenth century, the Ottoman theocratic class symbolized in the figure of the Sultan, began reforms to integrate those non-Islamic elements of the Empire: the "Tanmizat Reform" and subsequent "Constitutions of Midhat Pasha" (1876), denoted an opportunity to improve successfully the interaction with the Western ideas.[12] The main objective was to give a new place to the traditional minorities within the Empire and give them a more powerful role in relation to the Sultan's decisions.

During that era, the upper classes of Armenians had begun to interact defending the ideas proclaimed by the West, "Liberty, Equality and Fraternity." At the same time, the Grand Masonic Powers or Jurisdictions (whether Grand Lodges or Grand Orients) planned the mission of westernizing the region and founding as many Masonic lodges as they could. The Grand Orient of Italy, the Grand Lodge of Scotland, the United Grand Lodge of England and the Grand Orient of France worked actively to spread the formation of Masonic lodges in the heart of the Empire.[13]

At the same time, the Armenian society needed to gestate and declare that internal change that was taking place after the new reforms. The Armenian "Millet," (word used to refer about the religious minorities administration), organized, among the Armenians the so-called "Armenian National Constitution", which generated a secular administration and representation in provinces that were populated by them, changing the traditional power that always have been given to the Armenian Apostolic Church or the wealthier "Amirá-Elite"[14] classes. The reformists that supported the

"Armenian National Constitution"[15] thought and believed that it would bring significant social modifications in the relation of the historic Armenian Patriarchate of Istanbul, the strong conservative sectors composed of the "Amirá" and the citizens of the neediest Armenian classes. Armenian intellectuals, merchants and professionals needed a change for the Armenian society of the Empire. It was a time for unifying the Armenians, modernizing the ideas in order to have an opportunity to emulate those first nations of the world that moved themselves toward Freedom and Independence.

That movement was came on with the right moment for the Armenians to plant the foundation of the first Armenian-speaking Lodge. That first Lodge was born in Izmir (Smyrna) on June 5, 1864. The Lodge "Metzn Tigran" (or Decran Lodge) No. 1014 was installed under the auspices of the United Grand Lodge of England. Then on February 22nd, 1866, in the district of Pera, Istanbul, the foundation of the Lodge "Ser" (Love) took place under the patronage of the Grand Orient of France (Regular at the time). Hundreds of Armenians were initiated in both Lodges, which worked continuously until the first years of the last decade of the nineteenth century, when Sultan Abdul Hammid II[16, 17, 18] started the terrible repression of the Armenian Nation throughout the Empire (1894-1986).[19] The members of these lodges had been the lights in the cultural revival of the Armenian nation with a net influence up to these days.[20]

II. The Young Turk Revolution and the Birth of a National Freemasonry: The Ottoman Grand Orient.

Created during the last years of the XIX Century, the Young Turk movement wanted to generate a revolution designed to bring to power a multiracial and multi-ethnic parliament that would rule the whole Empire. Started as a movement of medical students, their first intention was to bring Jews, Armenians, Greeks and Arabs in a new structure of power.

Historian Şükrü Hanioğlu explains the genesis of this movement:

> Injecting European institutions and technology as a tonic to revitalize the decadent Ottoman Empire was a much discussed topic among the Turkish intellectual circles since the Era of *Tanzimat*. To this end, the Ottoman leadership sent students abroad, brought in European instructors and established counterparts of many Western institutions in Turkey.

Yet, these measures, especially sending students to the West, from the ruling elites point of view, brought with it the apparent danger of introducing European ideas and ideals in Turkey.

The Committee was found according to the system of cells used by various underground organizations of the time. Its activities were very limited, and were confined to discussions among the members in the first five years of its existence. In 1894, the title of the Committee was changed to the Ottoman Committee of Union and Progress (Osmanlı ittihad ve Terakki Cemiyeti). This change was due to the suggestion of Ahmed Rıza who came under the spell of the teachings of Auguste Comte.[21]

Taking the failed "Tanmizat" attempt and the "Constitutions of Midhat Pasha", they began to outline a real plan to accomplish the idea of taking Abdul Hammid II out of the throne. Since the early 20th century, within this new political Movement, the "Committee of Union and Progress" (Ittihad ve Terakki) was devising year after year, from Salonica[22], the plan to seize power in a coup against the "Red Sultan". From that city, now in Northwestern Greece, the Masonic lodges under the auspices of the "Grand Orient of Italy" and the "Gran Oriente Español", started to join in pursuit of such goal. Specially, the Lodge Macedonia Risorta (Grande Oriente D'Italia), headed by the Sephardic lawyer Emanuel Karasso (Karasu)[23], had recruited the persons who would be the leaders of the Revolution. Among them, one of the figures of the "Dönmeh" community in Salonica, Mehmet Talat [24], then historically known as Talat Pashá. In July 1908, the Young Turks Revolution took place and the feared "Red Sultan Abdul Hammid II" was removed from its throne.

Although the European Grand Lodges kept the lodges founded during the 19th century; the Young Turk revolutionaries wanted and needed its own Grand Lodge representative of the Ottomans. The main plan-idea of the Committee "Union and Progress" was to stop the western influence within the Empire; therefore, the advance of the European Grand Lodges was not welcome anymore. Is remarkable the explanation of Dorothe Sommer about this situation:

"As has been observed in relation to European lodges and their evolution during the nineteenth century, attempts to nationalize freemasonry took place everywhere, with the

Ottoman Empire being no exception. When in power, the Young Turks were keen to have their own lodges under their own obedience, which would oppose the foreign influence that they perceived as "masonic colonization". This endeavor naturally triggered alarm among the Western masonic bodies, which consequently decided no to accept and recognize the Ottoman Grand Orient as a regular masonic body." [25]

Master Masons working in lodges dependent on the "Grande Oriente D'Italia" and the "Grand Orient de France" got together helping to establish the Ottoman Grand Orient. But, on the other hand, the Grand Lodge of Scotland and the United Grand Lodge of England were not very convinced about the birth of this new Masonic Grand Jurisdiction. Citing the famous postscript to the letter from Sir G. Lowther to Sir C. Harding:

> "...P.S.—It has been said above that the Grand Lodge of Scotland refused to recognize the new 'Grand Orient Ottoman', whose Masonry it pronounced 'spurious'; but I learn that efforts are being made to indirectly get round this difficulty by inducing the Grand Lodge of England to recognize the new Turkish creation. In view of the curious developments in Egyptian Masonry, it would seem desirable that the Grand Lodge of England should follow the example of its Scotch sister and refuse its imprimatur to an institution so coloured by politics." [26]

That is how on March 3rd 1909, the Ottoman Grand Orient was founded and in October, its Supreme Council for the 33°rd Grade.

The first Officials of the Ottoman Grand Orient was composed by the following members: [27]

- Grand Master: Talat Pasha.

- Deputy Grand Master: Miralay Galip.

- Second Deputy Grand Master: Emmanuel Carasso.

- Grand Senior Warden: Mehmet Ali Baba.

- Deputy Grand Senior Warden: Eduardo Denari.

- Grand Senior Warden: Osman Fehmi.

- Grand Orator: Riza Tevfik.

- Assistant Grand Orator: Michael Noradunkian.

- Grand Secretary: Osman Talat.

- Grand Tresurear: Sarim Kibar.

The first Lodges that were born under the auspices of this new Grand Orient were:[28]

- Lodge Vatan (Homeland)

- Lodge Muhabani Hürriyet (Freedom's Fellows)

- Lodge Vefa (Perseverance)

- Lodge Shafak (Dawn)

- Lodge Rezne

- Lodge Ittihad ve Terakki (Union and Progress)

- Lodge Uhuviyet Osmani (Ottoman Brotherhood)

- Lodge Ziayi Shark (Eastern Light)

It is notable that the Ottoman Grand Orient would not refer their works to the Grand Architect of the Universe just in case of not provoking any offense to the muslim Brethren. That's is why, this new Grand Jurisdiction will only refer their works to the "Grand Architect", as a symbolic idea of it.

The Armenians[29], almost all of them as well as the rest of the minorities of the Empire, sustained and believed in the revolutionary and constitutional movement of the Young Turks. As Bedrós Haladjian, Diran Kelekian or Krikor Zohrab[30], all of them strong supporters of the movement, many other Armenian intellectuals observing the reformist politic composition of the Committee of Union and Progress, decided to support this new trend. Others chose, beyond the political support to the Constitutionalist Revolution, to "initiate" themselves in the Ottoman lodges.

The self-called "Ottoman" freemasonry reached the power.

III. THE "EUPHRATES" CONCEPT IN KHARBERD: AN ARMENIAN COLLEGE AND A MASONIC LODGE.

One of the most significant cities of the Historic Armenia and demographically most populated of Armenians during the Ottoman era was the city of Kharberd (or Kharpert). (Old Tsopk/Harput – Current Elazig) Kharberd, was one of the cradle for the Armenians since ancient times and one of the most active commercial centers of the Ottoman Empire, with a wide connectivity between other cities. Built on top of a low mountainous area, Kharberd expands over a plain of great extent, which its inhabitants traditionally called "the Golden Plain".[31] Moreover, the Euphrates River, with deep symbolism for the inhabitants of the region, escorts the whole surrounding region. Kharberd has also an old distinctive castle that brought together its residents for centuries, but because of its narrow streets during the mid-nineteenth century, the problems of water supply in the city generated that a large part of the population to move to the adjacent city of Mezre (Meziréh). In 1861,[32] Mezireh was renamed Mamuret-Al-Aziz, in honor to the Sultan Abdul-Aziz. Until the end of the Ottoman Empire, the Vilayet (province) took that name and brought together the neighboring populations of Husenig, Keserig, Bazmashen, Tadema, between others.[33] Beyond its commercial importance in the manufacture of silk and kilims (carpets), Kharberd was known for hosting the first "American Board of Commissioners for Foreign Mission"[34] which operated in Ottoman Turkey. Like many other missions within the Empire, and especially operating in Kharberd, they were distinguished by erecting schools and hospitals to provide support and christian education to the local Armenian society.

The "American Board of Commisioners for Foreign Missions in Kharberd," brought together thousands of Armenians under the wing of evangelical Protestantism, which by 1859 founded the First Evangelical Theological College in Kharberd. In 1865, thanks to this foundation, the Armenian Evangelical Church of Kharberd had great acceptance in the Armenian society of the time. After years of planning, a general "Fundraising Committee" was created to accomplish the dream of erecting a high level education College that would be baptized under the name of "Armenia College" (1878), being its first director the Rev. Howard Crosby Wheeler (principal 1878-1893). For ten years they could keep that name until the Ottoman Government demanded its change. Finally, the name "Euphrates College" was chosen.

In his nearly four decades of history the Euphrates College stood out as one of the most important cultural and educational institutions of the Armenian modern history. The legacy of the Euphrates College was to give hundreds of professionals and men of culture who have left their mark on the pages of Armenian history.

The Euphrates College also allowed many of its graduates the possibility to specialize their studies abroad (Ann Arbor, Edinburgh, Yale, Princeton). Several teachers of the college, previous graduates of it, managed to be members of the first and only Armenian Masonic lodge located in the town of Kharberd, which existed until 1915:

> Among the best known graduates of Euphrates College, many of whom returned to teach there, were Professors Nikoghos Tenekedjian, Khachadur Nahigian, Garabed Soghigian, Hovhannes Boujikanian, Donabed Luledjian (another graduate of Yale University, biologist and writer), and Mudrgitch Vorperian (geology). Sadly, all of these men died during the 1915 Genocide.[35]

Yeprad (Euphrates) Lodge No. 1078, Hyusenig, Kharpert. 1912. Published by Armenag Fenerjian in "Hayrenik" newspaper, Boston, 1954-1955. Courtesy of Melkon Lulejian & Lulejian Family.

In 1909, the following Brother Masons met in the village of Hussenig[36]: Brother Vartan Vezneian ("Widow's Son" Lodge No. 1 – Connecticut), Brethren Serovpé Vartabedian, Dr. Vosgan H. Topalian, Haroutioun Giragos Terzian and Hovhanness Giragos Terzian (all belonging to "Peace" Lodge No. 908, Grand Lodge of Scotland in Beirut-Chapter), Brethren Kaspar Haroutiounian and Khachatour Manouelian (both of the Lodge

"National" No. 209 - New York) and Brother Mardiros Onanian ("Logan" Lodge No. 575, Indianapolis). The meeting took place in the mansion of the commercial magnate, Bro. Serovpé Vartabedian with the objective of asking the Grand Lodge of Scotland, the permission for raising columns of a Lodge for the city of Kharberd. It is so that, after the steps taken and the proper letters send, that in 1910 the "Euphrates" Lodge No. 1078 was Regularly constituted as such.

The "Euphrates" Lodge No. 1078 was born to bring together the most distinguished characters of Kharberd, Mezireh and Hussenig areas. Its members, unlike other lodges of the Ottoman Empire, were all Armenians. For a long time, the meetings were held in one of the rooms of the mansion of Bro. Serovpe Vartabedian in the town of Hussenig. After some months, due to the increasing number of members, bought a land to erect their own temple in Mezireh.

Since their First Initiation Ritual dated on October 29th, 1910 until June of 1915, the "Euphrates" Lodge No. 1078 gathered the following several distinguished personalities, including[37]:

- Bro. Donabed Lulejian: Professor of Biology of the "Euphrates College." Graduated from the same school and then traveled to the United States and specialized his studies in University of Yale.

- Bro. Manoug Terzian: Banker.

- Bro. Khachatur Nahigian: Professor of Science of the "Euphrates College" and Director of Student for several years.

- Bro. Haroutioun Misakian: State employee.

- Bro. Garabed Soghigian: Librarian and Head of the Press of the "Euphrates College." Professor of Armenian language at the College.

- Bro. Hovhannes Kambourian: Medical Doctor.

- Bro. Pylos Cartozian: Hotelier.

- Bro. Melkon Lulejian: Pharmacist. Manager at the American Pharmacy of Kharberd.

- Bro. Karekin Gostanian: Professor of Armenian language at the "Euphrates College".

- Bro. Samuel H. Manougian: Reverend Pastor of the Armenian Evangelical Church in Hussenig.

- Bro. Samuel Donabedian: Teacher and medical doctor specialized at the University of Beirut.

- Bro. Sarkis Momdjian: Medical Doctor.

- Bro. Hampartzoum Gulesserian: Medical Doctor.

- Bro. Tovmas Mugurditchian: Official translator of the British Consulate at city of Diyarbekir.

- Bro. Khosrov Tembekijian: Professor of History and a prominent member of the Armenian Liberal Party.

- Some brethren engaged in commerce and trades were also members of this Lodge: Serovpé Vartabedian, Khoren Tchilingirian, Hovagim Mantarian, Krikor Takakjian, Asdour Barsamian, Sarkis Boghossian, Aghabab Vartabedian, Pilibos Movsesian, Hadji Avedis Barsamian, among others.

In 1912, during one of the Lodge meetings in the house of Seropvé Vartabedian, a mythical photograph is taken, in which several members of the Lodge Euphrates No. 1078 appear.[38] Thanks to one of the surviving Brethren of the Lodge (Melkon Lulejian) many documents were saved. In addition to that mythical picture, and thanks to the Lulejian-Melcon-Yaralian-Hedison[39] families, the Mark Mason Diploma of Donabed Lulejian and the Master Mason Diplomas of Karekin Gostanian and Melkon Lulejian had been saved as part of the a real archive of this Lodge.

Unfortunately the history of this Lodge had a tragic end. Although continued to appear as active until 1926, according to the archives of the Grand Lodge of Scotland, the lodge Euphrates No. 1078 was short-lived, just because in June of 1915, the major number of its members disappeared.[40]

One of the founders, Worshipful Brother Vartan Vezneian, grade 32° at that time, in 1912 proposed that the Lodge Euphrates should leave the auspices of the Grand Lodge of Scotland and join the newly born "Ottoman Grand Orient". His idea was based on being eventually "protected" if any hostilities may suffer the Christian elements of the Empire. In this case, for any eventuality, Ottoman "Brethren" would protect them as members of the same Institution. Brother Khachatour Nahigian opposed that idea and insisted that the Lodge Euphrates should remain under the Scottish wing.[41] Brother Vezneian decided to leave the Lodge Euphrates

No. 1078 and entered into the ranks of the Ottoman Grand Orient, looking for a future protection that would never appear. [42]

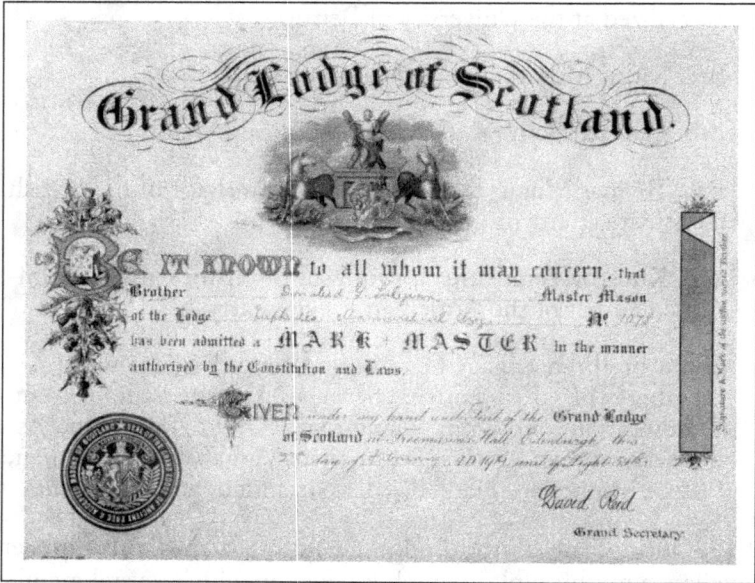

Original Mark Master Masonic Diploma of Bro. Donabed Luledjian issued by the Grand Lodge of Scotland. Courtesy of David Lulejian-Melcon-Yaralian-Hedison families.

IV. THE "TEHCIR LAW" AND REAL CONCEPT OF FRATERNITY.

For any Freemason originally Accepted and Initiated in a Masonic Lodge there is no real explanation to describe what the concept of "Fraternity" brings. In the common and secular life a person can be called as "Brother" because of a meaningful close relation and, on the opposite, in the Masonic world the title "Brother" refers to every member, perhaps without even knowing who that person is. Fraternity let us know the true concept of the Royal Arch and the way in which every Freemason must carve himself to carry out a global idea or mission in Brotherhood.

There are times when "the story behind the story" allows us to see more deeply the seek of the truth. And the History of Freemasonry allows just that. It let us see a little more of what is written in the official version.

The case of the Tehcir Law signed by the Grand Vizir and First Grand Master of the Ottoman Grand Orient, Bro. Talaat Pasha, is one of the most terrible pictures in the history of mankind and not only that, it also has jeopardized the concept of Brotherhood and Fraternalism. What's more, it has provided an absolute confusion about the whole role of the Freemasonry in this époque of the History.[43]

Once carried out the Young Turk Revolution and the Ottoman Grand Orient was born, their first Grand Master, Mehmet Talat Pasha, soon would "leave the gavel" and would dedicate himself to his duties as Minister of the Interior and Grand Vizier of the Empire. Meanwhile, the world itself was trying to be prepared for the tragic "Great War" (World War I), which would face the Ottoman Empire and the German Empire against the Allied Forces, from mid-1914 until the end of 1918. At that vein, Talat Pasha would rely on two military to govern: Ahmed Cemal (Djemal) and Enver Pasha. The triumvirate of the "Three Pashas" was ready for the belligerent action.

After the start of World War I, the Turkish army suffered a disastrous and calamitous loss of men against the Russians in what was called the "Battle of Sarikamich" (January 1915), the same that generated the wrath of General Enver Pasha, who blamed the Armenian populations on fighting against the Ottomans and in favor of the Russians. Even historians can not determine whether the disastrous campaign Sarikamich was the trigger for what was going to come to come but, it is historically determined that from April 1915 the Turkish Ottoman government began to implement a plan of extermination of the entire Armenian population in Anatolia.[44]

The April 24th, 1915, in Constantinople hundreds of Armenian intellectuals were arrested, including Brethren Diran Kelekian and well known Lawyer Krikor Zohrab, who belonged to the Ottoman Grand Orient. Afterwards, the same month the Tehcir Law is signed,[45] although it was already in practice in various parts of Empire. The aim of this law was to relocate and move the entire Armenian population of Anatolia to the southern deserts of the Empire (Deir al-Zawr). This displacement of the entire population has been historically translated as a plan of mass extermination in which the eternal death marches would end the lives of hundreds of thousands of Armenians in the deserts of Northern Syria. This plan derived from mass arrests to a mega-general deportation that has been called and catalogued as "the Armenian Genocide". It is estimated that between 1915 and 1923 more than one million Armenians have been killed, and even today its recognition by the Turkish State carries a profound debate in the International Community:

"Beginning in early June 1915, hundreds of thousands of Ar-

menians were turned out of their homes at hun and bayo-
net point. For months to come, on roads across the length of
Anatolia could be seen processions, some small, others large,
some just a handful of individuals, men, women, and children, their only belongings what they could carry on their
backs, with literally nowhere to go. Tens of thousands would
die of starvation and exposure; other tens of thousands would
succumb to disease, most particularly typhus. Often their
bodies were left to decompose where died. More sinister, off
in distant fields or gullies would be found rows of corpses,
Armenians of both genders and all ages shot out of hand by
Turkish soldiers. A sort of frenzy overlook the Ottoman Army
units assigned to the task of removing the Armenians from
their homes, and scenes of wholesale rape and slaughter were
common as Turkish troops moved through Armenian villages
and towns."[46]

Last photograph of Bro. Donabed Luledjian with his entire family.
Courtesy of David Lulejian-Melcon-Yaralian-Hedison families.

In May 1915, the imposition and orders signed by Talaat Pasha reached
the city of Kharberd where many of his masonic Armenian "Brethren" of
the Masonic Lodge Euphrates, as well as all the Armenian population of
that city, suffered persecutions and death. Almost all of the members of
Euphrates Lodge died because of tortures and mass executions in the city.
Others, because of the help of influential Turkish Brethren, would survive.

JUAN AUGUSTO ABADJIAN

At the beginning of June several of the teachers of Euphrates College are arrested, many of them members of the Euphrates Lodge as well. Thanks to the relation between Melkón Luledjian (member of the Lodge Yeprad and survivor) and the mason researcher Armenag Fenerdjian[47] many historic information about this lodge could be saved. Melkón's brother,[48] Donabed Luledjian, one of the most important teachers of the College who had studied in the University of Yale in the United States, had one of the most unfortunate fates. Upon deportation from the city, he was questioned, jailed and tortured by the mayor (Kaimakan) Mehmet Asim Bey, freemason from the Ottoman Grand Orient. Being both masons, though from different legitimacy and legality, political factors exceeded the situation and Bro. Donabed Luledjian almost succumbed to the tortures inflicted by the mayor and his soldiers.[49] Donabed survived because he was helped[50] by another Turkish mason, Hasan Tahsin who, by that time, had been appointed as director of the hospital of the Ottoman Red Crescent[51] in Kharpert. He took care of him and offered refuge, but Professor Luledjian decided to keep on traveling, save his family and reach Erzurum where he would be under Russian protection. Thanks to his descendants, today reliably documented, a letter written in the city of Erzincan, on August 14, 1916 by the late professor can be read:

> "I apply to the brotherly heart of a Freemason if you are one, to the kind heart of a Christian and a civilized gentlemen to save my family. I would apply to the Scottish Lodge of F&A Masons in Edinburgh, but by the lack of telegraphic connection and correspondence I apply to your highness and to you noble to find means by which my family may enjoy the protection of the American Flag by the American Consulate in Harpoot." [52]

As one of the first in saving hundreds of orphans, he contracted typhus and died in Erzurum, utterly desolate, away from his relatives, just trying to perform his work rescuing Armenian orphans.

Other Brethren that were tortured and murdered were, Khachatur Nahigian, Seropvé Vartabedian, Garabed Sohigian, Khosrov Tembekijian, Hovagim Mantarian, Harutioun Missakian and Vartan Vezneian, who years earlier had embraced the ranks of the Ottoman Grand Orient.

The testimonies collected by James Bryce describes what happened to some of these individuals, some of them professors of the Euphrates College:

(Written by the last Principal of the College, Mr. Ernest Riggs. 19 July, 1915)

I shall try to banish from my mind for the time the sense of great personal sorrow at losing hundreds of my friends here, and also my sense of utter defeat in being so unable to stop the awful tragedy or even mitigate to any degree its severity, and compel myself to give you concisely some of the cold facts of the past months, as they relate themselves to the College. I do so with the hope that the possession of these concrete facts may help you to do something there for the handful of dependents still left to us here.

Buildings.—Seven of our big buildings are in the hands of the Government, only one remaining in our hands. The seven buildings in question are empty, except for twenty guards who are stationed there. I cannot tell you exactly the amount of loss we have sustained in money by robberies, breakages and other means, and there is no sign that the Turks will ever return these buildings to us.

Constituency.—Approximately two-thirds of the girl pupils and six-sevenths of the boys have been taken away to death, exile or Moslem homes.

Professors.—Four gone, three left, as follows.

Professor Tenekedjian.—Served College 35 years; representative of the Americans with the Government, Protestant "Askabed," Professor of Turkish and History. Besides previous trouble, arrested May 1st without charge; hair of head, moustache and beard pulled out, in vain effort to secure damaging confessions; starved and hung by arms for a day and a night, and severely beaten several times; taken out towards Diyarbekir about June 20th, and murdered in general massacre on the road.

Professor Nahigian.—Served College 33 years, studied at Ann Arbor, Professor of Mathematics. Arrested about June 5th, and shared Prof. A.'s fate on the road.

Professor Vorperian.—Taken to witness a man beaten almost to death; became mentally deranged; started with his family

16

about July 5th into exile under guard, and murdered beyond Malatia. Principal of Preparatory Department; studied at Princeton; served College 20 years.

Professor Boudjikanian.—Served College 16 years, studied at Edinburgh. Professor of Mental and Moral Science. Arrested with Prof. A. and suffered same tortures; also had three finger nails pulled out by the roots; killed in same massacre.

Professor Soghigian.—Served College 25 years. Arrested May 1st; not tortured, but sick in prison; sent to Red Crescent Hospital, and after paying large bribes is now free.

Professor Khatchadourian.—Served College for over 15 years, studied in Stuttgart and Berlin, Professor of Music. Escaped arrest and torture, and thus far escaped exile and death, because of favour with the Kaimakam secured by personal services rendered.
Professor Donabed Lulejian.—Served College about 15 years, studied at Cornell and Yale (M.S.), Professor of Biology. Arrested about June 5th, beaten about the hands, body and head with a stick by the Kaimakam himself, who, when tired, called on all who loved religion and the nation to continue the beating; after a period of insensibility in a dark closet, taken to the Red Crescent Hospital with a broken finger and serious bruises. Now free.[53]

A happier case is the one of Bro. Pilos Cartozian of Euphrates Lodge. He was "saved" from the deportations by another Turkish Mason, who sheltered him for weeks. In 1920, Brother Clarence D. Royse, wrote in the official newspaper of the Scottish Rite in America, "New Age Magazine", an article called "Armenia and Armenians", which recounted that:

"... Several months ago a boy about 16 years of age, an Armenian by the name of Nerses Cartozian, arrived in Portland, Oregon, from Armenia, bringing with him a Masonic emblem which he said his father had roughly hammered from some old metal and had given to the son as a possible aid to him in his long journey ..."[54]

Nerses was the son of Pilos Cartozian, member of Lodge No. 1078 Euphrates.

Original Master Mason Diploma of Bro. Melkon Luledjian issued by the Grand
Lodge of Scotland. Courtesy of David Lulejian-Melcon-Yaralian-Hedison families.

Pylos Cartozian was protected by Hayri Bey and Halis Bey, both Brethren
of Ottoman Grand Orient. Brother Halis Bey sheltered Pilos for several
days at his house, putting on risk his own life. An article about the life of
Pilos is published in the journal "The Sunday Oregonian" of Portland on
August 5, 1920. In that article he confesses how Halis Bey, the Turkish
Mason helped him survive:

> "Pilos is my brother and you must kill me first before you can
> approach him."[55]

Other cases of survival are the ones of Doctor Hovhaness Kambourian[56]
and his wife Elizabeth who who saved tens of Armenian orphans who
had been kidnapped to be brought up in Turkish families. Bro. Samuel
Donabedian, also a doctor, could survive and install himself in Beirut,
being his son Avedis Donabedian,[57] one of the world pioneers in Public Health.[58] On the other hand, tirelessly in his persecutory mind, on
November 29, 1914, again the "Brother" Talat Pasha, who had ordered
the express arrest of Bro. Thomas Mugurditchian[59] (Euphrates Lodge No.

1078), can not succeed, since he could manage to escape and write his memoirs in Cairo.

Finally, two survivors who are much owed of being the living archive of the Euphrates Lodge Brethren were Karekin Gostanian and Melkon Lulejian (blood-brother Donabed). Both were arrested and taken to the outskirts of the city of Kharberd along with eight hundred Armenian men. All were tied in groups of three and shot on the spot. Melkon saw how his own nephew was killed. He escaped unleashing their hands from the ropes during the shooting. For many years, the philanthropic association of the Grand Lodge of Scotland helped the orphans of many members of the Lodge "Yeprad" No. 1078.[60]

Once again the political situation make this lodge of Armenian members disappear, and in this case, in the most turbulent way.[61]

The Government of the Young Turks ended when the Allied Forces defeated the Ottomans at the end of the WWI and partially invaded the Ottoman Empire, before the birth of the era of Bro. Mustafa Kemal and the birth of the modern Republic of Turkey.[62]

Trying to imitate the "Carbonaries" in Italy, the Young Turks tried to establish a Masonic State that was absolutely irregular and far from the rules extolled by Freemasonry. As stated by one of the most important specialist in the field, Paul Dumont, who affirms that "... Cynically, the Young Turks used freemasonry precisely to avoid it ..."[63]

Original title of the article about Bro. Pilos O. Cartozian which appeared in the Sunday Oregonian. August, 1920.

19

V. CONCLUSIONS

The intention of this work was to pay tribute to a group of Armenian Free-masons who have suffered a hundred years ago their physical disappearance. A group of men that only wanted to bring progress and prosperity to the society in which they lived.

Also this work shows an attempt to demonstrate that the true Fraternity lives in those hearts full of goodness. That's why Freemasonry, like all man-made institutions, can generate good works as well as terrific situations.

In difficult times it is when you can test how far the concept of Fraternity-Fraternalism can be taken. The case of the Euphrates Lodge No. 1078, a hundred years after his death, has been a clear example of that.

NOTES

1   For a deeper knowledge on these brotherhoods see: Dadoyan, Seta B.: *"The Fatimid Armenians: cultural and political interaction in the Near East"*. Brill, New York. 1997. Chapter III.

2   Regarding the interaction of the Kingdom of Cilicia and the Templar Knights see: *"Mutafian, Claude, "Le Royaume Arménien de Cilicie, XIIe-XIVe siécle"*. CNRS ÉDITIONS, Paris. 1993, 2001.

3   Dadoyan, pp. 72-75.

4   Barkhurtaryan, *"Armenian Architects and Stonecutter Masters from the Middle Ages"* Բարխուդարյան, Ս. «Միջնադարյան Հայ Ճարտարապետներ և Քարգործ Վարպետներ». Երեվան. Հայկական ՍՍՌ ԳԱ Հրատարակչություն. Erevan. 1963. Specially Chapter V.

5   See: Baladouni Vahé, Margaret Makepeace, East India Company. *"Armenian merchants of the seventeenth and early eighteenth centuries: English East India Company sources"*. American Philosophical Society, Philadelphia.1998.

6   Berberian, Ruben. *"The Armenian Freemasons and the Lodge SER of Constantinople"* Բերբերեան, Ռուբէն. «Հայ Մասոնները և «Սէր» Օթեակը Պոլսոյ Մէջ», Հայրենիք. Պոսթըն. Մարտ-Յունիս 1937. Hayrenik Newspaper. Boston. April edition, p. 128.

7   See Gould, Robert Freke. *"A Library of Freemasonry : comprising its history,*

antiquities, symbols, constitutions, customs, etc., and concordant orders of Royal Arch, Knights Templar, A. A. S. Rite, Mystic Shrine, with other important Masonic information of value to the fraternity derived from official and standard sources throughout the world from the earliest period to the present time," John C. Yorston Publishing Company. London. Philadelphia. Montreal. 1906. P. 125.

8   By the end of 1848, there existed fifteen members in the Lodge "Armenia". See Rev. Malden, C.H.: *"A History of Freemasonry (Under the English Constitution) on the Coast of Coromandel together with histories of the Old Madras Lodges which were founded before the Union, together with Appendices and a Map"*. Madras: Addison, 1895. P. 94.

9   More data on this Lodge in *"India."* Freemason Quarterly Review. 30 Sep. 1837: p.109.

10 Haffner, Christopher. *"The Craft in the East"*. Hong Kong: District Grand Lodge of Hong Kong and the Far East, 1977. p. 64.

11 Tachjian, Vahe. *"Ottoman Armenians: Life, Culture, Society. Vol. 1."* Houshamadyan e.v. Germany. 2014.

12 Both processes excellently explained in Beylerian, Arthur."*Freemasonry in the decline of the Ottoman Empire and the Lodge 'Ser' of the 19th century"* (in Armenian) Պէյլէրեան, Արթիւր. «Ազատ-Որդմաղրութեան Մուտքը Օսմանեան Կայսրութիւն և Պոլսոյ Հայկական «Մէր» Օթեակը ԺԹ. Դարուն», Պէյրութ, Հայկազեան Հայագիտական Հանդէս, ԻՍ. հատոր, in Haigazian Armenological Review. Haigazian University. Beirut. 2001. pp. 147-154.

13 This topic is clearly dealt with in Dumont, Paul: *"Freemasonry in Turkey: a by-product of Western penetration"* European Review, Cambridge University Press, vol. 13(03), pages 481-493, July, 2005.

14 Ottoman Armenian elite representing the upper class of bankers and merchants who opted for a conservative and non-reformist Armenian society. A/N.

15 Dadian, Megerditch B. (Le Prince), "La Société Arménienne Contemporaine" in Revue des Deux-Mondes. Librarie A. Franck, Paris. June 1867. pp. 803-827.

16 Anduze, Eric. *"La Franc-maçonnerie De La Turquie Ottomane: 1908-1924"*. Paris: Harmattan, 2005. pp. 28-40.

17 Kologlu, Organ: "Abdulhamid ve Masonlar". Istanbul: Pozitif Yayınları, 2004.

18 Locci, Emanuela. *"Il Cammino Di Hiram: La Massoneria Nell'impero Ottomano."* Foggia: Bastogi, 2013. pp. 33-35.

19 Between 1984 and 1896, Sultan Abdul Hammid II conducted the first generalized massacres of the Armenian population in the Ottoman Empire, which later became known as "Hammidian Massacres" and baptized Abdul Hammid II as

the "Red Sultan". See specific information on: Various Authors. *"Les massacres d'Arménie: Témoingnages des victimes, with the Preface of Georges Clémenceau"*. Paris: Édition du Mercure de France, 1896.

20   Other Lodges of less relevance at the time were "Armenak" (1872, Izmir, Grande Oriente d'Italia) and "Ararat" No. 76 (1882, Cairo, National Grand Lodge of Egypt).

21   Hanioğlu, Şükrü: *"Genesis of the Young Turk Revolution of 1908"* in *The Journal of Ottoman Studies III.* Istanbul. 1982. pp. 277-300.

22   Mazower, Mark: *"Salonica, City of Ghosts: Christians, Muslims and Jews 1430-1950"*. New York: Vintage, 2005.

23   One of the most prominent figures of the Ottoman Freemasonry. He was the Worshipful Master of "Macedonia Risorta" Lodge and became a deputy in the Ottoman Parliament after the Revolution. See Iacovella, Angelo: "Il Triangulo e la Mezzaluna", Instituto Italiano di Cultura Di Istanbul, 1997. Note on p. 56.; Locci, Emanuela. *"Il Cammino Di Hiram: La Massoneria Nell'impero Ottomano."* pp 69-77.

24   Born in Edirne in 1874, had been the head of the postal office in Salonica before 1908. He was initiated in "Macedonia Risorta" Lodge on June 12th 1903 and later (1909) he would be the founding leader of the Ottoman Freemasonry. Like many other Turkish Freemasons he was also involved in the practice of the Bektashism, a spiritual Order linked to the Dervish Ottoman tradition. Later called "Talat Pashá", he would be the "Grand Vizier" of the Ottoman Empire during the World War I and one of the "Three Pashas" during the WWI. He is catalogued as one of the master mind of the planning and execution of the "Armenian Genocide". In 1921, during his exile in Berlín, he ended his life assassinated by Soghomon Tehlirian, an Armenian who had lost 14 members of his family during the Armenian Genocide. See Bogosian, Eric. *"Operation Nemesis: The Assassination Plot that Avenged the Armenian Genocide"*. Little, Brown and Company. New York. 2015.

25   Sommer, Dorothe. *"Freemasonry in the Ottoman Empire: A History of the Fraternity and Its Influence in Syria and the Levant"*. I.B. Tauris. London: 2015. p. 78.

26   Kedourie, Elie. *"Young Turks, Freemasons and Jews"* in Middle Eastern Studies, Vol. 7, No. 1 (Jan., 1971), p. 103.

27   List of the first Officials in Locci, Emanuela. p. 80.

28   List of Lodges numbered in Fenerdjian. p. 80.

29   During a counter revolution made by the Ottomans supporting Abdul Hammid against the Young Turks in 1909, more than 30.000 Armenians lost their lives in the city of Adana. As a result of it in the "Proceeding of the Grand Lodge of New York" (1910) appears that: "The National Grand Lodge of Egypt has addressed an appeal, supporting that of its subordinate Lodge "Ararat" No. 76 of Cairo, to

Masonic powers and brethren the world over to subscribe to the fund to succor the stricken Armenian population in the vilayets of Adana and Aleppo, in Asia Minor, the scene of recent harrowing massacres".

30 All of them arrested and killed during the april of 1915. Fenerdjian. p. 81.

31 The most important works about this city are: Vahé Haig: "*Kharberd/Harput and its Golden Plain: Historic, Cultural and Ethnographic Memory Book*". New York. 1959. 1500 pages; Various Authors, Hovanissian, Richard (Editor): "Armenian Tsopk/Kharpert". Mazda Publishers. California. 2002. 469 pp.; Köker, Osman; Calumeno Orlando Carlo. "Armenians in Turkey 100 years ago : with the postcards from the collection of Orlando Carlo Calumeno", Birzamanlar Yayıncılık, Istanbul, 2005.

32 Hewsen, Robert H: "*Golden Plain: The Historical Geography of Tsopk/Kharpert*" in "Armenian Tsopk/Kharpert". Mazda Publishers. California. 2002. p. 45.

33 More distant but no less important towns were Malatia, Arapkir and Dersim, and other 2000 villages that integrated the whole province. Ibid. p. 49.

34 Andrews Stone, Frank: "*The Heritage of Euphrates (Armenia) College*". in "Armenian Tsopk/Kharpert". Mazda Publishers. California. 2002. p. 209.

35 Ibid. p. 218.

36 Documents provided thanks to Bro. Robert L. Cooper, curator of the Grand Lodge of Scotland. The Archives about this Lodge remark the extraordinary effort of Brother Vartan Vezneian sending several letters to the Grand Secretary of the Grand Lodge of Scotland, Bro. David Reid, in order to obtain the permission to open a new Masonic Lodge under the Scottish auspices. A/N.

37 List provided by Fenerdjian, Armenag. "*Freemasonry in the Middle East within the entire Armenian people*" Ֆենէրճեան, Արմենակ. «Ազատ Որմնադրութիւնը Մօտաւոր Արեւելքի Հայութեան Մէջ». Կեանք Եւ Արուեստ, Է. Տարի, Փարիզ.Life and Arts Paris, 1935.; and "Freemasonry amidst the Armenian", «Ազատ Որմնադրութիւնը Հայոց Մէջ». Հայրենիք. Պոսթըն. Հոկտեմբեր 1954-Դեկտեմբեր 1955. Hayrenik Newspaper, Boston. Eight articles from October 1954 to December 1955; and Lulejian, Melkon. "The Freemasons" Լիւլէճեան, Մելքոն. «Ազատ Որմնադիրները». Հայրենիք. Պոսթըն. Օգոստոս. Hayrenik Newspaper, Boston. August, 1958. pp. 96-98.

38 Published by Armenag Fenerjian in "Hayrenik" newspaper, Boston, 1954-1955. Courtesy of David Lulejian-Melcon-Yaralian-Hedison families.

39 Notes and documents of descendants of the Lulejian family in the United States. Courtesy of David Lulejian-Melcon-Yaralian-Hedison families.

40 The Lodge Yeprad appeared in the list of regular lodges until 1926 inclusive. See List of Regular Lodges of F.A.F.M. for the Grand Lodge of New Jersey, 1926. Pantagraph Printing and Stationary Co., Illinois, March 1926.

41 Lulejian, M. p. 97.

42 Paradoxically, Bro. Vartan Vezneian was one of the first victims of the deportations and massacres that took place in the Kharberd province since June 1915.

43 For any Armenian that wanted to be part of the Freemasonry this topic has been an obstacle. For many scholars Talat Pasha is one of the fathers of the Ottoman Freemasonry and, at the same time, is one of the main responsible for the Genocide of the Armenian Nation. That is why both good decisions and errors must be ascribed to the persons (masons) and not to the institution itself (Freemasonry). It is a common mistake in the tendentious historic analysis of the events that took place in those years.

44 On this issue there are plenty of books. For the most important works see: Dadrian, Vahakn. *"The History of the Armenian Genocide: Ethnic Conflict from the Balkans to Anatolia to the Caucasus"* Oxford: Berghahn Books, 1995.; Kevorkian, Raymond: *"The Armenian Genocide: A Complete History"*. London: I.B. Tauris, 2011; Ackam, Taner: *"The Young Turks' Crime Against Humanity: The Armenian Genocide and Ethnic Cleansing in the Ottoman Empire"*. Princeton University Press. 2012.; Bryce, James and Arnold Toynbee: *"The Treatment of Armenians in the Ottoman Empire, 1915–1916: Documents Presented to Viscount Grey of Falloden, Uncensored ed"*. Edited and with an introduction by Ara Sarafian. Princeton: Gomidas Institute, 2000.; Ohanian, Pascual C. *"Turquía, Estado Genocida (1915-1923) Documentos"*: Buenos Aires. Akian Ediciones, 1986.

45 The "Tehcir Law" translated from the Ottoman Turkish as "Temporary Deportation Law", Raymond Kevorkian explains: The fact that the "temporary deportation law" was not adopted until late May indicates either that it took time to implement the measures adopted by the Central Committee or that the CUP felt the need to create a legal cover for its plans. It is also significant that official publication of this governmental law-by-decree came one month after its adoption and that it was released even then in bowdlerized form. Five of the eight paragraphs of the law—those bearing on the confiscation of Armenian property and the settlement of muhacirs in Armenian homes—seem to have been censored. Not until passage of the Law of 26 September 1915 did the Ottoman government give presentable legal form to the confiscation of Armenian property, at a time when the deportation process was virtually complete. Although the Armenians were never mentioned by name, the wording of the censored paragraphs of the "temporary law" was no doubt too explicit; it must have seemed to go too far toward revealing the Ittihad's true objectives. Publishing rules for the immediate installation of muhacirs in Armenian homes came down to admitting that the "displacement toward the interior" of the Armenian population had nothing "temporary" about it, but that it was meant to be permanent. Kevorkian pp. 244-245.

46 Butler, Daniel Allen. "Shadow of the Sultan's Realm: The Destruction of the Ottoman Empire and the Creation of the Modern Middle East". Potomac Books Inc. Washington D.C. 2011. p. 154.

47 Bro. Armenag Fenerdjian was one of the first scholars interested in Armenian Freemasonry. He was Secretary and Worshipful Master in several periods for the Lodge "Hayastan" No. 1185 (Grand Lodge of Scotland), later the Lodge Paros No. 1184. Thanks to the articles cited by Fenerdjian and his assiduous researches and publications, much more valuable information could be obtained to complete this history as a global idea of the history of masons of Armenian origin. A/N.

Fenerdjian, Armenag. "*Freemasonry in the Middle East within the entire Armenian people*" Ֆէնէրճեան, Արմենակ. «Ազատ Որմասադրութիւնը Մօտաւոր Արեւելքի Հայութեան Մէջ». Կեանք Եւ Արուեստ, Է. Տարի, Փարիզ. Life and Arts Paris, 1935.; and "Freemasonry amidst the Armenian", «Ազատ Որմասադրութիւնը Հայոց Մէջ». Հայրենիք. Պոսթըն. Հոկտեմբեր 1954-Դեկտեմբեր 1955. Hayrenik Newspaper, Boston. Eight articles from October 1954 to December 1955.

48 The story is narrated in first person by himself in Lulejian, Melkon. "The Freemasons" Լիւլէճեան, Մելքոն. «Ազատ Որմասադիրները». Հայրենիք. Պոսթըն. Օգոստոս. Hayrenik Newspaper, Boston. August. 1958.

49 Lulejian, M. p. 98.

50 Notes and documents of descendants of the Lulejian family in the United States. Courtesy of David Hetison (Hedisian) and Lulejian family.

51 See Tahsin Bey's appointment in Hüsnü, Ada. "THE FIRST OTTOMAN CIVIL SOCIETY ORGANIZATON IN THE SERVICE OF THE OTTOMAN STATE: The Case of the Ottoman Red Crescent (Osmanlı Hilal-i Ahmer Cemiyeti)". Sabancı University, September 2004. p. 32.

52 It is a heartbreaking letter, today guarded by the Hedisian-Lulejian family.

53 Bryce, James and Arnold Toynbee: "*The Treatment of Armenians in the Ottoman Empire, 1915–1916: Documents Presented to Viscount Grey of Falloden, Uncensored.*" Edited and with an introduction by Ara Sarafian. Princeton: Gomidas Institute, 2000. pp. 305-306.

54 Royse, Clarence D.: "Armenia and the Armenians" in the New Age Magazine. Volume XXIX. Number 10. October 1920. p. 435.

55 "*Tale of Miraculous Escape told by Armenian Refugee: Masonic Brother, at Risk of His Life, Shelters Pilos O. Cartozian, Brother of Cartozian Brothers, of Portland*" at the "The Sunday Oregonian." Portland. August 5, 1920.

56 Andrews Stone, Frank: "*The Heritage of Euphrates (Armenia) College*". in "Armenian Tsopk/Kharpert". Mazda Publishers. California. 2002. p. 231. While researching about his descendants I have discovered that his great grandson J. Kambourian is a Master Mason who works in Australia. He was totally touched when he knew that his Great Grandfather Dr. Hovhanness Kambourian was a Masonic Brother. N/A.

57   Europa Publications, Sleeman Elizabeth (Editor): "The International Who's Who. 2004, 67th Edition." Europa Publications Limited. Surrey. 2003. p. 443.

58   http://www.fadq.org Avedis Donabedian Foundation.

59   Mugerdicthian, Thomas: "*Dikranagerdee Nahankin Charteru yev Kurderou Kazanioutounneru*" (Massacres in the Province of Dikranagerd-Diyarbekir). Cairo. Djihanian. 1919.

60   One of the works established by the philanthropic association of the Great Lodge of Scotland was to help the orphans of many of the members of the Lodge "Yeprad" No. 1078. See Fenerdjian, Armenag. Ֆէնէրճեան, Արմենակ. «Ագատ Որմադրութիւնը Սոտատր Արելելքի Հայութեան Մէջ». Կեանք Եւ Արուեստ, Ե. Տարի, Փարիզ.

61   The Lodge Yeprad appeared in the list of regular lodges until 1920 inclusive. See List of Regular Lodges of F.A.F.M. for the Grand Lodge of New Jersey, 1920. Pantagraph Printing and Stationary Co., Illinois, March 1920.

62   In 1919, the Worshipful Master Siotis of the Lodge "La Renaissance" of Istanbul sends a terrible note about the Masonic situation of the members of the Young Turk Goverment and catalogues them as a "Regular meeting of assassins": "Vous savez sans doute que toutes les personnes qui formaient ce Grand Orient sont plus ou moins mêlées à tous les massacres et toutes les persécutions qui ont eu lieu contre les non musulmans de Turquie, et que le Grand Maître actuel est Djavid Bey qui faisait partie du ministère Talat de sinistre mémoire. Pour ces raisons, notre L:. a pensé qu'elle ne saurait en aucun cas entrer en relation avec les L:. turques. Nous attendons votre avis là-dessus et nous agirons en conséquence, tout en pensant que le G:.O:.D:.F:., ne peut reconnaître comme puissance Maç:. régulière une réunion d'assassins." Anduze, Eric. "*La Franc-maçonnerie De La Turquie Ottomane: 1908-1924*". Paris: Harmattan, 2005. pp. 106-107.

63   See Dumont, Paul: "Freemasonry in Turkey: a by-product of Western penetration," European Review, Cambridge University Press, vol. 13(03), July. p. 493.

II

A CONTEMPORARY LOOK AT THE VARIOUS FORMS OF FREEMASONRY AMONG AFRICAN-AMERICANS IN THE UNITED STATES

DR. ELQUEMEDO OSCAR ALLEYNE

INTRODUCTION

There have been men of color among the ranks of speculative masonry for ages. Brother John Pine, the designer of the frontispiece of Anderson's 1723 Constitutions, was said to be of African ancestry and a member of the lodge that met at the Horn Tavern in West-minster,[1] which was one of the founding lodges that formed the Grand Lodge of England in 1717. Brother Joseph Bologne, known as the Chevalier de Saint-Georges of France, was initiated in the mid-1700's into the Paris-based Lodge of the 9 Sisters (Les Neuf Sœurs) under the Grand Orient of France. He was a skilled and well-respected composer, conductor, violinist, swordsman, equestrian and soldier[2] and of African descent. He assisted with the founding of the Olympic Lodge Orchestra which was sponsored by l'Olympique de la Parfait Union lodge, where the musicians were all Masons.

Brother Angelo Soliman, of African ancestry and a well-known friend of Brother Amadeus Mozart, is recorded as joining the Vienna Masonic lodge "True Harmony" in 1783.[3] In New Jersey, Alpha Lodge No. 116 rose to infamy in 1871 when it introduced a mostly African American

---

1   Prescott, Andrew. "John Pine: A Sociable Craftsman." *MQ Magazine*. Issue 10, July, 2004.

2   Monsieur de Saint-George: Virtuoso, Swordsman, Revolutionary: A Legendary Life Rediscovered by Alain Guédé.

3   Paul Nettl. Angelo Soliman--Friend of Mozart. *Phylon (1940-1956)* Vol. 7, No. 1 (1st Qtr., 1946), pp. 41-46. Clark Atlanta University. http://www.jstor.org/stable/271283

membership causing outcry and backlash from other U.S grand lodge jurisdictions.[4] The world champion boxer Jack Johnson was initiated into Lodge Forfar and Kincardine No. 225 in Dundee, Scotland on October 13, 1911, causing a major uproar with many US grand lodges issuing protests and threats to pull their recognition of the Grand Lodge of Scotland.[5, 6] Records also indicated that men of color were admitted to an Edinburgh Masonic lodge in 1904 and other Scottish-chartered lodges in Africa, such as the Lodge Morality, No. 1362 (Ghana), in 1930.[7]

Historical and current data were collected and reviewed on African Americans and Freemasonry by the author. It was best to characterize predominantly African American Freemasonic organizations into three categories: Prince Hall Affiliated, Prince Hall Origin and Non-Prince Hall. The term "predominantly African American" is used in this review to refer to Masonic organizations whose majority membership is comprised of African Americans.

PRINCE HALL AFFILIATED

Prince Hall, born in or around the year 1738, is known as the "Father of Black Masonry." He was a staunch proponent for equal treatment for blacks, education for black children and the abolition of slavery and slave trade. His additional legacy to American history came when Prince Hall and fourteen other free black men were initiated into Lodge No. 441 under the Irish Constitution, attached to the 38th Foot Regiment of the British Army, and garrisoned at Castle William (now Fort Independence) Boston Harbor on March 6, 1775, with John Batt serving as its Master.

When the British Army left Boston in 1776, the Lodge No. 441 granted Prince Hall and his brethren a "permit" to meet as African Lodge No.1 and to bury their dead; but they could not confer degrees nor perform any other Masonic "work". Another permit was granted by the Provincial

4 J. Hampton Harley. Alpha Lodge No. 116 F & AM. Transactions of the A. Douglas Smith, Jr. Lodge of Research #1949, Volume 2. August 16, 1989.

5 Gordon Vincent. The Black Boxer & The Scottish Craft. Gordon Vincent. *The Black Boxer & The Scottish Craft.* http://www.lodge76.wanadoo.co.uk/the_black_boxer.htm Date Accessed, December 28, 2009.

6 The New York Times. *Johnson's Initiation Angers Freemasons.* October 29, 1911. Section Cable News, Wireless and Sporting Sections, Page 51.

7 The Grand Lodge of Scotland. Black Freemasons. The Grand Lodge of Scotland. *Black Freemasons.* http://www.grandlodgescotland.com/masonic-subjects/black-freemasons. Date Accessed December 29, 2009.

Grand Master John Rowe to walk in procession on St. John's Day. For eight years these brethren, together with others who had received their degrees elsewhere, assembled and enjoyed their limited privileges as Masons. By January 14, 1779, thirty-three Masons were listed on the rolls of African Lodge No.1.

On March 2, 1784, WM Prince Hall petitioned the Premier Grand Lodge of England with the help of WM William Moody of the Lodge of Brotherly Love No.55 in London, England for a warrant or charter. The two established correspondence after a Brother from African Lodge No. 1 was in need of aid and assistance while in England. When he returned to the US, he told Prince Hall how he was received and helped by Brothers from Lodge of Brotherly Love No.55. On September 29th 1784, a warrant was granted by the Premier Grand Lodge of England to 15 men in Boston, Massachusetts forming them into African Lodge, No. 459 on the English Register. It must be noted that the actual Warrant did not arrive until 1787.

At the creation of the United Grand Lodge of England with the merger of the Antients & Moderns in 1813, African Lodge and many others were omitted from the Premier Grand Lodge's register. Some of these lodges were renumbered or remained stricken from the register, there having been no contact for many years.[8]

In 1827, African Lodge No.459 declared itself to be an independent Grand Lodge: the African Grand Lodge of Massachusetts which was later renamed Prince Hall Grand Lodge of Massachusetts. All Prince Hall Grand Lodges are descended from what is now the Prince Hall Grand Lodge of Massachusetts.[9] History is rife with the issues and controversies surrounding the acceptance of the origins, legitimacy and recognition of Prince Hall Affiliated Masonry.[10] The objective of this paper is not to become immersed in the pros or cons of those arguments then or now.

In 1994, the United Grand Lodge of England's Grand Registrar released

8   George Draffen. Prince Hall Freemasonry. May 13, 1976.

9   Ralph McNeal, Jr. The Phylaxis Society–PHA Commission on Bogus Masonic Practices; Conversations with the author, January 2010.

10 Tony Pope. Our Segregated Brethren, Prince Hall Freemasons. http://www.free-masons-freemasonry.com/pope_OSB_1.html Date Accessed January 29, 2010.

a resolution which stated that the Prince Hall Grand Lodge of Massachusetts should be accepted as regular, and be recognized. The administrations of the Grand Lodges of Ireland and Scotland also agreed in principle that the Prince Hall Grand Lodge of Massachusetts should be recognized.

To clarify its position, the UGLE stated that by the standards of today (i.e., the requirement of three lodges being necessary to form a Grand Lodge), the formation of the Prince Hall Grand Lodge of Massachusetts was irregular. However in the 18th century, three grand lodges in North America were formed by not three but *two* lodges, with the Grand Lodge of New Jersey being formed simply by a Grand Convention of Masons. Therefore the UGLE ruled that by the standards then prevailing, the formation of the Prince Hall Grand Lodge of Massachusetts could have been seen as merely eccentric, and of acceptable regularity. In spite of the unusual transformation of its original lodge into a grand lodge, the philosophy and practice of Prince Hall Masonry today are of exemplary regularity.[11]

Since the UGLE's resolution, there are 42 mainstream grand lodges in the US that have established or voted in favor of recognition of the Prince Hall grand lodge in their state. Nine grand lodges still at this time do not recognize Prince Hall Masonry as regular or legitimate for a number of reasons. Those states are Arkansas, Alabama, Florida, Georgia, Louisiana, Mississippi, Tennessee, South Carolina and West Virginia.[12]

With over 5,000 lodges and 47 grand lodges that can be traced back to the African Lodge No.459, Prince Hall Affiliated has a membership of at least 300,000 brothers worldwide. With several notable and famous members known for their contributions to science, law, politics, civics, sports and entertainment,[13] Prince Hall Affiliated continues to be a major gateway to men of color interested in becoming Freemasons. While the organization is predominantly African American, PHA has several members who have joined that are non-African American and from other culturally diverse backgrounds.

---

11 The United Grand Lodge of England, *1994 Resolution on Prince Hall Freemasonry.* Proceedings of December 14, 1994.

12 Paul M. Bessel Masonic Research website Map of US Recognition Status http://bessel.org/masrec/phamap.htm

13 MW Prince Hall Grand Lodge of New York. http://princehallny.org/

Prince Hall Origin

The Prince Hall Origin organization, which can be said to be regular by lineage, is an unrecognized body. Its current governance structure is lead by a National Grand Master (Clyde L. Shepard) with its headquarters in Jackson, Mississippi.[14] In order to understand the complexity surrounding Prince Hall Origin and Prince Hall Affiliated, an additional historical context is required. On May 8, 1843, the mainstream grand lodges of New Hampshire, Massachusetts, Rhode Island, New York, Maryland, Virginia, North Carolina, South Carolina, Georgia, Mississippi, Florida and Ohio held a convention in the city of Baltimore, Maryland.

The purpose of this convention was to preserve the ancient landmarks and develop a uniformity of work among US grand lodges reeling from the impact of the Anti-Masonic movement. The result of this convention lead to the first known introduction of "dues cards", the introduction of initiation fees from candidates prior to receiving degrees, the conducting business on the third degree only, the establishment of suspensions for non-payment of dues, and the adoption of several ceremonies, such as those for a funeral, the constitution of a lodge, the dedication of Masonic halls, amongst others. One of the proposals also evaluated at the Baltimore Convention was the establishment of a General Grand Lodge, which failed to get support. The attendees instead chose to recommend that the several grand lodges of the United States enter into and form a National Masonic Convention.[15]

Similarly, on June 24-26, 1847, there was a Prince Hall convention in Boston, Massachusetts, with delegates from African Grand Lodge of Massachusetts, the First Independent African Grand Lodge of North America (Pennsylvania), Boyer Lodge of New York, and Hiram Grand Lodge of Pennsylvania. The purpose of the meeting was to resolve a schism between brothers of the First Independent African Grand Lodge and Hiram Grand Lodge of Pennsylvania. Hiram Grand Lodge was created by a group of brothers who were expelled from First Independent African Grand Lodge. The attendees at this meeting however created the Most Worshipful National Grand Lodge of Ancient York Rite Masons (also known as Prince Hall Origin Compact).

This conceptually created one National Grand Lodge (NGL) over all ex-

14 The National Grand Lodge PHO Compact http://mwnationalgrandlodge.org/ Date Accessed January 29, 2010.

15 Allen E. Roberts. The Convention that changed the face of Freemasonry. Masonic Service Association, Short Talk Bulletin. October 1986.

isting Prince Hall grand lodges. The National Grand Lodge is said to have created 23 other subordinate grand lodges between 1848 through 1877. It is credited with developing the uniformity of work among early Prince Hall Masonry and solidifying the network of lodges assisting in the Underground Railroad, which began towards the end of the 18th Century, and was an organized system and vast network of people who helped hundreds of fugitive slaves escape to the North and to Canada.[16]

However, there was discord within this newly established NGL. Boyer Lodge of New York withdrew from the NGL jurisdiction on June 7, 1848, and reclaimed their independent sovereignty. Hiram Grand Lodge of Pennsylvania left on November 9, 1849. The First Independent African Grand Lodge of North America (Pennsylvania) left on June 28, 1850. Prince Hall Grand Lodge of Ohio left in 1867, and Prince Hall Grand Lodge of Massachusetts (originally African Grand Lodge of Massachusetts) left in 1873. Most Prince Hall grand lodges withdrew from the NGL between the years 1871-1879. They generally joined forces as independent sovereign grand lodge counterparts and later adopted the name Prince Hall Affiliated at a convention of grand lodges in 1944.[17]

Although several noted Prince Hall Affiliated historians wrote that the National Grand Lodge disintegrated and disbanded at the exit of these grand lodges from the Compact, the NGL continued to form new grand lodges after 1877, in addition to maintaining that it held jurisdiction over the other grand lodges that did not leave with the PHA grand lodges. The National Grand Lodge still exists today and is known as the Most Worshipful National Grand Lodge F & AAYM, Prince Hall Origin, National Compact, USA with subordinate grand lodges listed in at least 20 states.[18]

The National Grand Lodge is regarded as unrecognized because conventional Masonic practice maintains that there is no authority under the Ancient Charges or Masonic law, nor is there any Masonic justification to have a grand lodge subordinate to another. Many have tried to draw similarities to the United Grand Lodges of Germany (UGLG), which is comprised of five constituent grand lodges. The UGLG, which is recognized as regular, solely exists to represent German Freemasonry to foreign

16 David L Gray and Ralph L. McNeal Jr., *The National Grand Lodge FAQ*, Dr. Charles Wesley Masonic Research Society. http://www.hariam.org/CHWR/nglfaq.html Date Accessed December 28, 2009.

17 Ralph McNeal, Jr., The Phylaxis Society–PHA Commission on Bogus Masonic Practices; Conversations with the author, January 2010.

18 The National Grand Lodge PHO Compact, http://mwnationalgrandlodge.org/. Date Accessed January 29, 2010.

grand lodges and to the German public. The member grand lodges remain sovereign and autonomous in order to conduct their internal affairs and their manner of teaching Freemasonry. In the case of the PHO National Grand Lodge, the subordinate grand lodges are not afforded the latter.

Conversely, it can be said that the practice of Masonry within Prince Hall Origin can be considered regular (notwithstanding its governance structure) as some PHO grand lodges can trace their lineage directly back to African Lodge No.459—as is the example of the Compact Grand Lodge in Delaware.[19] There exists an acrimonious relationship between the two organizations as neither group recognizes each other, and there have been instances where Prince Hall Affiliated lodges have absorbed a number of PHO lodges or "healed" PHO members into PHA.[20] The unofficial term *healing* refers to the ceremonial and/or administrative process by which an unrecognized Mason may become a member of a regular lodge based on the policies and procedures of the grand lodge approving his membership.

In recent years, there have been members of the NGL and at least one PHA researcher who have openly called for the recognition of PHO as a legitimate and recognized Masonic organization.[21] Two roadblocks prevent this from being a reality: The National Grand Lodge's governance structure claiming sovereignty over other grand lodges, and no mainstream grand lodges in amity or recognition with their sister Prince Hall Affiliated grand lodges will enter into recognition with another grand lodge in their state. Bewilderment will continue to the uninformed as many Masons do not comprehend the difference between the two groups that lay claim to the use of Prince Hall in their names separated only by a vowel. Evidence of this is shown in some states where the NGL uses Prince Hall in their title while the Prince Hall Affiliated grand lodge does not (e.g., the Mississippi PHA Grand Lodge is the Most Worshipful Stringer Grand Lodge, PHA, while the PHO Grand Lodge is the Most Worshipful Prince Hall Grand Lodge State of Mississippi). To add to this multifaceted landscape, we must also examine the groups known as the Non-Prince Hall Masons.

19 William G. Emery. A Brief Narrative History Of the M.W. African Harmony Grand Lodge, Free and Accepted, Ancient York Masons, Prince Hall Origin - National Compact. http://www.mwnationalgrandlodge.org/GLHistory.htm. Date Accessed January 2010.

20 Mastermason.com Prince Hall Affiliated Web Forum To Heal or Not To Heal http://forum.mastermason.com/forum_posts.asp?TID=10304&PN=2. Date Accessed September 2011.

21 Alton G. Roundtree, Paul M. Bessel. Out of the Shadows, The Emergence of Prince Hall Freemasonry in America, 225 Years of Endurance. 2006.

NON-PRINCE HALL

This unrecognized group of Masons is primarily comprised of bodies that many within regular Freemasonry classify as *bogus, clandestine, spurious* or *irregular*. As each grand lodge can derive their own definition for these terms, for the purposes of this paper, the author defines a *clandestine lodge* or grand lodge as a body of Freemasons, or of those improperly claiming to be Freemasons, uniting in a lodge without the consent of a grand lodge, or although originally legally constituted, continues to operate as a lodge after its charter has been revoked. *Spurious* is defined as coming from an illegitimate birth or falsely attributed origin. *Irregular* encompasses those groups that are not acting in accord with laws, rules, or established Masonic custom. *Bogus* refers to those groups that present themselves as a Masonic organization, but are fake or fraudulent business schemes.

One historic figure central to the development and existence of these groups is John George Jones, also known as the *Father of Bogus Masonry*. Jones was born on September 18, 1849, in Ithaca, New York, but at an early age, his family relocated to Chicago, Illinois. A lawyer by profession, he was admitted to the Illinois Bar on March 24, 1881, and was later elected as a state representative of the 5th District of Cook County. Jones had a stellar Masonic career: he was a member of the Most Worshipful Prince Hall Grand Lodge (PHA) F&AM, of the State of Illinois when he was initiated, passed, and raised in John Jones Lodge No. 7. This lodge was named after his uncle, a former Grand Master of Illinois.

He served as Master, was elected Grand Secretary in 1873 and 1874, and even went on to be elected as Deputy Grand Master in 1875. In 1876, he became very active in Scottish Rite Masonry where he was coroneted a 33° and served as the Chairman of the Committee on Foreign Correspondence. He entered into communication with many international Scottish Rite councils in order to present the case of the legitimacy of Scottish Rite for men of color.[22] Jones is regarded as being principally responsible for the creation of the Prince Hall Shriners organization when, on June 3, 1893, he founded the Ancient Egyptian Arabic Order Nobles Mystic Shrine of North and South America and its Jurisdictions, Inc.

22 John G. Jones. *The Origin of Scottish Rite Masonry.* Unpublished Manuscript, Chicago, IL. 1888.

Unfortunately, his impressive Masonic resume was checkered with issues. In 1887, he was suspended by J.W. Moore, the Prince Hall Grand Master in Illinois, for contumacy (contemptuous resistance to authority) but was later reinstated. In 1895, he ran for Sovereign Grand Commander of the United Supreme Council, Southern Jurisdiction PHA and lost to another Prince Hall leader, Thornton Jackson. After contesting and losing the election, he then broke off with his *own* Scottish Rite Council and declared that he was the Sovereign Grand Commander of the United Supreme Council of Southern & Western Jurisdiction.

Jones was tried in 1903 by a grand lodge commission for fraudulently conferring Masonic degrees without authority upon persons who had not petitioned any lodge in the PHA Jurisdiction. He was found guilty, suspended indefinitely, and expelled from Prince Hall Masonry. Since that date, he and the leaders of his organization proceeded to set up multiple clandestine lodges, grand lodges and supreme councils in direct competition to the Prince Hall Affiliated groups.[23] John Jones' legacy in the State of New York alone is staggering: in 1908, he helped form grand lodges in upstate New York and New York City. A look at the historical sketch of these bodies is very revealing:

Hiram Grand Lodge AF&AM

"On Aug 20, 1908 three Lodges, Keystone No.1 chartered by the Grand Lodge of Pennsylvania, MW HT Brodis Grand Master, **Seneca Lodge No.2 chartered by the Grand Lodge of Illinois, MW John G. Jones Grand Master** and St John Lodge No.3 chartered by the Grand Lodge of Massachusetts, MW H.C. Scott Grand Master, met in a place called Abbots Hall located in the city of Buffalo, State of NY, and organized Hiram Grand Lodge of Ancient Free and Accepted Masons. **The meeting was presided over by MW John G. Jones, Grand Master of the Illinois Grand Lodge.**

The officers for the Grand Lodge were MW Benjamin Lane (GM), RW Clem Smith (DGM), RW Robert Buree (GSW), RW Charles Chatman (GJW), RW Washington Takett (GS) and RW Joseph Moon (GT)."[24]

23 Ralph McNeal, Jr. The Phylaxis Society–PHA Commission on Bogus Masonic Practices. http://www.thephylaxis.org/bogus/index.php. Date Accessed December 2009.

24 Hiram Grand Lodge AF&AM New York, Inc. Constitution & By Laws September 30, 2008.

Groups that have originated from Jones and similar men have created the largest number of unrecognized, irregular and clandestine grand lodges with their headquarters in New York than in any other state in the US.[25] Some of these newer groups have even been founded within the early 21st century (see Table 1).[26]

THE THREE LETTERED VS. FOUR LETTERED PHENOMENON

There are many Masons who do not have a clear picture of nomenclature assigned to their lodge and grand lodge names. Lodges descending from Antients, the Grand Lodge of Ireland, and the Grand Lodge of Scotland tend use the name Ancient Free & Accepted Masons (AF&AM) in their title. Lodges descending from the Premier Grand Lodge of England from 1717-1813 use Free & Accepted Masons (F&AM) in their title.

Among the mainstream Grand Lodges in the United States there are 25 F&AM Grand Lodges, 24 AF&AM Grand Lodges, 1 AFM Grand Lodge (Ancient Free Masons); South Carolina) and 1 FAAM (Free Accepted Ancient Masons; District of Columbia). Prince Hall Affiliated has 47 F&AM Grand Lodges. In essence, there is no bearing on recognition or regularity among regular and recognized grand lodges when it comes to this naming scheme except for the fact that many non-Prince Hall grand lodges refer to themselves as AF&AM because of the belief that they are Scottish Rite Masons, and are therefore distinguished from the other F&AM named groups.

This self-professed distinction by the non-Prince Hall groups is based on their misinterpretation of the Ancient and Accepted Scottish Rite (A&ASR), which is (essentially) French in origin and not Scottish. The Scottish Rite as a concordant body in American Freemasonry covers Masonic degrees that number 1 through 33. However, there is a strict agreement that the A&ASR will not confer their first three Scottish Rite degrees, out of deference to the recognized supreme authority of the grand

---

25 Edward L. King. Fake Masonry. http://www.masonicinfo.com/fakemasonry.htm Date Accessed December 28, 2009.

26 New York State Department of State, Division of Corporations; the PHA Commission on Bogus Masonic Practices, http://www.thephylaxis.org/bogus/; Paul M. Bessel Masonic Research website, http://bessel.org. Date Accessed December, 2009.

lodge in each state. These first three degrees are often referred to as the *red lodge* or *Craft degrees*. There are some lodges in the mainstream Louisiana Grand Lodge (F&AM) that use red lodge ritual for their Entered Apprentice, Fellow Craft and Master Mason degrees. Puerto Rico has mostly red lodges, while other mainstream US grand lodges also have a few subordinate lodges that exemplify red lodge or Craft degrees (CA, HI, NY & WI). In NY, examples of these are Garibaldi, Alba and a few of the former Cerneau Lodges.

Many of these non-Prince Hall groups originated either from former expelled or disgruntled Masons who were mostly from F&AM jurisdictions and then started new lodges and grand lodges as AF&AM in order to stylize themselves as having Scottish Rite origins. In many instances, they formed a large number of irregular supreme councils, which in turn "chartered" subordinate blue lodges. As in the case of New York, they additionally registered their groups as business entities with the Secretary of the New York State Department of State, Division of Corporations in order to obtain a certificate of incorporation.[27]

These certificates of incorporation are then used as charters empowering them to work as a Masonic organization. The dilemma lies in the fact that in actuality, these groups do not know of nor practice *any* of the Craft or red lodge degrees associated with the Scottish Rite. Those that they use are actually copies of exposures such as, *Duncan's Ritual* or Lester's *Look To The East*.[28]

The following are a few other examples of these non-Prince Hall groups. Between 1917 and1921, Jerry Baxter Baldwin and others organized 17 lodges throughout Alabama, Mississippi, and Georgia. They applied and received a charter from Jefferson County and the State of Alabama on November 17, 1921, for the creation of the "Free and Accepted Colored Masons of America." On April 4, 1955, they amended their certificate of incorporation changing the name to the Supreme Grand Lodge, Modern Free and Accepted Masons of the World, Ancient and Accepted Scottish Rite.

---

27 The NY State Department of State, Division of Corporations. Business Entity Search Tool. http://www.dos.ny.gov/corps/bus_entity_search.html. Date Accessed January, 2010.

28 Ralph P Lester, Harold Sander. Lester's Look To The East: A Revised Ritual Of The First Three Degrees Of Masonry. Fitzgerald Publishing Corp. (1927). Malcolm C. Duncan, Duncan's Ritual of Freemasonry, Three Rivers Press (April 12, 1976)

This affiliation with Scottish Rite was due to that fact that Mr. Baldwin (then the Grand Master of Modern Free) and his group were successfully sued in court by John Wesley Dobbs, the Grand Master of the Prince Hall Grand Lodge of Georgia.[29, 30]

INTERNATIONAL FREE AND ACCEPTED MASONS

The demise of Modern Free and Accepted Masons gave rise to the International Free & Accepted Modern Masons, Inc. and Order of Eastern Star, Inc. in 1950, created by William V. Banks. Banks joined and was also expelled from the Modern F&AM Masons group when he attempted to split the organization into two factions in order to be gain power and control. Banks incorporated and chartered the IFAMM organization in August of 1950 in Detroit, Michigan, and later in Wilmington, Delaware, stating that this empowered International Masons to practice Freemasonry, and operate as a Masonic Order, throughout the United States, its possessions and territories. To quote the organization's marketing material: "This American issued charter empowers, International Masons to the same rights as those charters issued directly from the Grand Lodge of England or the Grand Orient of France".[31]

Two unique features make International Masons readily recognizable. First, their logo features an upside down skeleton key beneath the Masonic square and compasses. This was a direct result of the lawsuit with the Modern Free and Accepted Masons group. The ruling stated that the organization could not use the signs and symbols traditionally associated with legitimate Masonic organizations. Secondly, members of the IFAMM don a fez as part of their symbolic lodge regalia. In regular and recog-

---

29 Ralph McNeal, Jr. The Phylaxis Society–PHA Commission on Bogus Masonic Practices. http://www.thephylaxis.org/bogus/index.php. Date Accessed December 2009.

30 MWPHGL of GA (F&AM) v. Supreme GL (MF&AM) Colored Masons of the World. US District Court for the Middle District of Georgia, Columbus Division. December 28, 1951.

31 Ralph McNeal, Jr., The Phylaxis Society–PHA Commission on Bogus Masonic Practices. http://www.thephylaxis.org/bogus/index.php. Date Accessed December 2009.

nized American Freemasonry, fezzes are traditionally worn in the Shriner or Grotto organizations and are not representative of symbolic blue lodge regalia.

In 1943, 19 men created Williamsburg Masonic Circle No. 1. This group then organized with other lodges to be known as Mecca Grand Lodge, which is now known as the Empire State Grand Council, Ancient and Accepted Scottish Rite Masons, Inc. The organization purchased the Brooklyn Masonic Temple in 1977. The Brooklyn Masonic Temple was originally built in 1909, and by 1912, it was home to 35 regular New York lodges. Many of the GLNY subordinate lodges in New York City sold or consolidated their properties and now meet in the rooms of the Grand Lodge of New York building on West 23rd Street in Manhattan.

Unfortunately, it is very easy for one to mistake the Brooklyn Masonic Temple building as belonging to a regular grand lodge. Its outer façade is impressive and is used for entertainment venues in addition to being the home of a number of irregular lodges in Brooklyn, NY. The group also has a Facebook page frequently visited and "liked" by many Freemasons throughout the world, and who are not aware that it does not fall under the jurisdiction of a recognized Masonic organization.

In keeping with the tradition of the mainstream and Prince Hall Affiliated's development of inter-fraternal Conference of Grand Masters, the unrecognized and irregular groups also participate in similar organizations. There is a self-styled umbrella grouping of the various grand lodges from 16 states and D.C. united under the General Grand Masonic Congress, Ancient Free and Accepted Masons of the United States of America.[32]

This group hosts an annual convention, discusses issues, and develops agreements. Ironically, there are actually seven different General Grand Masonic Congresses throughout the country each claiming to be the original legitimate Congress. In New York, there is an additional organization calling itself the Brotherhood of Grand Lodges. By their outward appearance, it is difficult for both Masons and the public to differentiate between these groups.

The African American Day Parade Dilemma

Adding to this public confusion, one only needs to look to the African American Day parade that has been held every September in Harlem, NY

---

32 The Chancellor Robert R Livingston Masonic Library of the Grand Lodge of New York, Cusick Collection.

since 1969. The parade features a Masonic Parade Section. Entrants to this section are represent at least 18 individual grand lodges in which only one (The Most Worshipful Prince Hall Grand Lodge of New York) is accepted as regular and recognized.

THE MECHANICS

As another example of the age-old legend of fraternal differences, the Independent United Order of Mechanics was founded in Lancashire, England, in 1757 "due to a schism" within a couple of their Masonic lodges. From there it spread to the Caribbean, the Netherlands, Central America, South Africa, and was founded in the United States in 1910. The order is still active today especially in those regions. The members meet as a lodge but do not refer to themselves as Masons, preferring to be called *Mechanics*.

The Mechanics' first six degrees are almost identical to the Masonic symbolic lodge degrees. There are other degrees that follow which are almost identical to the York and Capitular Rites of Freemasonry (e.g. Mark degrees, Royal Arch, and Knight Templar). Membership in the Mechanics is open to both males and females. With a presence in New York City, at the onset it is relatively easy to associate the Mechanics with styles traditionally worn by Masons.

This author estimates there are over 300 predominantly black Non-Prince Hall grand lodges in the United States that cannot prove their lineage to African Lodge No. 459. This compares with over 70 predominantly Caucasian or mainstream grand lodges that are also considered irregular, unrecognized, or clandestine (e.g., Grand Orient of the USA, Accepted Freemasons, Grand Lodge of All England, Grand Lodge of Ancient & Esoteric Freemasons, and the Regular Grand Lodge of England).[33]

THE REGULAR GRAND LODGE OF ENGLAND

The Regular Grand Lodge of England (RGLE) is also known as the Masonic High Council of the Ancient and Honourable Fraternity of Free and Accepted Masons, is said to have formed according to the Old Constitutions granted by His Royal Highness Prince Edwin at York A.D. 926. This High Council states that it derives its regularity from the "Act of Regularity" issued at Freemasons Arms, Covent Garden, London on 25

---

33 Paul M. Bessel. Email correspondence with author, 2010.

January 2005.[34]

The RGLE is of great interest as it has created the Masonic High Council of The United States of America for the purpose of establishing grand lodges in the US in recent years, as well as chartering many other clandestine/irregular Masonic organizations. This move served a mutual benefit because the unrecognized groups whose charters were not from a grand body of competent jurisdiction jumped at the opportunity to be associated with the RGLE so that they could claim that they had obtained "official charters from England" despite the fact that these English charters are no more legitimate for recognition as their previous state certificates of incorporation.

At their 2010 International Grand Assembly on November 11-14 in Virginia Beach, Virginia, the RGLE lists the following Grand Lodges as falling under their jurisdiction:

Regular Grand Lodge of Virginia	Regular Grand Lodge of Nevada
Regular Grand Lodge of Illinois	Regular Grand Lodge of New Jersey
Regular Grand Lodge of N. Carolina	Regular Grand Lodge of New York
Regular Grand Lodge of Texas	Regular Grand Lodge Of California
MHC of Utah	MHC of Florida

Regular Grand Lodge of Maryland

In 2005, the United Grand Lodge of England (UGLE) Grand Secretary, R. Morrow, issued a letter to the grand secretaries of grand lodges in amity with the UGLE warning them about the presence of this self-constituted irregular and unrecognized group. There is a dynamic problem posed by the RGLE to mainstream and PHA Masonry: in states where recognition does not exist between the mainstream and PHA Grand Lodges, this organization has appeared as a solution for those men who simply want to dwell together in unity without the entrapping issues of territory or cultural separation.

---

34 The Regular Grand Lodge of England. http://www.rgle.org.uk/RGLE_Act.htm Date Accessed January 29, 2015.

CONCLUSION

Despite conventional thinking, Freemasonry among the African American community should not be regarded as monolithic. While Prince Hall Affiliated is the oldest form of the Freemasonic fraternity in the African American community, estimates suggest that there are over 245 other Masonic organizations that exist and operate as such. Prince Hall Origin shares a unique relationship with the Prince Hall Affiliated groups with respect to common and disputed origin, and with divergence on the topic of recognition and regularity. The Non-Prince Hall groups are comprised of a vast number of unrecognized organizations that can be considered to be spurious, irregular, or clandestine, yet they operate and conduct themselves quite visibly in the African American community as legitimate Masonic entities.

Significant differences in the practice and presentation of Freemasonry exist within the African American population. This poses unique issues with respect to regularity and recognition. Most US mainstream grand lodges recognize Prince Hall Affiliated as their regular and legitimate counterpart; however, the differences illustrated here point to the need for systemic education and improved awareness among the rank and file members and leadership of both organizations. Many in mainstream Masonry make the error in categorizing this as a "Prince Hall problem", and one that does not impact or threaten the mainstream.

The ascendancy of social media, smartphones, Masonic discussion boards and forums, and other advances in telecommunications has removed the cocoon of isolation that once existed in the Craft. There are anecdotal reports of regular Masons interacting, and even inadvertently sitting in tiled meetings, with irregular Masons because they automatically assumed that the brother was a member of a recognized grand lodge, or was Prince Hall Affiliated. In addition, mainstream lodges are experiencing an increase of a generation of men who are looking for an integrated lodge experience that mirrors the diversity of their life course and experiences. With the frequency of travel and other opportunities for increased contact, the Masonic mindset might consider this a problem for all regular and recognized Masons.

It is also important to educate the community as to the differences and benefits of membership in recognized vs. unrecognized Masonic organizations. While Freemasonry does not recruit, it is important to develop initiatives that can allow a man to make a well-informed decision when he does choose Freemasonry so he can knock on the appropriate door. The findings underscore the need to use a unified approach among grand lodges to provide necessary education and dynamic opportunities for action from a universal perspective.

POSSIBLE SOLUTIONS

Data has shown that New York State has the distinct "honor" of having the largest number of unrecognized, irregular and clandestine grand lodges in the United States. A review of the official incorporation dates reveals that some of these groups have been around as early as 1907, while others have been created as recently as 2010. There is no clear answer as to why New York possesses so many unrecognized and irregular groups, but their impact and presence can continue to cause great confusion among the Craft and in the overall community. This issue, however, exists in every state in the Union.

As more men become attracted to Freemasonry, the topic of regularity will remain an area of important concern. Unfortunately, men are being duped into joining various clandestine, bogus, and irregular organizations all over the United States, believing that they are being regularly initiated into the world's largest and oldest fraternity. In fact, it was only within the last decade that concise information has been made available publicly in order to identify many of these groups and educate the membership on the importance of regularity.

However, significant damage has already been done: with the outward appearance of these groups mirroring that of recognized jurisdictions, many Masons and the general public simply cannot tell the difference. Members of the irregular groups have a resounding belief that they are Freemasons, practicing the tenets of the fraternity with corresponding concordant and appendant bodies, charities, conventions, councils, etc.

They continue to exist, and in some cases grow, despite having irregular charters that are based upon their incorporation (as in the case of NY under the New York State Division of Corporations, and not a just and duly constituted body of competent jurisdiction). Others are detestable money-making schemes that defraud men in order to obtain "Masonic degrees." Those initiated into these groups soon find that there are substantial deficiencies and discrepancies with respect to practice and experience. An additional cost to our fraternity's legacy is the fact that the public develops a false impression of Freemasonry based upon the actions of those affiliated with bogus groups.

Once this issue is brought to light, the natural reaction has always turned to what can be done. The author does not purport to have authority to develop, plan, or implement policies for any grand lodge jurisdiction. The following are only recommendations, which may serve as possible solutions that can be adopted for a unified response to this issue.

A UNIFIED RECLAMATION OF REGULARITY PROGRAM

The outcomes of this suggested program may improve the healthy practice of speculative Freemasonry in each US state via the enhanced awareness, and reduction, of the risk of membership in irregular organizations.

The aims of the *Reclamation of Regularity Program* would be to:

Aim 1: Increase awareness of the general population to the inherent advantages of choosing regular Freemasonry for themselves and their families.

Aim 2: Assist these communities in their understanding of how to achieve regular membership for themselves and their families.

Aim 3: To provide necessary tools and products to ensure that residents can have a safer and healthier Masonic experience as a result of the Program.

In order to continue to obtain the programmatic aims and goals, objectives should be set forth to ensure that they are being met and reviewed on a continual basis. Programmatic objectives should be specific, measurable, achievable, realistic, and time-bound. For example, in states where the mainstream and Prince Hall Affiliated grand lodges share amity, the two may:

- Develop, monitor and improve the *Reclamation of Regularity Program* within their state over a 5-year period implementation.

- Expose all in the target communities to consistent and repeated messages using multimedia presentations, internet-based marketing/educational tools, and other resources such as featured links, web/pod casts and related information on both of the official websites of the mainstream and Prince Hall Affiliated grand lodges where amity exists. This creates a method to actively engage and educate the irregular Mason on the path to and advantages of regularity without embarking in direct Masonic interaction.

Goal 1: Internal Awareness

- Increase the internal education on the two regular and recognized Masonic grand lodges in each state.

- Improve the internal awareness of the irregular, unrecognized and clandestine practices that exist in a state through the implementation of unified lodge education and presentations in the various regular and recognized Masonic districts.

- Increase the number of visitations and interactions among the two recognized jurisdictions in order to improve fraternal solidarity and provide a visible deterrent to the confusion and misperceptions of Masonic regularity and irregularity.

Goal 2: External Public Knowledge

- Increase the number of men and families who have a better understanding of what regular Freemasonry is through the implementation of speaking engagements and presentations at Masonic events.

- Educate state residents on the risk of joining irregular and unrecognized groups and bogus organizations.

- Decrease the number of inadvertent errors of joining irregular and unrecognized Freemasonry through the distribution of unified written and online educational messaging on the benefits of a regular path to membership.

Goal 3: Target the Irregular Mason Tactically and Tactfully

- Increase their education on regularity in each state through the implementation of unified mass media, multimedia messaging and various educational resources available highlighting the benefits of joining regular and recognized Freemasonry.

- Outline the methodology in place for the irregular Mason if he so desires to renounce his membership in an irregular, bogus and clandestine lodge and, if found worthy, to petition a just and duly constituted lodge under either of the two regular and recognized grand lodges in each state.

LONG TERM ASSESSMENT AND OUTLOOK

The program will continue to target all areas of each state that are in high risk categories for the above mentioned concerns of the *Reclamation of Regularity Program*. The use of an established low cost but effective online educational and referral system remains key. This unified approach will secure that appropriate procedures are in place whereby activities are monitored and reviewed on a quarterly basis.

The intended outlook of the *Reclamation of Regularity Program* is to consistently demonstrate the capacity for furthering the advantages of regular Freemasonry in all areas of planning, programming and community service development and it will become well recognized for the benefits it will produce. We should remain dedicated to new initiatives and fervently seek new collaborative opportunities for the overall betterment of our Craft and the community as a whole.

Table 1:

Name of Grand Lodge	Year Founded
MW King Solomon Grand Lodge AF&AM of New York, Inc.	1907
MW Hiram Grand Lodge AF&AM	**1908**
Grand United Masonic Orient	1928
Serenisima Gran Logia De Lengua Espanola Para Estados Unidos	1933
Grand Lodge, Ancient Universal Mysteries, Grand Orient of America Inc.	1935
MW Enoch Grand Lodge of New York, Inc.	1944
MW Mount Carmel Grand Lodge of Ancient York Rite, Inc.	1949
Universal Grand Lodge	1954
MW Alpha Grand Lodge of New York, Inc.	1957
MW Athenian Grand Lodge of New York, Inc.	1961
MW Mt. Nebo Grand Lodge of New York	1964
Tyree Grand Lodge	1966
St. John's Grand Lodge	1968
MW Orient Grand Lodge of New York, Inc.	1969
MW Canaan Grand Lodge,	1969
Oriental Grand Lodge AF&AM of the State of NY	1969
Omega Grand Lodge, AF&AM, New York State, Northern Jurisdiction, Incorporated	1970
Empire State Grand Lodge	1973
MW King George Grand Lodge	1974
Supreme Council Of The 33rd Degree Of The AASR Of Free Masonry Of The State Of Louisiana	1974
St Jude Grand Lodge	1975
King David Grand Lodge	1975
Mack Wright GL of AASRM	1979
Cornerstone Grand Lodge	1982

MW Grand Lodge of AF&AM	1983
GL Haitienne de St. Jean des Orients d'Outre-Mer	1983
MW Herbert C. Lee Grand Lodge	1986
MW Independent Bethlehem Grand Lodge, AF&AM, Inc	1986
MW Henefer GL	1987
MW United Orient Grand Lodge	1990
Grand Lodge of the Ancient and Primitive Oriental Rite of Memphis, Misraim, Memphis-Misraim, Inc	1990
MW Mystic Tie Grand Lodge	1991
MW Doric Grand Lodge, Inc. AF&AM	1991
MW New Amsterdam Grand Lodge	1991
International F&A Masons & Eastern Stars, Inc.	1991
St Johns Grand Lodge & Harriet Tubman Grand Chapter	1993
Excelsior State Grand Lodge Of Ancient Free Mason	1994
Harmony Supreme Council A&ASR	1996
MW Moorish Grand Lodge AF&AM,	2001
Sons of Heskeith Grand Lodge	2002
Royal International Supreme Council, Western Hemisphere	2003
MW Grand Corinthian Lodge, Inc.	2003
Royal International Supreme Council, Western Hemisphere	2003
New Amsterdam GL AF&AM	2004
Sovereign Moorish Grand Lodge of the Americas	2008
Regular Grand Lodge of New York	2008
Grande Lodge Nepthali	2010
Regular Grand Lodge of NY, Ancient & Honorable Fraternity of Free Masons, Inc	2010
French Speaking Grand Lodge of Haitian Masons	
Guyanese Grand Lodge	
MW Mt. Ephraim Grand Lodge	
MW Edwin Sturrup Grand Lodge of New York, Inc.	
St Raphael Grand Lodge	
MW Sons of Zebedee Grand Lodge AF&AM, Jurisdiction of New York	
Superior Grand Lodge Jurisdiction of New York, Inc.	
MW Sons of Haiti Grand Lodge	
United Moorish Grand Lodge	
Waset Grand Lodge	
Nimrod Grand Lodge	
Sons of Light Grand Lodge	
Continental Grand Lodge	
MW St. Mark Grand Lodge	
MW Mt. Calvary Grand Lodge	
MW Hiram Abif Grand Lodge	
MW Zerubbabel Grand Lodge	
MW St. Andrew Grand Lodge	
Nuwaupian Grand Lodge	
King James Grand Lodge	
King Cyrus Grand Lodge AF&AM	
Unity Grand Lodge AF&AM	
Mecca Grand Lodge AASR	
Esoteric Grand Lodge of America, Inc.	

Source: New York State Department of State, Division of Corporations; the PHA Commission on Bogus Masonic Practices: http://www.thephylaxis.org/bogus/; Paul M. Bessel Masonic Research website: http://bessel.org.

III

THE CITY OF LONDON AND ITS MEDIEVAL GUILDS AND ITS INFLUENCE ON THE STRUCTURE FREEMASONRY

YASHA BERESINER

DISCLAIMER

The presentation looks at the origins of the organisational *structure* of Freemasonry at the time of its foundation in London 1717.

There are two subjects which this paper is *not* intended to cover:

a) It is not to be confused with the ongoing arguments as to the relationship of the Craft with medieval trade guilds and

b) It avoids the question of the supposed foundation of organised freemasonry on 22 June 1717 as reported—for the first time—by James Anderson 21 years later, in his 2nd Constitutions published in 1738.

GRAND LODGE OF ENGLAND

The Grand Lodge of England, as the Governing Body of Craft Freemasonry controlling subordinate Lodges, was set up sometime prior to June 1717. It consisted then, as it does now, of a Grand Master at its head, his Grand Wardens and Grand Officers, *inter alia,* ruling over a number of Lodges, each with its own accountable Worshipful Master, Lodge Officers and members. The activities of the Lodge, following the ritual, revolve around convivial dining and charity.

ADOPTED & NOT PROGRESSIVE

The contention in this paper is that the format of this initial structure of

Freemasonry did not develop or progress in stages, but was 'lifted' in toto from the structure that comprised the medieval City of London in the previous century.

CITY GUILDS

The 17th Century saw the culmination of the City Guilds system that had previously been in total control of social, commercial and administrative aspects of City Life. The Liverymen elected the Lord Mayor from amongst their own membership. The Lord Mayor and his Sheriffs (a much older institution as will be shown), ruled over the City Livery Companies, each of which had an independent Master and Officers presiding over their trade membership and intent on work -practice, festivities and charity.

ANALOGY

The analogy is obvious and the time frame is as clear: organised Freemasonry began in 1717, the City structure as described, is discernible at the start of Norman England in the 11th Century. How, then, did the City structure, adopted so comprehensively by Freemasonry, originate?

PREMIER GRAND LODGE

Considering first, the foundation of the Premier Grand Lodge on 22nd June 1717, there are no contemporary sources of any kind available on the supposed events that took place at the time. The first and only source for these events is James Anderson (1680-1739), in his second Constitutions published more than two decades later in 1738, on whose account all historians have had to rely. As mentioned at the start of this paper, this is an argument not to be pursued now.

CONSTITUTIONS & REGULATIONS

The first Constitutions of 1723 have a fictitious, at best legendary, history of Freemasonry which mentions Prince Edwin as Grand Master of the Masons assembled in York in 926 AD. Although most the Old Charges also mention Edwin, son of King Athelstan, none make a reference to a 'Grand Master.' The General Regulations incorporated into the first Constitutions, were the creation of George Payne (d. 1757) in 1720, as evidenced by the entry on page 58 of the Constitutions themselves.

UNDEFINED STRUCTURE

In the thirty-nine Regulations that follow, there are no references to the structure of the newly formed Institutions, outside of Regulation XII, which states:

> The Grand Lodge consist of, and is form'd by the Masters and Wardens of all the regular particular Lodges upon Record, with the Grand-Master at their Head, and his Deputy on his Left-hand, and the Grand-Wardens in their proper Places; [...]

The paragraph continues with the now familiar composition of Grand Lodge, the appointment of a Secretary and Treasurer, Tyler etc. It is worth noting that the term 'Grand Master' is here used for the first time and, as mentioned above, none of the documentation, the ancient charges and regulations, including the Scottish William Schaw (c1550-1602) Statutes of 1599, speak of a 'Grand Master' prior to these Constitutions of 1723.

CITY STRUCTURE

The structure of the City of London, meanwhile, which culminated with the election of the first Mayor, Henry Fitz-Ailwin de Londonestone in 1189, traces its origins to the Anglo-Saxon period of King Alfred the Great (849-899). Governance of Saxon Society revolved around the King, elected by the Witan, the Council of wise-men selected from the nobility. As the Kingdom grew, the King could only rule and collect taxes due to him by the appointment of 'ealdorman,' a concept very familiar today.

NORMAN LONDON

With the advent of the Norman conquest of England—but not of the walled City of London—special privileges were granted to the citizens, which in time included the election of their own Mayor. The City of London, its boundaries still identified by the Roman wall, was the only region in England that enjoyed such a privilege, granted because the commercial power of the City was recognised by the King. Throughout the rest of the Kingdom, in the Shires or Counties of England, the Monarch's appointed Shire Reeves, the familiar Sheriffs of today, who played their part in communicating the King's wishes, collecting taxes and enforcing the King's law.

EARLY GUILDS

By the mid-12th century, the Guild system, which had began as friendly and fraternal societies in Saxon times, had reached levels of sophistication and power that allowed them to control the City. The division of the City of London into 25 wards allowed for the administration to be divided into 25 Aldermen and a number of Councilmen for each ward. Concepts that eventually led to the establishment of the House of Lords and House of Commons respectively.

GUILD INFLUENCE

Meanwhile the Guilds or Livery Companies ruled in the City by legislation that allowed them to elect their own Lord Mayor, supported by his own two Sheriffs and given the responsibility of heading the City Guilds, each of which had its own Master, independently responsible with elected members of the Livery.

DECLINE OF THE GUILDS

This system was in place for the best part of six centuries and came to an end with the expansion of trade to nations beyond the seas, the final blow coming in the form of the devastating fire of London of 1666, which put an end to the trade monopoly of many of the guilds.

WORK IN PROGRESS

The subsequent history of the City guilds, their survival to this day as charitable if somewhat sophisticated organisations, is beyond the scope of this paper. However, the possibility, even likelihood, that George Payne adopted the well established City Guild structure, to give the newly born organised body an acceptable and guaranteed format, must be realistically feasible.

CREDITS AND BIBLIOGRAPHY

John Belton

Brent Morris

Andreas Rizopoulos

Berchin, Derek, *Discovering London Series,* London: MacDonald, 1969.

Beresiner, Yasha, *City of London —A Masonic Guide,* Lewis, 2003.

Corporate Authors, *City Livery Companies,* London: Guildhall, 2006.

Unwin, George, *The Gilds and Companies of London,* Frank Kass, 1963.

Vibert, Lionel, [Introduction] *The Constitutions of Freemasons 1723: Reproduced in Facsimile from the Original Edition [...],* London: Quaritch, 1923.

IV

FREEMASONRY—THE MISSING LINK BETWEEN JACOBITISM AND THE AMERICAN REVOLUTION?

SAMUEL BIAGETTI

"WHY IS THERE NO JACOBITISM IN AMERICA?" This question, to my knowledge, has never been asked, let alone adequately answered—although it may turn out to be as significant to scholars' understanding of the eighteenth century as Werner Sombart's famous question about the lack of socialism in America is to the nineteenth. It has never been asked, presumably, because the Jacobite party—the movement that sought to restore the deposed Stuart dynasty to the English and Scottish throne—was traditionalist, royalist, rife with Roman Catholics, and vaguely Francophile, and hence was the antithesis of everything that we take early Anglo-America to be—Protestant, Whiggish, Enlightened, and proto-democratic. Hence, Jacobite sentiments are assumed, rather than argued, to be alien to American soil. Scholars have held to this assumption despite the awkward fact that American patriots in the 1760s and early 1770s asserted the supremacy of the Crown over Parliament, closely echoing Jacobite arguments; historians have shown the same squeamishness that William Knox, the colonial agent for Georgia, expressed in 1769, when he wrote that the American Whigs "must see, that if they reject parliamentary authority, they make themselves still to be subjects of the abjured Stuart race. This however is too delicate a matter to say more upon."[1]

We may, two and a half centuries later, violate Mr. Knox's sense of delicacy by asking what relationship Jacobitism, which spawned two major rebellions in Britain, might have had to the more successful uprising in America. The historian Brendan McConville points out that the Stuart dynasty experienced something of a vogue of popularity in North America after 1750, with colonial assemblies displaying portraits of the Stuart kings in

---

1 William Knox, *The Controversy Between Great Britain and her Colonies, Reviewed* (London, 1769) 138, quoted in Eric Nelson, *The Royalist Revolution* (Cambridge, Mass.: Harvard University Press, 2014) 43.

their chambers while miniatures sold briskly on colonial streets—but he denies that this fashion for the Stuarts reflected any desire to restore their descendants to the throne.[2] Nonetheless, in the small colony of Rhode Island, records suggest that colonists were fascinated with Jacobitism. For instance, when the Providence Library Company, founded largely by Freemasons, burned down in 1758, only those books checked out at the time survived; these sixty titles included no fewer than five books on the Jacobite movement, in addition to two by the Chevalier Andrew Michael Ramsay, a famous Jacobite and Masonic author who promoted the notion that the Fraternity was descended from the Crusading knightly orders.[3] In addition, in 1775, the Reverend Ezra Stiles of Newport recorded hosting an Irish Protestant minister from Nova Scotia who claimed to have met Charles Edward Stuart, the so-called "Young Pretender," three times and asserted that the exiled prince was secretly a Protestant.[4]

Whatever we might make of the private feelings of American colonists toward the House of Stuart, we can easily establish that participation in the Jacobite cause in the earlier half of the eighteenth century did not preclude active support for the American Revolution in the latter half. The example of Hugh Mercer, a Scottish physician who migrated to America, is sufficient to demonstrate this point: after serving as a surgeon for the Jacobite forces in the failed uprising of 1745, Mercer relocated to Fredericksburg, Virginia, where he practiced medicine. A close friend of George Washington, during the Revolution he took up the office of Brigadier-General in the Continental Army before dying of wounds sustained in the Battle of Princeton in 1777.

Precisely how Hugh Mercer squared his Jacobite past with his Revolutionary actions in America may be impossible to know—but any hope for an answer must be sought in the more private and secretive sphere that our friend Mr. Knox considered too delicate to discuss in print. Specifically, Hugh Mercer was a Freemason, and affiliated in 1761 with the Fredericksburg Lodge, of which he later served as Worshipful Master. It is a long-established fact that Freemasonry has a peculiarly close relationship to Jacobitism, with British Jacobite exiles founding most of the earliest lodges on

---

2 Brendan McConville, *The King's Three Faces* (University of North Carolina Press, 2007) 193-205.

3 "The Providence Athenaeum: The Sixty Titles (71 Volumes) Saved from the Fire in 1758," Providence Athenaeum, <http://www.providenceathenaeum.org/collections/founders.pdf>, retrieved June 10, 2013, <http://www.librarything.com/catalog/ProvidenceAthenaeum>, retrieved June 10, 2013.

4 Franklin Bowditch Dexter, ed., *The Literary Diary of Ezra Stiles* (New York: Scribner and Sons, 1901), vol. 1, p. 534-6.

the European continent and the Jacobite Prince of Wales, Charles Edward Stuart, joining the Fraternity some time before 1745. However, historians have been just as reluctant to discuss and make sense of this Jacobite strain in eighteenth-century Masonry as William Knox was to discuss the Jacobite implications of American patriotism. Jessica Harland-Jacobs, in *Builders of Empire*, acknowledges the strange abundance of Jacobite Masons, but avoids the matter by concluding that Masonry had a "protean nature" and an "ability to accommodate a range of political positions in the eighteenth century."[5]

In fact, the connection between Jacobitism and Freemasonry was much more than a mere accident of eighteenth-century politics, and the strong overlap between the two movements should not be surprising, considering their shared commitment to kingship. The foundational documents of eighteenth-century Masonry reveal that the so-called "Royal Art" was positively obsessed with the sanctity of kingship. Masonic myths trace the formal organization of stonemasons to Solomon and Hiram of Tyre, divinely sanctioned monarchs who stood as intermediaries between the earthly and heavenly realms; as the "Master's Song" in Anderson's *Constitutions* declares of the Solomonic age, "The Royal Art was then divine, / The craftsmen counsell'd from above," and, "[n]o wonder then if Masons join, / To celebrate those Mason-Kings."[6] (Indeed, remarkably for a pamphlet that supposedly promoted proto-democratic Whiggism, the first edition of Anderson's *Constitutions* uses the word "royal" at least 29 times and "king" at least 36 times.) Similarly, Jacobite propaganda emphasized the sanctity of monarchy and the divine right of kings, associating the monarch with the pagan gods of virility and spring; the Stuart claimants in exile even continued the old custom of the "king's touch" as a cure for ailments.[7]

The obsession with kingship extended to all branches of eighteenth-century Masonry, including the Whiggish branch centering on the Grand Lodge in London. Although the leaders of the Premier Grand Lodge rejected the Stuarts' claim to the throne, they sought royal patronage from the House of Hanover, which they obtained with the initiation of Frederick, Prince

5   Jessica Harland-Jacobs, *Builders of Empire: Freemasons and British Imperialism, 1717-1927* (University of North Carolina Press, 2007) 109.

6   James Anderson, ed., *Constitutions of the Free-Masons* (London: William Hunter for John Senex, 1723) p. 77.

7   Paul Monod, *Jacobitism and the English People* (Cambridge University Press, 1993) 15-69, 127-8.

of Wales in 1737.[8] James Anderson, who penned the *Constitutions of the Free-Masons*, was a fervent monarchist who also published the obsessively thorough *Royal Genealogies; or, the Genealogical Tables of Emperors, Kings, and Princes, from Adam to these times.*[9] Although he was a Whig, Anderson was eager to proclaim his reverence for kingship: he published the sermon "No King-Killers" in 1715, in order to deny the Presbyterians' role in the execution of Charles I sixty-five years earlier; he dedicated the work to his mentor, Daniel Williams, "a profess'd and firm friend of monarchy and Presbytery, [who] ever asserted them to be highly consistent."[10]

Our Scottish physician, Hugh Mercer, was, like James Anderson, born in Aberdeen, Scotland, and his father was, like Anderson, a Presbyterian minister. Their similar backgrounds suggest that a similar Scottish brand of royalism could cross over from the Jacobite to the Hanoverian wing of British politics, with Freemasonry serving as the common denominator. Moreover, Hugh Mercer's migration to America and his entry into revolutionary politics suggest that Masonry might have further served as a connecting link between the Jacobite movement and the American Revolution. Indeed, most North American Masons who did take part in the Revolution practiced the Ancient Rite, the branch of Masonry that had been founded in the 1750s by largely Jacobite Irish Masons.

Nonetheless, the rites and ceremonies of "Ancient" Masonry were hardly distinguishable from their "Modern" counterparts. If Masonry transmitted any distinctively Jacobite ideas or practices to Revolutionary-era North America, they must be sought in the higher degrees. Indeed, the Fredericksburg Lodge over which Hugh Mercer presided was one of the first in the world known to confer the Royal Arch degree, the germ of all higher-degree systems, which developed among Jacobite circles in France or Ireland. More dramatically, the Rite of Perfection, an elaborate system of twenty-five higher degrees, developed among Jacobite Masons and their allies in France in the mid-eighteenth-century, and can be seen to reflect the Jacobites' anxieties over royal legitimacy. The Rite of Perfection spread from metropolitan France to the West Indies in the 1760s, where it continued to attract men connected to the Jacobite cause—so much so that one lodge of Perfection in Saint Domingue even took the name of

---

8   Harland-Jacobs, 109.

9   James Anderson, *Royal Genealogies; or, the Genealogical Tables of Emperors, Kings, and Princes, from Adam to these times.* London: James Bettenham, 1732.

10   W. J. Chetwode Crawley, "The rev. Dr. Anderson's non-Masonic Writing, 1712-1739," *Ars Quatuor Coronatorum*, (London: H. Keble), vol. 18, 1905, p. 30.

"Édouard Stuart" in honor of the exiled British dynasty.[11] The Rite spread eventually to North America; the first two Lodges of Perfection on the American mainland were at New Orleans and Albany, but each of these collapsed fairly quickly by 1774.

Shortly after these failed higher-degree lodges, Masons in Newport, Rhode Island, took up the Rite of Perfection in the 1770s. It was here, in Newport, that the Rite would survive the Revolution and find a permanent home. Moses Michael Hays, a Jewish merchant who had attained the degrees of Perfection several years earlier in New York, opened a lodge in Newport in June 1780, which he called "King David's." The founding members of King David's Lodge were mostly Jewish, Quaker, and Anglican merchants, along with a smattering of Continental Army officers. On July 10, 1780, just three weeks after the lodge's opening, a French expeditionary force under General Rochambeau arrived in Newport harbor and began quartering several thousand soldiers in the town. Nine days later, Jean-Louis de Sybille, the secretary to General Rochambeau, asked for admittance to the lodge. Not only was Sybille approved and soon after initiated, but over the ensuing year, while the French forces resided at Newport, thirteen French military officers followed Rochambeau's secretary into the lodge.[12] Claude Blanchard, the commissary to the French forces, remarked on the openness with which American Masons marched and displayed their regalia in public—a spectacle unknown in France. On February 7, 1781, Blanchard himself was initiated by his own secretary, M. de Jumecourt, a "zealous free mason," and attended two more receptions at an American lodge; as he remarked in his journal, "I was then nearly 39 years old. This was beginning rather late."[13]

Blanchard's and Sybille's initiations into Masonry in Rhode Island suggest that the Fraternity served as a social cement to the Franco-American alliance. What is more, the makeup of King David's Lodge—Anglicans, Quakers, and French Catholics, allied in opposition to a Hanoverian king—perfectly mirrors that of the Jacobite-Masonic circles in France that originally conceived of the Rite of Perfection. The Rhode Island Masons could hardly have missed this remarkable concordance.

More specifically, the French expeditionary force stationed in Newport comprised four regiments, one of which hailed from Saintonge, a rural

11 André Kervella, *L'Effet Morin* (Ivoire-Claire, 2010) 172-3.

12 King David's Lodge Log Book, 1780-1790, Saint John's Lodge no. 1, Portsmouth, R. I.

13 Thomas Balch, ed., *The Journal of Claude Blanchard* (Arno Press, 1969) 88.

region north of Bordeaux that had long been a hotbed of mystical het-
erodoxy; at least one French officer who joined King David's Lodge in
Newport, Major de Fleury, is known to have belonged to the Saintongeais
regiment.[14] Saintonge was also the homeland of Bernard Palissy, the six-
teenth-century Huguenot potter and alchemist who had come to symbolize the encoding of esoteric beliefs in primitive forms. Benjamin Franklin,
during his diplomatic mission to Paris to procure French support for the
American Revolution, took on the persona of a rustic artisan, and French
printers posited a "great analogue" between Franklin and Palissy.[15] Franklin, of course, went on to affiliate with the famous Loge des Neuf Soeurs
in Paris.

In sum, Freemasonry can be seen to bring a greater emotional depth to the
Franco-American alliance by evoking the past, including the Jacobite legacy. More specifically, the Rite of Perfection offered a means of reconciling
the conflict between the royalism of Freemasonry on the hand and revolutionary republicanism on the other. The outbreak of revolution in North
America in 1775-6 triggered a wave of iconoclasm, with previously loyal
subjects attacking statues, coats of arms, and other signs of royal authority,
suggesting a violent emotional break with the old order.[16] The myths and
rituals of the Masonic higher degrees could help to defuse the psychic
conflict of rebellion against an anointed king. The first nine degrees of the
Rite of Perfection (the 4th through the 12th degrees of Masonry, according
to this scheme) deal with the aftermath of the murder of Hiram Abiff,
dramatizing the month-long quest to avenge the master builder's death.
These degrees deal with the dilemmas of conflicting loyalties; their lessons
are ambiguous and inconclusive. For instance, in the 9th degree, "Master
Elected of Nine," the initiate plays the role of Joabert, a Masonic workman
sent to apprehend one of Hiram's three assassins. Joabert locates the fugitive in a cave but breaks King Solomon's commands by killing him on the
spot rather than returning him to Jerusalem to stand trial. When Joabert
reports to Solomon's palace, the king orders him executed, but his fellow
Masons intercede, obtaining clemency for Joabert on the grounds that, "it
was an excess of zeal and love for the memory of our respectable Master
H[iram] A[bif] that had certainly prompted him to disobey his orders."

14 "Etat des Logements dans la ville de Newport aux orders de M's le Comte de
Rochambeau Quartier-General." / "Winter Quarters of Soldiers under the Command of Rochambeau in Newport, RI," Vault A, Mss Box A-16, Rochambeau
and the French in Newport, Papers and miscellaneous, 1760s-1940, Newport
Historical Society, Newport, R. I.

15 Neil Kamil, *Fortress of the Soul* (Baltimore: Johns Hopkins University Press) 272-5.

16 Brendan McConville, *The King's Three Faces: The Rise and Fall of Royal America*
(Chapel Hill: University of North Carolina Press, 2006) 281-303.

The lecture following the ritual declares both the necessity of following orders precisely and "how easily the heart of a good king is influenced to be merciful," without resolving the tension between these two notions.[17]

The conflicts and ambiguities of the first nine degrees of the Rite are partly resolved by the Royal Arch and the degree of Perfection, which serve as the 13th and 14th degrees of the Rite. They recount the recovery of the lost true and ineffable name of God, which Masons find in a vault and deliver to King Solomon. After the destruction of Jerusalem by the Assyrians, the Masons preserve the true name among themselves. Taken together, the fourteen degrees from the Apprentice degree to the Perfection seek to preserve the holiness of kingship while gradually transferring it from monarchs to the Masons themselves. At the opening of the Perfection degree, the Worshipful Master anoints each candidate's eyes, lips, and heart with oil representing that which anointed "the penitent David and the wise Solomon." When The lecture of the degree declares that the Masons work "in secret places, to re-establish the edifice ruined by the traitors, under the protection of the sovereign and sublime princes," it may as well be describing the Jacobite movement. In the immediately ensuing degrees, the Masonic candidate begins to take upon himself the authority of earthly kings. Firstly, in the fifteenth degree, "Knight of the East," the candidate plays the role of Zerubbabel, a Jewish elder who successfully petitions the Persian emperor Cyrus for permission to return to Jerusalem and rebuild the Temple. The lecture of the following degree, Prince of Jerusalem, declares that, "For their great zeal, courage, and knowledge [the Masons] obtained the title of governors of the people."[18] Finally, in the twentieth degree, the candidate leaves behind the role of Zerubbabel and takes on that of the Emperor himself.

Ultimately, the conflict between a deep attachment to kingship and the new republican order could be reconciled through apocalypticism. Kings, in the apocalyptic world-view, serve as temporary intermediaries, representing divine authority on earth; God's direct intervention in worldly affairs renders human kingship unnecessary. The Masons, according to the higher degrees, must prepare the world for a moral renovation and the millennium. The arrival of American envoys in Paris led some French observers to describe the American Revolution in apocalyptic terms, with Franklin standing in for the primitive artisan who, like the Prophet Elijah, would reveal the secrets of nature and herald the restoration of Eden.[19]

17 Francken Manuscript 1783, 76, 80.

18 Francken Manuscript 1783, p. 201-2.

19 Kamil, *Fortess of the Soul*, 272-3.

The same train of thought—the questioning of royal authority leading to apocalyptic hopes—can be seen in the later degrees of the Rite of Perfection. The candidate ascends the political ladder at the same time that he climbs a spiritual ladder, approaching an enlightenment that renders the political order obsolete. The ritual of the seventeenth degree, "Knight of the East and West," takes place in a lodge illuminated by sun and moon figures. The Master of the lodge draws objects one by one out of a chest or trunk with seven compartments, re-enacting the breaking of the seven seals described in the Book of Revelations. On the opening of the sixth compartment, the sun goes dark and the moon "is stained with blood." The breaking of the seventh seal reveals seven trumpets which are sounded as the candidate receives the apron, jewels, and crown of the degree, "to show that a good mason is equal to the most high prince."[20] The Masons' future dominion is represented in the trestle board of the nineteenth degree, that of "Grand Pontif," as a heavenly Jerusalem, whose walls are a perfect square pierced by twelve gates, and at the center of which grows, as in the Garden, the Tree of Life.[21]

In the culmination of the Rite of Perfection, the 23rd or "Knight of the Sun" degree, human and earthly institutions are superseded by God's representatives: the candidate is instructed to cultivate an alchemically purified body, "from which must come a new king and a revolution in fullness of time, filled with glory." The Mason himself becomes the instrument of a divine mandate to re-establish the peace and harmony of Eden and the "one and true religion, and the same which Adam received from God." [22] The overthrow of worldly authority, which the Hanovers embodied for the American revolutionaries as well as for the Jacobites, went hand in hand with a religious restoration and the return of human affairs to their prelapsarian innocence. A "revolution" was the completion of both a political and a cosmic cycle.

The Rite of Perfection embodies a stream of thought connecting the Jacobite movement with the American Revolution, and in so doing, it illustrates the depth of the revolutionaries' dilemma. The break with the Crown demanded deep mental, emotional, and philosophical change. The ritual texts show the influences of eighteenth-century religious writings, such as Andrew Michael Ramsay's *Travels of Cyrus* of 1727, which depicts the Persian prince voyaging through the ancient world and discerning the primitive religious truth underlying all religions, including the unity of

---

20 Francken Manuscript 1783, p. 207-9.

21 Ibid, 219-20.

22 Ibid, 248.

God and humanity's fall from grace and eventual redemption. Likewise, elements of the higher degrees echo the teachings of the English mystic William Law, a nonjuring Jacobite, who identified the Sun with God's undying creative fire. Law rejected the notion of creation *ex nihilo* in favor of an eternal, cyclical universe; the lecture of the twenty-first degree similarly claims that, "9000 years before the era of Adam this world did exist."[23] Law's 1726 *A Practical Treatise Upon Christian Perfection* probably supplied the title of the Rite of Perfection. The revolutionary restoration envisioned by Ramsay, Law, and the authors of the higher degrees was anti-political rather than democratic or egalitarian, looking to the institution of a divine, spiritual authority on earth.

These observations on Freemasonry in general and on the Rite of Perfection in particular do not demonstrate that any American Revolutionaries were Jacobites per se—that they actually wished for a Stuart restoration. However, they are intended to suggest that a set of myths and rituals, developed in response to an earlier crisis of the British monarchy, later helped American colonists to cope with the breakdown of royal authority in America. Freemasonry was the vehicle for these myths and rituals, which helped to make sense of both American independence and the Franco-American alliance as stages in an unfolding millennium. The Jacobite legacy and its influence both on Freemasonry and on the American Revolution must be explored and taken seriously; academic historians have long ignored the persistence of Jacobitism in both Europe and America, preferring a progressive history of continual secularization and democratization. This Whiggish mythology must give way to an appreciation of how those who made history continually re-enacted the past.

---

23 Young, *Religion and Enlightenment*, 130-5; George Henderson, *Chevalier Ramsay* (Nelson, 1952): 124-9; Francken Manuscript 1783, 236-7.

V

RESHAPING VIRTUE: THE CASE OF EIGHTEENTH-CENTURY FRENCH AND ITALIAN MASONIC POETRY

GIULIA DELOGU, PH.D
Università degli studi di Trieste

ABSTRACT

Virtue appears to be a central theme in eighteenth-century masonic poetry. Following Voltaire's lead, who affirmed: "À chanter la vertu j'ai consacré ma voix. / Vainqueur des préjugés que l'imbécile encense,/ j'ose aux persécuteurs prêcher la tolérance" (Épître à Boileau ou mon testament, 1769), French freemason poets devoted their poetic efforts to virtue. The very same *leit-motiv* can be found in Italy: Tommaso Crudeli, the first martyr of Italian Freemasonry, solemnly committed his "lyre" to "virtue" in *Il Trionfo della Ragione* (1767). But what did this devotion to virtue imply? For many it meant putting poetry to the service of the common good, composing poems which on on hand disclosed the vices of society, on the other hinted virtuous models to be followed. This is the case of Emmanuel Carbon Flins des Oliviers. The French poet, who belonged to the renowned Parisian lodge des *Neuf Sœurs*, harshly criticized the Church, while making the great *philosophe* "un apôtre de la liberté politique et de la tolérance" in his poem *Voltaire* (1779). Conversely, virtue meant also retreat from the everyday *mêlée*, the ability to detach oneself from the basest human passions and to live accordingly a pristine ingenuity; in short virtue was the attribute of the Golden Age people. The freemason poets Jean-Baptiste Gresset, Jacques Delille, Aurelio de' Giorgi Bertola and Ippolito Pindemonte all longed for the (lost) Age of Astraea, but they also tried to find possible modern replicas in the virtuous and simple "vie champêtre" of shepherds and farmers. Similarly, masonic *chansons* celebrated lodges as the true return to a natural egalitarian status and thus as 'Schools of Virtue'. Between the late 1770s and the early 1780s new tendencies emerged, chiefly a syncretic and encyclopedic will, whose aim was to embrace the reality (and the super-reality) in its wholeness. Antoine Roucher and Antonio Jerocades well incarnate this new 'poetry of fusion', which applies also to virtue. In their poetic masterpieces, *Les Mois* and the *Lira Focense* respectively, the two freemason poets tried to present an 'ecumenical' version of virtue, blending together Enlightenment, masonic, Christian and classical motives.

My aim is to reconstruct the process through which freemason poets reshaped the concept of virtue in novel and productive ways. In fact, I believe that they contributed to create a new masonic morality, which combined spiritual and secular values. Moreover, I am convinced that a new model of Great Man stemmed from this renovated *ethos*: the virtuous freemason. Between the late Eighteenth-Century and the early Nineteenth-century, freemason *savants* such as Voltaire, Lalande, Dupaty, Filangieri and Mascheroni became the object of a true cult, thanks to the poetic composition of their Brothers, anticipating the revolutionary secular cult of Marat and Napoleon's personal propaganda.

FREEMASONRY, VIRTUE AND POETRY

My research deals with Freemasonry, poetry and virtue and I think we should start by asking ourselves why Freemasonry? Why poetry? Why virtue?

Italian historian Gian Mario Cazzaniga affirmed: it is impossible to study the Eighteenth century and the Enlightenment without taking into account Freemasonry.[1] For instance we can remember the importance of Freemasonry in shaping the routes of the *Grand Tour*, an importance which has been well established, particularly by Pierre-Yves Beaurepaire.[2] Freemasons travelled all over the Continent, meeting Brothers and *savants*, bringing new ideas with them. In other words, during the eighteenth century Freemasonry was a key player. Freemasonry had a European dimension, which fostered contacts between Brethren from different countries.

---

1   Cazzaniga, Gian Mario. *Symboles, signes, langages sacrés: pour une sémiologie de la franc-maçonnerie. Actes du Colloque franco-italien, Paris, le 25 mars 1994.* ETS : Pisa, 1995. 11: "Il devrait être très difficile de s'occuper de la modernité, et en particulier des Lumières, sans se poser le problème de la signification et du rôle de la Franc-maçonnerie. Il s'agit d'une institution qui a eu une remarquable fonction d'organisation culturelle, [...] une vrai République des lettres, qui visait à devenir république tout court."

2   Beaurepaire, Pierre-Yves. "Grand tour, République des lettres e reti massoniche: una cultura della mobilità nell'Europa dei lumi." *La Massoneria. Storia d'Italia, Annali. XXI.* Ed. Gian Mario Cazzaniga. Einaudi: Torino, 2006. 31-89.

The fascination for the square and compass affected 'great men' from Europe to the Americas. Voltaire, Lalande, Dupaty, Montesquieu, Mirabeau, Franklin, Washington, Hamilton, Pope, Lessing, Goethe, Herder, Maffei, Bertola and Filangieri all were freemasons.

As far as poetry is concerned, during the Eighteenth century it was a fundamental and powerful medium. Poems, often oral and occasional in character, were less subject to censorship and thus circulated widely. Consequently, they were a perfect instrument for the diffusion of ideas. The traditional view of the age of the Enlightenment as an era of rationalism, and therefore not poetic, strongly contrasts with the reality of eighteenth century culture, in which poems and songs were composed for all manner of events (birth, baptism, graduation, marriage, monacation, victory, death) and countless people fancied themselves poets. In a word, poetry was epidemic.[3] But why poetry was so powerful? Italian historian Luciano Guerci observes that while treatises and discourses spoke to the "mind", poems were able to speak to the "heart,"[4] or, as Hans Ulrich Gumbrecht puts it: "poetry can make things 'present.'"[5] In addition, as the French scholar Béatrice Didier maintains poetry could reach even the lowest social classes, thus having the "privilege to address even the illiterate."[6] Finally, Amedeo Quondam, referring to eighteenth and nineteenth century Italy, spoke of "supremacy of poetry."[7]

Coming finally to virtue, the Eighteenth century was obsessed with the concept of virtue. The freemason poet Tommaso Crudeli solemnly committed his "lyre" to "virtue," Brissot glowed to emulate the ancient virtues of Phocion, the Greek hero portrayed by Plutarch, and young Alessandro Manzoni identified the pillars of both morality and poetry in truth and virtue. In other words, virtue was omnipresent. Now, eighteenth-century virtue is a complex and multifaceted concept which embraces secular and spiritual meanings. It is therefore very difficult to grasp. Many underlined

---

3   Darnton, Robert. *The Devil in the Holy Water or the Art of Slander from Louis XIV to Napoleon*. University of Pennsylvania Press: Philadelphia, 2010: "By 1789, France had developed a large subculture of indigent authors—672 poets alone, according to one contemporary estimate".

4   Guerci, Luciano. *Istruire nelle verità repubblicane. La letteratura politica per il popolo nell'Italia in rivoluzione (1796-1799)* Il Mulino: Bologna, 1999.

5   Gumbrecht, Hans Ulrich. "Presence." *The Princeton Encyclopedia of Poetry and Poetics*. Princeton University Press: Princeton, 2012. 1105.

6   Didier, Béatrice. *La littérature de la Révolution française*. Presses Universitaires de France Paris, 1988. 89.

7   Quondam, Amedeo. *Risorgimento a memoria. Le poesie degli italiani*. Donzelli: Roma, 2011. 10.

its secular character, reconstructing the disenchantment process which led towards a rediscovery of the ancient virtue of the Greeks and the Romans. This rediscovery, began during the Humanism and after that the Renaissance, had certainly a great influence in the way eighteenth-century people perceived virtue and ethics. However, religion continued to play a very important part: secularized though some intellectuals might have been, the vast majority of eighteenth century people still had a strong connection with religious beliefs.

MASONIC POETRY, OR THE PATH TOWARDS VIRTUE

I believe (and I'll try to convince you too) that the best way to understand eighteenth-century virtue is analyzing it through masonic poetry. Masonic poems were exactly that kind of poems able to "speak to the heart" and therefore to show people the path towards virtue. The majority of the texts were, in fact, combined with a musical score. Hence the poems-songs were designed to be performed, usually in public ceremonies. All these characteristics made the language simpler and often repetitive, always insisting on recurring key-concepts. Masonic poetry had a long-standing and illustrious tradition related to virtue. From its very onset, in fact, both Italian and French masonic poetry were closely related to virtue. Voltaire, for instance, had composed an Épître à Boileau ou mon testament, a poetic manifesto, where he affirmed his guiding principles: "À chanter la vertu j'ai consacré ma voix. / Vainqueur des préjugés que l'imbécile encense, / j'ose aux persécuteurs prêcher la tolérance."[8] Similarly, Italian freemason Tommaso Crudeli solemnly committed his "lyre" to "virtue" in his collected poems, and in particular in the ode *Il trionfo della ragione*, published only many years after his death in 1767:

> You that mitigate and correct the turbid turmoil of hard hearts, and bend atrocious souls and uncultivated spirits to the laws of Reason, I want you, Lyre, to love peace and to be resounding of virtue.[9]

Crudeli himself was a true symbol of masonic virtue having been imprisoned and mistreated because of his belonging to Freemasonry by the Florentine Inquisition. Although later freed, he never recovered and died

---

8   Voltaire. Épître au Boileau ou mon testament [1769], Œuvres complètes, t. X. Garnier: Paris, 1877.

9   Crudeli, Tommaso. *Poesie*. Napoli, 1767: "Te, che i torbidi tumulti / d'aspri cor calmi e correggi, / ch'alme atroci e spirti inculti / di Ragion pieghi alle leggi, / di virtù, di pace amante, / te, vogl'io, lira sonante."

shortly afterwards, becoming the first martyr of Italian Freemasonry.[10]

But what did this devotion to virtue imply? For many it meant putting poetry to the service of the common good, composing poems which on one
hand disclosed the vices of society, on the other hinted virtuous models to
be followed. This is the case of Emmanuel Carbon Flins des Oliviers. The
French poet, who belonged to the renowned Parisian lodge of the *Neuf
Sœurs*, in his poem *Voltaire*, harshly criticized the Church, while making
the great *philosophe* "un apôtre de la liberté politique et de la tolérance":[11]

> Ce Poète ennemi de l'erreur / qui des Tyrans pieux réprima la
> fureur. [...] Liberté, tu renais au tombeau de Voltaire; / Vol-
> taire dans la tombe a fait citer les Rois / au tribunal sacré des
> peuples et des Loix.[12]

Conversely, virtue meant also retreat from the everyday *mêlée*, the ability
to detach oneself from the basest human passions and to live accordingly a
pristine ingenuity; in short virtue was the attribute of the Golden Age people.[13] So the freemason poets Jean-François de Saint-Lambert, Jean-Baptiste Gresset, Jacques Delille, Aurelio de' Giorgi Bertola and Ippolito Pindemonte longed for the (lost) Age of Astraea, but they also tried to find
possible modern replicas in the virtuous and simple "vie champêtre" of
shepherds and farmers.[14] Similarly, masonic lodges were celebrated as the
true return to a natural egalitarian status and thus as 'Schools of Virtue':

> Dans nos Temples, tout est symbole / tous les préjugés sont
> vaincus, / La Maçonnerie est l'école / de la décence et des ver-
> tus. / Ici, nous domptons la faiblesse / qui dégrade l'Humani-

10 Conti, Fulvio. *La massoneria a Firenze: dall'età dei lumi al secondo Novecento*. Il
   Mulino : Bologna, 2007.

11 Porset, Charles, ed. *Une Loge maçonnique d'avant 1789. La Loge des Neuf Sœurs*.
   Edimaf: Paris, 1989. 181-182.

12 Carbon Flins des Oliviers, Emmanuel. *Voltaire*. Esprit: Ferney, 1779.

13 On the importance of the Golden Age Myth in Enlightenment France see Edel-
   stein, Dan. *The Terror of Natural Right: Republicanism, the Cult of Nature and the
   French Revolution*, University of Chicago: Press Chicago – London, 2009. 11-14.
   Print.

14 On Italian Poetry and the Golden Age Myth, see Di Benedetto, Arnaldo. "Imma-
   gini dell'idillio nel secolo XVIII: Bertola e le poetiche della poesia pastorale.", *Dal
   Tramonto dei Lumi al Romanticismo*. Mucchi: Modena, 2000. 9-37.

té / et le flambeau de la Sagesse / nous conduit à la volupté.[15]

THE POETRY OF FUSION

Between the late 1770s and the early 1780s new tendencies emerged, chiefly a syncretic and encyclopedic will, whose aim was to embrace the reality (and the super-reality) in its wholeness. Antoine Roucher and Antonio Jerocades well incarnate this new 'poetry of fusion', which applies also to virtue.[16] In their poetic masterpieces, respectively *Les Mois* and *La lira focense*, the two freemason poets tried to present an 'ecumenical' version of virtue, blending together Enlightenment, masonic, Christian and classical motives.

Roucher belonged to the Parisian lodge of the *Neuf Sœurs*, and significantly, was referred to as the 'French Lucretius', an epithet forged by his 'brother' Nicolas Bricaire de la Dixmerie. Roucher composed *Les Mois* with the 'encyclopedic' intention of embracing all existence in a single poetic work. His lines are pervaded with an "Enlightenment sentiment" and characterized by faith in progress and science, love for truth and eagerness for knowledge.[17] Antoine Roucher depicted a very original Pantheon of virtuous men and women, including his father, his mother, Jeanne d'Arc, Dupaty, Voltaire and Rousseau. Moreover, if in Carbon Flins des Oliviers' already mentioned poem, Voltaire stands out as a gigantic figure, the defender of freedom and the enemy of error, Roucher went even further: alive Voltaire had been a *grand homme*, death not only has made him immortal, but it has also transformed him into a god:

---

15 *Stances chantées au banquet de la loge des Neuf Sœurs, Orient de Paris, le 7 juin 1778, après la réception du F. Voltaire, Une Loge maçonnique d'avant 1789. La Loge des Neuf Sœurs.* 33.

16 The category 'Poetry of Fusion' paraphrases the concept 'Politics of Fusion' as used by Robert Morrissey regarding Napoleon's political action (Morrissey, Robert. *The Economy of Glory: from Ancien Régime France to the Fall of Napoleon.* The University of Chicago Press: Chicago, 2014. 4). I believe, in fact, that the two very different cases have, nonetheless, common aspects: the will of harmonizing opposites and conciliating past and present, the respect of the tradition and the desire of creating something new.

17 Roucher himself declared to be moved by "violent amour pour la vérité" and "avidité de connaître" (Roucher, Antoine. *Les Mois.* Imprimerie de Quillau: Paris, 1779.). On Roucher as 'poet of the Enlightenment' see Guitton, Édouard. *Jacques Delille (1738-1813) et le poème de la nature en France de 1750-1820.* C. Klincksieck: Paris, 1974. 290-301.

GIULIA DELOGU, PH.D

Voltaire n'aurait point de tombe où ses reliques / Appelleraient le deuil et les larmes publiques! / Et qu'importe après tout à cet homme immortel / Le refus d'un asile à l'ombre d'un autel? / Le cendre de Voltaire en tout lieu révéré / Eût fait de tous les lieux une terre sacrée, / Où repose un grand homme un dieu vient habiter. [18]

Antonio Jerocades, fancying himself a modern Orpheus and following on the very first Italian masonic poems by Tommaso Crudeli, wished to educate people through poetry, thus he dedicated his compositions to unveiling the importance of masonic values such as fraternity, friendship, virtue and liberty.[19] The poem *L'Amico* is particularly significant because it is where the poet sketches a portrait of the ideal man, understood as amalgam of the virtuous freemason and the enlightened *philosophe*:

Two bodies and one heart, two minds and only one thought / two kingdoms and one throne: or two chains and one foot / two sons of two fathers and only one heir; / frankly speaking and sincerely thinking. / Freely thinking and speaking the truth; / not changing rules when changing place; / loyal silence, secret faith; / disregarding pride and respecting his commitment; / putting life and death in danger / to achieve freedom and peace, / through fortitude and wisdom / enlightening the shadows, without showing the light, / saving his country and bearing the exile: / this is the truthful image of

18 Roucher's few lines devoted to Voltaire's memory, were censored in the 1779 first edition. However, these lines circulated widely. They had, in fact, been recited in a successful masonic ceremony held by the lodge of the *Neuf Sœurs* in 1778. The full version of the poems was finally published in 1792. On this point see Gumbrecht, Hans Ulrich. "Who were the philosophes." *Making Sense In Life and Literature.* University of Minnesota Press: Minneapolis, 1991. 155-163: Gumbrecht argues that the period 1776-1788 is characterized by a "self-apotheosis of Enlightenment figures".

19 Porset, Charles. "Franc-Maçonnerie." *Dictionnaire européen des Lumières.* Ed. Michel Delon. Presses Universitaires de France: Paris, 1997. 487: "le lexique des Lumières a parfaitement été assimilé autour de quelques idées forces qui font de la vertu et de l'égalité les conditions nécessaires de l'amitié, cimentée à son tour par la fraternité qui fonde la bienfaisance source du véritable bonheur".

the Friend.[20]

BRUTUS AND EPICTETUS, WARRIOR AND PHILOSOPHER

Both Roucher and Jerocades meditated on the concept of virtue and subsequently depicted in their poems great and virtuous freemasons (real as Voltaire or ideal as the Friend), being the great man the very embodiment abstract notion of virtue.[21]

The masonic and poetic representation of virtuous men as powerful combination of opposing values had a long-standing tradition. At the very onset of French Freemasonry Élie-Catherine Fréron characterized the virtuous freemasons as the perfect synthesis of epicurean materialism and platonic spiritualism, while presenting himself as disciple of Horace—the

---

20 Jerocades, Antonio. *La lira focense.* Presso Gennaro Fonzo: Napoli, 1784: "Due corpi, e un cor, due menti, e un sol pensiero / due Regni, e un Trono; o due catene, e un piede, / di due padri due figli, e un solo erede; / un parlar franco, un ragionar sincero. / Pensar, e dir liberamente il vero; / non cangiar leggi col cangiar di sede; / il silenzio fedel, l'occulta fede; / sprezzar l'orgoglio, e tollerar l'impegno; / il vivere, e il morir porre in periglio / per ottener la libertà, la pace, / A prezzo della forza, e del consiglio, / dar lume all'ombre, e non mostrar la face, / salvar la patria, e ritener l'esiglio; / dell'Amico è l'immagine verace".

21 The 18th century fascination with great men (and women) traced back to the Renaissance rediscovery of Plutarch's *Parallel Lives* and to the widely successful French translation by Amyot (1559). Subsequently contemporary great men's biographies began to appear. Between 1697 and 1792 at least fourteen collective biographies were published in France. Finally, in 1758, the *Académie française* established to devote the eloquence competition to eulogies of "great men of the nation". Later the revolutionaries tried to give a tangible dimension to the cult of great men founding the Panthéon; see Bell, David. *The Cult of the Nation in France: Inventing Nationalism, 1680-1800.* Harvard University Press: Cambridge, Mass., 2001.; Bonnet, Jean-Claude. *La Naissance du Panthéon: Essai sur le Culte des Grands Hommes.* Fayard: Paris, 1998. The 'obsession' for great men was not a prerogative of France, it was, in fact, a more widespread sentiment: for a glimpse on eulogies in Italy and in the Holy Roman Empire see Trampus, Antonio. "Da Maria Teresa a Giuseppe II : gli ex-gesuiti e la tradizione letteraria degli elogi". *Ricerche di storia sociale e religiosa.* 1999. 59-89. On Napoleon's propaganda see Tulard, Jean. *Napoléon ou le mythe du sauveur.* Fayard: Paris, 1977.; Lentz, Thierry "L'officina della memoria". Bonaparte, Napoleone. *Memorie della campagna d'Italia.* Donzelli, Roma, 2012. Eighteenth-century virtue seems to bear a pronounced gender difference. In fact, while there is the category of great man, those of great women does not exist. After all, as David Bell noted "men citizens dominated the public arena and women remained in the private realm of the home" (*The Cult of the Nation.* 127).

very same poet who had inspired Boileau and later on Voltaire:

> L'heureuse liberté / à nos banquets préside / l'aimable volupté
> / à ses côtés réside. / L'indulgente Nature / unit dans le maçon
> / le charmant Epicure / et le divin Platon. / [...] / Mes frères,
> par ma voix / un élève d'Horace / jaloux de votre choix / vous
> demande une place / nul est bien plus épris / que de la confré-
> rie / de certains beaux esprits. [22]

The masonic portrayal of the great and virtuous man as the one able
to combine even opposites became very productive during the French
Revolution. While Jacques-Louis David painted his well known Christ-
like Marat,[23] Michel de Cubières, a freemason himself, celebrated the
martyr Jean-Paul Marat as the only one able to unite Epictetus, that is
to say speculative skills and research of truth, and Brutus, namely civic
engagement and fight for freedom:

> Ah! Du peu qui lui reste, / voyez-le à l'indigent faire l'offre
> modeste, / prendre soin de la veuve, adopter l'orphelin / [...] /
> et toujours distinguant les vices des vertus, / en lui seul réunir
> Epictète et Brutus.[24]

The path towards the representation of Napoleon as great man was open.
A few years later, in fact, Italian freemason Federico Todeschini would
have exalted the French Emperor as "sublime monarch, great philosopher
and excellent warrior" and as "prodigy of strength and wisdom".[25] The

---

22 "La lanterne à la main", *Chansons maçonniques des XVIIIᵉ et XIXᵉ siècles*. Ed. Daniel
Ligou. ABI : Paris, 1972. 7. The *chanson* was recited at the Parisian lodge Procope
on February 26, 1744 during Fréron's own initiation ceremony.

23 Jacques-Louis David, *The death of Marat* (1793).

24 Cubières, Michel de. *Les deux Martyrs de la Liberté ou Portraits de Marat et de Le-
pelletier*. Imprimerie de Ch. Fr. Patris, Imprimeur de la Commune: Paris, 1793.
Brutus designed two distinct Roman heroes: Lucius Junius Brutus, founder of the
Republic, and Marcus Junius Brutus, the leader of the Caesaricides. On Brutus'
fortune during the Revolution, see Giardina, Andrea, and André Vauchez. *Il mito
di Roma: da Carlo Magno a Mussolini*. Laterza, Roma-Bari, 2008. 127.

25 Todeschini, Federico. *I mali dell'Intolleranza*. 1807: "Ma il supremo del Mondo
Architetto / Alle stragi prefisse un confin, / E ministro al grand'uopo fu eletto /
Un Monarca che in mano ha il destin; / Un Monarca sublime Massone / Gran
Filosofo, e sommo guerrier, / Che a sua voglia del mondo dispone, / Ch'è un
prodigio di possa, e saper".

Italian poet made Napoleon into the ultimate incarnation of virtue, which unites both the meditative side of virtue, enhanced during the late Enlightenment, and the active one, exalted by the revolutionaries. The idea of virtue as union of even conflicting skills and values, firstly explored by the freemason poets, became therefore widespread and found an iconic representation in Antonio Canova's masterpiece *Napoleon as Mars the Peacemaker* (1806): a tangible sign of the Great man's divine ability to bring peace through war.

'The freemason poet' (Jerocades, Antonio. *La lira focense*. Presso Gennaro Fonzo: Napoli, 1784)

Antonio Canova, *Napoleon as Mars the Peacemaker* (the 1811 bronze copy of the original marble statue, sculpted in 1806)

VI

Rembrandt's Secret

Zhenya Gershman
Artist & Art Historian, Co-Founder & President, project AWE

Authors note:
Dedicated to Nikka—the light of my life. With deep gratitude to those who encouraged and advised me throughout the research, writing, or editing process: Irina Gershman, George Gershman, Amy Golahny, Harry Maslin, Evan Pepper, John Slifko, and Elizabeth Yochim.

Introduction

There are many mysteries surrounding Rembrandt's life. Many of his subjects remain in question. Rembrandt himself seemed either not to be concerned or was purposefully cautious about leaving any written document about his life or artistic practice. Paradoxically, he left more autobiographical paintings than any artist of his time, including over seventy self-portraits.

In addition, Rembrandt used his signature as another method of self-insertion—when signed, his presence was always proudly asserted. Over the years, he continually revised and honed a particular way of signing his work. By 1632, he had dropped all of the auxiliary information such as his hometown, his last name, and the reference to his father to focus primarily on what makes him unique, which he represented with his first name alone. Let us begin our investigation into Rembrandt's secret with an examination of his signature.

1. "D" FOR ... ?

Sometime in the early 1630s (probably around 1633), Rembrandt made a significant change to his identity that, mysteriously, remained uncommented upon by his contemporaries (image 1). For some reason, he added a letter "d" to his first name, changing Rembrant to Rem**brandt**. Despite the large number of paintings and etchings signed with this modified first name, most of the documents that mention him during his lifetime retain the original "Rembrant" spelling. While scholars have noted the change in the spelling of Rembrandt's name, they have not offered an explanation to account for it. This self-revision of Rembrandt's name was indeed of great significance. By adding the extra letter, though not making a phonetic change, the meaning of the word was entirely altered.

The name can be divided into two distinct words: "Rem" and "brandt" (in a number of his signatures after 1632, Rembrandt emphasized this duality by either capitalizing the letter "B" in the middle of his name or literally separating the word into two: Rem brandt). In Dutch, "Rem" stands for "brake" (or "obstruct") and "brandt" translates as "fire" (or "light"). The combination of these two words "rem" and "brandt" creates a wordplay that means "obstructed light." In fact, whenever Rembrandt's name is mentioned, one of the first associations with his art is the mastery of light and dark. The radiant light that illuminates his canvases, panels, paper, and copper prints, is accentuated by rich, dense, and velvety areas of darkness or obscurity. Thus, Rembrandt's revised name becomes a pun reflecting the quintessential ability of creating illuminated darkness or "dimmed light" (image 2).

What was the impetus behind Rembrandt's obsession with creating the illusion of illumination? We must go beyond the subject of light in art typically associated with the innovations by Renaissance masters such as Leonardo and Titian, culminating in the technical virtuosity of chiaroscuro technique of light and dark in Caravaggio. What lies beyond the visual illusionism of dark backgrounds accentuating luminous characters which seem to break free from the two-dimensional surface? Light has been used as a visual symbol of divinity, spirituality, creativity, knowledge, truth, purification, and birth across time and in cultures like those of ancient Egypt and Greece, as well as in Judeo-Christian traditions.

There is, another important scheme of thought that should be explored in connection with chiaroscuro: inspired both by kabalistic and Christian symbolism, as expressed by Albert Mackey, light is of great importance in Masonic rituals (chapter XXII). Among its numerous and reach symbolic meanings, it represents the divine truth and is believed to be a guiding principle that points the way for one's life pilgrimage. No wonder that Goethe, a brilliant writer as well as a Freemason, is believed to have uttered *"Mehr Licht"* (more light) as he was dying. In contrast, Goethe's famous line from Götz von Berlichingen, Act I (1773) states: *"There is strong shadow where there is much light."*

Naturally there can be no light without darkness. The shadow, or obscurity, serves as an important stage for the backdrop of illumination. Masonic rituals include significant references and experiences of light and dark. In Masonic images, moreover, this duality is often represented by black-and-white checkered floors. Rather than merely following in the footsteps of the Caravaggisti, who were imitating the rapidly spreading contagious formula of extreme chiaroscuro, Rembrandt was contemplating the symbolism and mysteries of the necessary polarities beyond the technique. Consequently, was the self-imposed silent letter "d" in his first name added to signify the extremes of light and dark, a hint for the initiated?

2. THE THREE POINT BROTHER : .

Rembrandt repeatedly added a beautifully rendered letter "f" after signing his name. Scholars have interpreted this to mean "fecit" or "made by." A master of multiple meanings, Rembrandt enjoyed the potential of this letter to also evoke the word "frater" or "brother." Thus his signature would be read as "Rembrandt, fraternally," or "Rembrandt, brother," implying his belonging to a closed fraternal society. Additionally, Rembrandt punctuated the letter "f" with three mysterious dots (image 3).

Albert C. Mackey, in his Encyclopedia of Freemasonry and its Kindred Sciences, recorded: "Abbreviations of technical terms or of official titles are of very extensive use in Freemasonry ... A Masonic abbreviation is distinguished by three points ... in a triangular form following the letter (11)." It was a specific form of coded communication by which one Freemason signaled to other Brothers. Mackey goes through the list of known abbreviations in which "f" stands proudly for "Brother," as can be seen in a document from Grande Lodge of France (image 4).

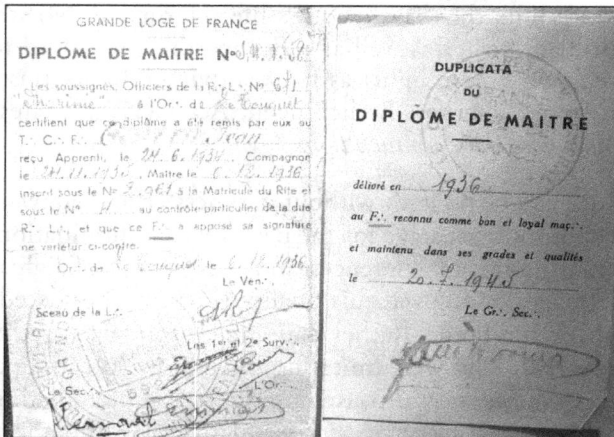

Jacques Huyghebaert in "Three Points in Masonic Context" specifies that this triple punctuation "also appeared in signatures, which explains why Freemasons are still called in French: 'Les Frères Trois Points.'" Looking at a great number of Rembrandt's signatures, three dots in a triangular pattern can indeed be visible following the letter "f". This type of public display that nonetheless remained invisible to the uninitiated seemed to appeal to Rembrandt, and we will see it again with his approach to self-portraits as well as the encoding of his name within the artwork.

3. Written in Stone ...

Rembrandt's preoccupation with his signature spills over to his unortho-

dox treatment of its placement. His signatures go beyond the basic purpose of claiming authorship and can be seen as an extension of self-rep-
resentation or self-insertion. Most often
the location of his signature deliberately
directs the viewer's attention to the key
aspects in his work. In addition, Rembrandt insistently adds his name to stone
surfaces, for example, at the base of a col-
umn in the painting of *Samson Threatened
his Father-in-law*, and in the rough stone
in *The Abduction of Europa* (image 5). In
Masonic ritual and legend, stone (as one
might expect) plays a leading role. Beginning with the new apprentice,
who is entrusted with polishing the rough stone with hammer and chisel,
and culminating in the variously shaped stones appearing in the Master
Mason Degree, there is hardly a ceremony in freemasonry that is not connected in some way with stone.

It is noteworthy that after completion of the initiation ceremony, the new
Brother is placed in a particular position within the Lodge and is usually
told that he represents the cornerstone on which freemasonry's spiritual
Temple must be built. Additionally, when joining Royal Arch Masonry,
the initiated is asked to create a signature "mark" which serves as a personal identifier carved into stone. On numerous occasions, Rembrandt
places the signature in his paintings as if written on stone for the viewer to
ponder. It is important to acknowledge this deliberate choice, which goes
beyond utilitarian use of the signature for identification purposes of the
artist's work.

4. "KNOW THYSELF"

Rembrandt's ongoing practice of self-portraiture is also akin to the Masonic philosophy of self-realization. Unlike most organized groups, Freemasons strive for the cultivation of individuality rather than adjusting to
fit in with the preexistent structure. Each member's task is to cultivate and
"polish" oneself, a process akin to polishing a rough stone to smooth perfection. This undertaking involves not only striving to perfect oneself and
thus realizing full potential, but understanding one's personal limitations.
The concept of initiating change in the world by changing oneself is at the
basis of the Masonic way of life. No wonder Masonic philosophy appealed
to such great and independent minds as Voltaire, Mozart, and Goethe.

Few painters have practiced the task of scrupulous self-examination as much as did Rembrandt. In just four years, between 1627 and 1631, he portrayed himself at least 20 times (Chapman, 3). He painted, etched, and drew his own likeness at least 75 times over 40 years in an astonishing number of roles, ranging from a street beggar to the Apostle Paul. Over time, one can observe the pretenses of an aspiring court painter being stripped away from the aging artist, allowing a more private and vulnerable self to come forward. This impulse of self-examination has been variously interpreted—as the practice of the humanistic tradition, as vanity, or a self-marketing tool, or even as a response to actors' exercises. However, it is important to consider Rembrandt's extraordinary contribution to self-portraiture in a new light, as it bears strong resemblance to the Masonic task of ongoing self-examination.

5. Are You Looking At Me?

What lies beyond the face in Rembrandt's self-portraits? There are often multiple metaphors in seventeenth-century Dutch painting. We know to look behind ordinary objects to read a deeper meaning or to take away a moral lesson. Gestures, clothes, backgrounds, poses, direction of gaze, and colors can all be indicative of a meaning that the artist is conveying to the viewer. Unfortunately, over time, these messages frequently are misread or overlooked. Often, myths attach themselves to paintings over the centuries. The heart of the matter, however, usually lies in a deceptively basic observation of the work of art.

Let's take a closer look at Rembrandt's Self-portrait (1636–38), now in the Norton Simon Museum (image 6).

At first glance it's a rather traditional bust-length portrait. Rembrandt portrays himself in a master's beret, with a penetrating gaze, which can be said to be either examining the viewer or, in contrast, drilling through his own image in the mirror. One barely detects the hint of a hand hidden in the lapel of the jacket. The chiaroscuro effect illuminates the face, inviting the viewer to scrutinize the persona as it obscures the hand gesture, making it easily unnoticeable. Remember that it is from the deep shadow that knowledge can be born.

This gesture may look familiar. Compare Rembrandt's self-portrait (either the painting or a related etching from 1638) to a portrait of George Washington from 1776 by Charles Willson Peale (images 7, 8).

The gesture is identical. In the case of Washington (who was a Freemason), we know exactly what it represents. The "hidden hand" is found in the rituals of the Royal Arch Degree of Freemasonry and communicates Masonic membership to other initiates (Duncan, 237–38). The hidden fingers also represent an internal disposition of faith illustrated by the Masonic diagram of this concept (image 9). Is the hiding of the hand in Rembrandt's self-portrait actually a way of revealing an important message?

6. OPEN SESAME ...

Another type of authorship can be seen in the form of "I"-witness in Rembrandt's famous Danaë (image 10). This masterpiece marks one of the first instances in which the artist presents himself in the act of creation within the depiction of a mythological scene. In the background, one can actually detect Rembrandt, wearing his signature beret and holding brushes and a palette perpendicular to his body, suggesting that the paint is still wet (image 11). It is surprising enough to discover Rembrandt inserting himself into a mythological painting as both the creator and a witness of the scene.

Even more intriguing is the combination of the artist's tools of the trade he is holding in his right arm—the palette and brushes together with the keys. There is no literal door to be opened in this painting. Rather, these keys are suggestive of an intellectual and perhaps a spiritual door that can be opened by and for the viewer. Setting the obvious story aside, the myth of Danaë is also an allegory of the boundless reach of divinity. While Danaë is locked away in a tower, God/Jupiter finds a devious way of entering the room in the form of a golden shower (in Rembrandt's interpretation this is represented by a golden luminous stream of light invading the scene from above). The keys traditionally symbolize a means by which secrets are obtained. Here we are invited by the artist to enter the sanctum sanctorum along with the divinity. Once again, we encounter an essential code in Freemasonry: the key as a symbol for unlocking the truth (Précieu, 87).

One more hint to consider. The shackled cupid in the background of the painting has served as a source of debate (image 12). The accepted interpretation was made by Erwin Panofsky, who claimed that it represented

Danaë's chastity (though hard to reconcile with Danaë's welcoming attitude towards the intrusion). It is interesting to observe what happens if we continue to apply a Masonic lens. As pointed out by Charles Clyde Hunt in his book *Masonic Symbolism*, to Freemasons, Cupid represents secrecy, based on the idea that love should be practiced in private (326). By adding handcuffs to Cupid, the symbol of privacy, is Rembrandt implying that secret knowledge is being exposed publicly? As viewers we are observing a nude woman on whom, according to the myth, no one was to cast eyes. Simultaneously, are we becoming privy to sacred and secret Masonic symbols (i.e., the key, the streaming light, the proximity of the artist to God as creator) that have been embedded by the artist? Is Danaë the center of this drama or is Rembrandt placing a seductive woman here as a distraction from another meaning?

7. MIRROR, MIRROR ON THE WALL ...

Going a step further, Rembrandt's famous print The Alchemist (c. 1652), which has been ascribed various titles (including Faust), is even more daring (image 13). It presents a visual riddle based on a synthesis of three sources: Christianity, Kabala, and Alchemy. A man draped in what appears to be a tallit (a Jewish prayer shawl) rises and turns towards the window. A radiating disk surrounded by three concentric circles appears in mid-air, obscuring a figure holding and pointing into a mirror (image 14). This levitating vision bears a secret inscription, which has been de-coded by using a mirror and deciphering the Latin anagram to read as Hebrew words that spell the name of God (Perlove and Silver, 63–65). The middle of the roundel bears a cross dividing it into four sections with the letters INRI (from New Testament: Iesus Nazarenus, Rex Iudaeorum or Jesus Christ, King of the Jews).

However, Rembrandt rotated the letters thus emphasizing the "R" residing prominently at the top, spelling RIIN clockwise. Riin is an equivalent way to notate Rembrandt's last name Rijn, since in Dutch the capital letters "I" and "J" can be written identically. Rembrandt also added a clever and daring spin to the abbreviation of the letter "R" from Rex (or King), identifying himself by either first or last name: "R" for Rembrandt or "R" for "Rijn." In alchemy and according to the kabala, the mirror reflects the image of God. The world can be seen as God's mirror (McHenry, 15). As we have seen, Rembrandt was intimately acquainted with the mirror through countless self-portraits. His work can be seen as an extension of another mirror in reflecting both Rembrandt and the Divine.

Once again, Rembrandt imbeds his presence while also aligning the artist with the carrier of light and secret knowledge. The presence of the skull, globe, books, and the mysterious writing embedded in the roundel of the apparition has led scholars to see the scene as the vision of the alchemist. Consider a new striking juxtaposition. Compare the Rosicrucian Cross (also prevalent in Masonic symbolism) to Rembrandt's image of the vision (image 14)—you will find the three concentric circles, the cross in the middle, Hebrew letters spelling God, and the letters INRI (image 15).

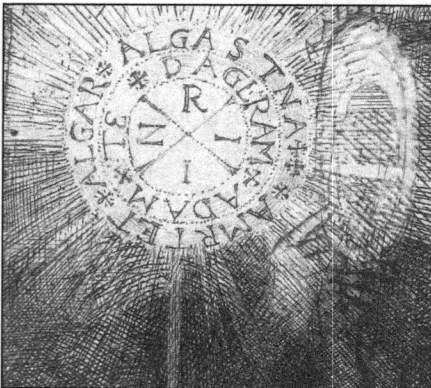

In *People of the Book: Christian Identity and Literary Culture*, David Lyle Jeffrey stresses that Goethe, as a Freemason, had a particular interest in a print by Rembrandt. In fact, Goethe went so far as to obtain "a reproduction, illustrating with it his 1790 first edition of Faust. (213)" Jeffrey suspects that the Alchemist's alternate title, *Doctor Faustus*, was probably inspired by this association. Further, Jeffrey concludes, "The light symbol which comes through the window does have significance for Freemasonry (213)." In addition to the Christian interpretation of the letters INRI signifying Christ, Jeffrey adds that "for Masons this came to signify *rather Igne Natura Renovatur Integra*—suggesting the sacred fire of Masonry that renews humankind naturalistically (213)." Goethe obviously saw something more than just a collectible item in this mysterious etching by Rembrandt.

7. SQUARING THE CIRCLE ...

Following Rembrandt's printmaking mysteries, Thomas E. Rassieur, in his essay on Rembrandt's printmaking techniques, mentions the artist's "reuse [of] plates previously worked by other printmakers (46)." Out of the two known cases, Rassieur describes the first as Rembrandt's "frugal recycling of an out-of-date mathematical diagram no longer having commercial value (213)." Fate has it that this copper plate survived and is now housed at the Rijksmuseum. It is on the verso of the plate for the famous 1636 *The Return of the Prodigal Son* (image 16). Careful observation reveals a squaring-of-the-circle diagram. This mathematical problem has puzzled great minds, including Leonardo da Vinci, over centuries. Contemplation of this problem remains an important practice for Freemasons today, though since 1882 it has been proven to be an impossible task.

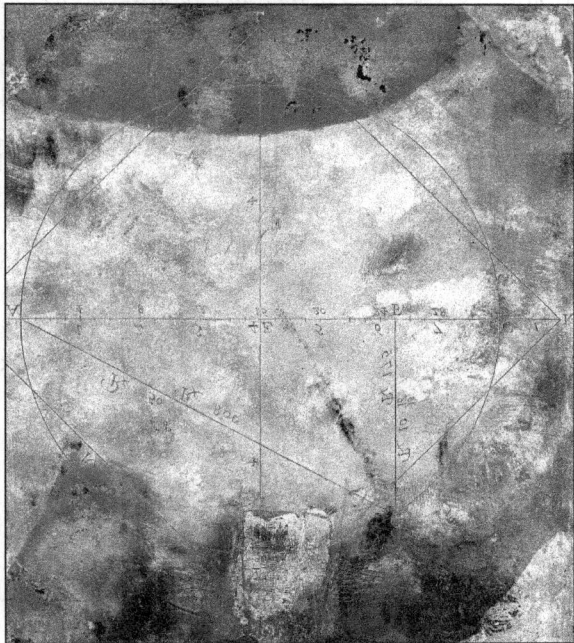

For Freemasons one's daily work includes the striving to comprehend the divine plan, with the understanding that such comprehension will never be possible. This paradox is reflected in the problem of the squaring of the circle. The goal is not to solve it, but to practice creative thinking. We know that Rembrandt spent an enormous amount of money on collecting other artists' work. It is premature to jump to the conclusion that he may have purchased this plate out of frugality. Rather, it gave him yet another source for a timeless esoteric geometric problem that may have resonated with his creative and philosophical endeavors.

8. ALL ROADS LEAD TO ... ?

Rembrandt had various sources for his esoteric quest. One of them was his fascinating involvement with Menasseh Ben Israel, or Manoel Dias Soeiro, who was a Portuguese rabbi, cabalist, scholar, writer, printer, publisher, and founder of the Hebrew printing press in Amsterdam in 1626. Rembrandt borrowed concepts from the kabala for numerous paintings and prints, and it is speculated that he had access to esoteric symbols through Ben Israel (Steven Nadler, 104–44).

There was evident collaboration when Ben Israel commissioned Rembrandt to create four illustrations for his publication Piedra Gloriosa (Glorious Rock)—*David and Goliath, Daniel's Vision of Four Beasts, Jacob's Ladder*, and *The Image Seen by Nebuchadnezzar*, published in 1655. In

combination, we have the glorified rock (the subject of this volume and one of the most important symbols for Freemasons), the borrowing from the kabala, and the geometric solution that is used to represent the relationship between God and men. All four images are strongly indicative of Masonic preoccupations. Specifically, I would like to focus attention on Daniel's Vision (image 17). Here we ought to look for: concentric circles surrounding the divine figure at the top and a compass shape spreading from the oculus, a symbol of divinity, pointing down to the Earth.

These two geometric applications are closely reminiscent of a key Masonic concept describing God as The Great Architect. The basic tools of measurement, a pair of compasses and the square, are considered the main two symbols of sacred geometry. Further, the circle as a product of the compass becomes a symbol of the divine and the creative.

It is noteworthy that the compass lines radiating from the oculus and the God figure at the top reach all the way to the ground to touch Rembrandt's signature. Rembrandt thus underlines the connection between the two creators in this image—God and the Artist. It is also fascinating that when the book was reprinted a different artist was commissioned (most likely unbeknownst to Ben Israel) to copy Rembrandt's etchings. While Daniel's Vision was replicated, it was altered by deleting the image of God and the compass lines. Was Rembrandt's visual solution too controversial?

9. The Circle of Trust

Who would have appreciated such nuanced symbolism in Rembrandt's time? It is noteworthy that his first known commission of 1625, *The Stoning of St. Stephen*, came from Petrus Scriverius (Peter Hendrickz Schrijver), a fascinating and politically controversial figure and a friend of Willem van Swanenburg (Rembrandt's first teacher's younger brother). A seventeenth century portrait engraving bears his name with an additional inscription "Lare Secreto" from the Latin for "Secret Home". In describing Scriverius, a Rembrandt scholar Gary Schwartz writes: "His album is enriched with drawings by three Haarlem artists he called friends [including] the imprisoned leader of [the] Rosicrucian movement Johannes Torrentius (25)."

There was another link between Scriverius and Rembrandt—Joost van den Vondel, one of the greatest Dutch poets of the seventeenth century. There are a number of Rembrandt paintings that have been suspected of reflecting scenes from Vondel's plays commissioned by Scriverius. One of which is Vondel's 1639 play Gebroeders (Brothers), staged in 1641, and Rembrandt's *The reconciliation of David and Mephiboseth* (1642). The main two subjects of the play and the painting are not brothers by blood but by compassion and conviction—a theme that would fit well with the Masonic Brotherhood. The inspiration worked both ways. Vondel's famous lines were written in response to Rembrandt's portrait of Cornelis Cllaesz Anslo: *"O, Rembrandt, paint Cornelis' voice. The visible part is the least of him; the invisible is known only through the ears; he who would see Anslo must hear him."* The subject of invisibility is described by David Stevenson: *"Masons, as many of the seventeenth-century references to the Mason word indicate, were not what they seemed, in that outsiders could not see anything distinctive about them which identified them as masons, but fellow initiates could detect 'invisible' emanations which identified them (172)."*

Vondel, indeed, may have belonged to a secret group that would have preferred to stay invisible to the authorities. A seventeenth-century Rosicrucian caricature survives, etched by Pieter Nolpe, with a verse below the image mentioning "a meeting of the brotherhood of the Red Cross". In this print, the clothing of two figures is decorated with a cross. And among those whose identities are suggested—Joost van den Vondel and Torrentius (image 18).

Though Holland was considered to be tolerant to the outsiders, in Rembrandt's time one could still risk being jailed or even tortured for belonging to an unsanctioned organization. Consider the example of the Torrentius whose paintings were ordered to be burned, after he was accused of being a Rosicrucian, arrested (in 1627), and tortured in prison. In his article on Torrentius, George Taylor writes: "The connection between Rembrandt and the Order, although perhaps tenuous on the surface, is reinforced by The fact that in the foreground of the *Nachtwacht*, a red rose was originally painted, though Frans Banning Cocq (who commanded the Company in the painting) later replaced it with an orange on the copy in the British Museum. It can also be shown that the geometrical basis of the composition of the Nachtwacht is founded on the aforementioned Rosicrucian symbols (19)."

10. THE SECRET AGENT ...

Let's consider one more suspect. It has been widely accepted that Rembrandt was introduced to the Dutch Court by Constantijn Huygens, who was a secretary to the two Princes of Orange. Huygens secured for Rembrandt a considerable number of commissions for the Prince's gallery in the Hague, including a five-part series of the Passion of Christ. Thus most art historians remark that Rembrandt's career was made overnight in his early twenties. How and why the paths of a miller's son and that of one of the most brilliant and erudite courtiers came to cross. It seems that this meeting was not accidental. The choice of Jacob Isaacsz Swanenburg as Rembrandt's first painting teacher was not random; it was an attempt to establish connections at the court. Jacob's cousin had married into Huygens's family; it, then, was only a question of time for the exceptionally talented student to be introduced to the art connoisseur. Who was Huygens beyond his official court identity? Here are some illuminating facts:

1. One of Huygens' friends and correspondents was the famous Freemason Christopher Wren.

2. Huygens collected rare treatises on Rosicrucianism and Kabalism.

3. He worked closely with operative Masons while designing his own house and contributing plans for the Mauritshuis in The Hague.

4. Huygens was known for frequently describing God as "the Great Architect."

5. In 1661, his son Christiaan paid several visits in London to Sir Robert Moray, a Scottish soldier, statesman, diplomat, judge, spy, Freemason and philosopher.

6. Moray sealed his letters to both Huygenses, father and son, with a Masonic seal.

7. Visual evidence points to possible Masonic associations as well: in Huygens' impressive portrait by Thomas Keyser, the artist portrays him at his desk with Huygens's left hand prominently resting on a pair of compasses.

11. OH BROTHER ...

The Freemasons left behind tangible clues of their existence—predominantly in architecture. In the Netherlands, Jacob van Campen (1595–1657), an artist and an architect (and a friend of Constantijn Huygens), adopted Vitruvian principles (based on the work of Roman architect Marcus Vitruvius Pollio) to help design the Mauritshuis. To underscore the importance of the Masonic implication, consider Stevenson's evaluation: *"Vitruvius' concept of the architect was vital to the changing perceptions of the mason craft ... which helped to lead to the emergence of freemasonry"; and again: "It would seem, then, that some men joined lodges through identifying masonry with Vitruvian concepts of architecture (106, 113)."* In addition, van Campen's work was influenced by Christopher Wren, the English architect and Freemason, evidenced in the famous example of Nieuwe Kerk in Haarlem. Intriguingly, a Masonic Lodge under the name of Jacob van Campen was established in 1875 in Amersfoot (in the province of Utrecht) in honor of van Campen's symbolic legacy in architecture.

It is Van Campen who is credited with the redesign of Rembrandt's house on Sint-Anthonisbreestraat around 1627–28 (image 19). This addition included a new façade with a triangular pediment. A pediment including an oculus in the center is strongly evocative of Masonic architectural design. The delta triangle, which masons greatly revere, is a symbol of Freemasonry adopted from the Egyptians. Among its many profound meanings, it represents the presence of God as the Great Architect. Part of the importance of this symbol is that for the uninitiated it looks like an archetypal geometrical shape; but to the initiated, the sacred meaning is evident, for as Stevenson notes, "Playing the mason was being invisible (170)." This element in Rembrandt's house provides an interesting comparison when seen side-by-side with Masonic architecture [such as the 1866 Masonic Lodge of Dublin and the 1895 Masonic Temple in Canada (image 20)].

12. ... Who Is There?

Our inquiry into the secret world of Rembrandt may not answer every question here and now. Rather, by opening an esoteric Masonic umbrella, it provides a novel way of looking at his work and life. Anyone can visit Rembrandt's house today. You do not need a special key to open the front door; just present a ticket to enter what is now a museum. Inside one will find a reconstructed shelf in Rembrandt's painting studio that boasts a beautiful pair of compasses, square, delta triangle with a circular opening, and a skull (image 21). An entry awaits one prepared to use the key that Rembrandt left us through his work—are we ready to open that door?

Works Cited List

Chapman, H. Perry. *Rembrandt's Self-Portraits A Study in Seventeenth-Century Identity.* New Jersey: Princeton University Press, 1990.

Duncan, Malcolm. *Masonic Ritual and Monitor.* New York: Dick & Fitzgerald, 1866.

Huyghebaert, Jacques. *Three Points in Masonic Context.* Huffington Post, 2014.

Hunt, Charles Clyde. *Masonic Symbolism*, Montana: Kessinger, 1939.

Jeffrey, David Lyle. *People of the Book: Christian Identity and Literary Culture.* Michigan: Eerdmans, 1996.

Mackey, Albert. *The Symbolism of Freemasonry, Illustrating and Explaining Its Science and Philosophy, Its Legends, Myths and Symbols*. South Carolina: District Court, 1882.

Mackey, Albert. *Encyclopedia of Freemasonry and its Kindred Sciences*. New York and London: The Masonic History Company, 1914.

McHenry, Deni McIntosch. *Rembrandt's Faust in his Study Reconsidered: A Record of Jewish Patronage and Mysticism in Mid-Seventeenth-Century Amsterdam*. Yale University Art Gallery Bulletin, 1989.

Nadler, Steven. *Rembrandt's Jews*. Chicago: University of Chicago Press, 2003.

Perlove, Shelly and Larry Silver. *Rembrandt's Faith*. Pennsylvania: Pennsylvania State University Press, 2009.

Précieu, Recueil. *Ceremonies of the Masters Degree in the Adonhiramite Rite*.

Rassieur, Thomas. *Rembrandt's Journey: Painter Draftsman Etcher*. Massachusetts: Boston Museum of Fine Arts, 2003.

Schwartz, Gary. *Rembrandt His Life, His Paintings*. New York: Viking Adult, 1985.

Stevenson, David. *The Origins of Freemasonry*. United Kingdom: Cambridge University Press, 1988.

Taylor, George. "Torrentius." Rosicrucian Beacon 2.1, March 2012.

List of Images

1. Evolution of Rembrandt's signature from 1626 to 1633, Rijksmuseum, Holland.

2. Rembrandt van Rijn, *Philosopher in Meditation*, 1632, Musée de Louvre, Paris.

3. Rembrandt van Rijn, *Adam and Eve*, 1638, The Museum of Fine Arts, Houston.

4. Diplôme Maçonnique Français de 1945, Grande Loge De

France. ©2008 Christophe Dioux, used under a Creative Commons Attribution-ShareAlike license.

5. Rembrandt van Rijn, *Samson Threatened his Father-in-law* (detail showing the signature), 1635, Gemäldegalerie, Berlin.

6. Rembrandt van Rijn, *Self-Portrait*, c. 1636-38, Norton Simon Museum, Pasadena.

7. Rembrandt van Rijn, *Self-portrait in a Velvet Cap with Plume*, 1638, National Museum of Wales.

8. Charles Willson Peale, *Portrait of George Washington*, 1776, Brooklyn Museum.

9. Sign of the Master of the second veil, Figure 34, Duncan's Masonic Ritual and Monitor, Malcom C. Duncan, 1866.

10. Rembrandt van Rijn, *Danaé*, 1636, Hermitage, St. Petersburg, Russia.

11. Rembrandt van Rijn, *Danaé* (detail showing the background character), 1636, Hermitage, St. Petersburg, Russia.

12. Rembrandt van Rijn, *Danaé* (detail showing the cupid), 1636, Hermitage, St. Petersburg, Russia.

13. Rembrandt van Rijn, *A Scholar in His Study (The Alchemist)*, 1650-54, Rijks-museum, Amsterdam.

14. Rembrandt van Rijn, *A Scholar in His Study* (detail showing the text in the roundel).

15. Rosy Cross, Francis King, 1975, Magic—the Western Tradition, Art and Imagination series, ed. Jill Purce, Thames and Hudson, London.

16. Rembrandt van Rijn, Verso of the etching plate for *The Prodigal Son*, c. 1636, Rijks-museum, Amsterdam.

17. Rembrandt van Rijn, *Daniel's Vision of Four Beasts*, 1655, Rijks-museum, Amsterdam.

18. Peiter Nolpe, *Satire met het schilderen van de Antichrist*, ca. 1650, Rijksmuseum, Amsterdam.

19. Rembrandt's House, detail showing triangular roof, Rembrandthuis Museum, Amsterdam.

20. Masonic Temple in Canada, detail showing triangular roof.

21. Rembrandt's shelf in his studio, Rembrandthuis Museum, Amsterdam.

VII

FLAME OF ENLIGHTENMENT:
FREEMASONRY AND THE FEAR OF METAPHOR

KLAUS-JÜRGEN GRÜN
Professor of Philosophy at Frankfurt University; Freemason since 1992;
Master of the research-lodge Quatuor Coronati Bayreuth (Germany)

When I ask students in my seminars at Frankfurt University if they ever have seen a sunset, they assure me that they have. If I further ask more precisely if they really have seen the sun setting down, nearly all of them change their minds immediately and declare that they have not. The two different states of mind are the two meanings of metaphors. On one side there is the meaning that could be understood literally and on the other side metaphors must be understood metaphorically. One who believes in the Golden Rule can never mean it in a literally sense, because rules don't have any colour at all. And as a few days after gunmen murdered in January 2015 a dozen people at the offices of the French magazine *Charlie Hebdo* in Paris, Moslems got upset because of the new cover showing a cartoon with crying Muhammad. They were upset because they did not understand the metaphorical sense of caricatures and opposed that Muhammad doesn't cry. The same inability to understand metaphors metaphorically affected the painter George Grosz after *World War I* when he was accused of blasphemy because of his caricature *Jesus wearing a gas mask* showing Christ on the cross wearing a gas-mask and soldiers' boots saying "Shut Your Mouth and Keep on Serving." Only a few years later many modern painters in Germany were prohibited from painting by the Nazis because Hitler demanded paintings to display "the true German spirit" and he preferred the work of artists such as Franz von Defregger, who was specialised in genre and history paintings. But modern painters usually paint their objects not like a mirror reflects them. There still is a great fear of Metaphors like it has been in history of thought ever since. Metaphor as the most important aim of art reminds us that our concepts of the world do not need to be exact copies of the world.

As an anecdote from the famous painter Pablo Picasso shows, art is an efficient instrument of enlightenment. Picasso once painted a woman's portrait. Her name was Gertrude Stein. Picasso made some portraits of her, but one day she complained that the portrait doesn't look like her. "Just wait a while", Picasso answered, "and it will." Art tells us something we do not take account of if we only recognise the positive facts in the world. Picasso tells the model Gertrude Stein something she will not be able to recognise if she only looks in the mirror. Art brings another perspective before our eyes that we are not usually made aware of. Art makes us familiar with the metaphorical sense of meaning. One who expects art —like the Nazis did—only to picture the world like it always appears to his eyes, is not interested in art, but in an illustration of his opinion about an ever lasting and not to be criticised truth.

Generally, we can describe the process of enlightenment as the transformation of concepts from their literal meaning into their metaphorical meaning. Whenever we observe a glimpse of enlightenment it is based on this transformation. A staunch defender of enlightenment was David Hume. His *A Natural History of Religion* published stories like the following:

> "A famous general, at that time in the MUSCOVITE service, having come to PARIS for the recovery of his wounds, brought along with him a young TURK, whom he had taken prisoner. Some of the doctors of the SORBONNE (who are altogether as positive as the dervishes of CONSTANTINOPLE) thinking it a pity, that the poor TURK should be damned for want of instruction, solicited MUSTAPHA very hard to turn Christian, and promised him, for his encouragement, plenty of good wine in this world, and paradise in the next. These allurements were too powerful to be resisted; and therefore, having been well instructed and catechized, he at last agreed to receive the sacraments of baptism and the Lord's supper. The priest, however, to make everything sure and solid, still continued his instructions: and began the next day with the usual question, How many gods are there? None at all, replies BENEDICT; for that was his new name. How! None at all! cries the priest. To be sure, said the honest proselyte. You have told me all along that there is but one god. And yesterday I eat him." (Hume, 484)

"Such are the doctrines of our brethren the Catholics," Hume commentates of this caricature. The poor Benedict took the story of "this is my body, which is given for you ..." literally. (In Latin this is rendered as 'hoc est corpus meum ...' which sounds very close to 'hocus-pocus.' (Cf. Grün (b))

We are amused by this joke because we do not believe in the identity of God and the consecrated wafer. But Benedict took the words in the Lords Supper: "this is my body" literally. Especially to Protestants this sentence only has a metaphorical meaning. Benedict unfortunately followed the exact and literal meaning which the Roman Catholic Church attributed to the metaphor "this is my body". It was formulated at the important Council of Trent (held between 1545 and 1563 in Trento (Trent) and Bologna) and has never been revoked. The Council states that Christ is "really, truly, substantially present" in the consecrated host. Everybody who denied this literal meaning of the real-present of the body in the host was (and still is) damned.

The development of Freemasonry in the early eighteenth century is based on a new interpretation of holy and sacred scriptures. Philosophers and scientists denied the indispensable assumption of metaphysics and miracles within the aristotelian scholastic theology which is necessary to understand the consecration of the wafer. We find enlightenment in the eighteenth century being engaged with the change in the understanding of causation. Newtons laws put a totally different interest into the meaning of causality and influenced the deistic understanding of Christianity. Even if most of the philosophers and poets did not believe in the universe as a mechanical clockwork they were convinced that superstition and the notion of miracles as a causal-factor did not explain anything in the world. Miracles only explain something about the thinker who is convinced, that miracles can be a causal factor. Like many other notions the word "miracle" and teleology as a concept of causation had lost their explicit meaning in favour for their metaphorical meaning. (It still causes remarkable danger if the two concepts of causation—the religious and the scientific concept—clash together. It is a matter of enlightenment if one really believes that the naked volcano tourists—the few tourists posing in summer 2014 naked on Mount Kinabalu in Malaysia which the Kadazan Dusun people believe is a sacred place—were actually causing an earthquake that killed some other people because of their nakedness on the sacred volcano. (The Guardian)

What we expect from explanation depends on our believes. If you pose the question: "Where do all those poor people come from?," religious teleology and final causation in aristotelian metaphysics answers: "From the Poverty." Scientific thinking since the enlightenment believes that this explanation explains nothing.

But we still do not know exactly what the nature of causation really is. What do we mean by saying, that one occurrence causes another one? Let me give a current example: The Cambridge mathematician and physicist Stephen Hawking declared some weeks ago, he doesn't believe that humans will make it through another millennium. Some headlines wrote, that in 1000 years there will be no human anymore on earth. What kind of knowledge is this? Should we take it as a prediction? Should we accept it as true? To explain the problem of historical truth in enlightenment, we can imagine for the time being that there will be no human being anymore in 1000 years. So we take the prediction literally. Does that mean *because* of Hawking's saying there will be no humans? Or did he know the law of history that made that only possible development necessary that there will be no humans?

But the most probable explanation of the possible human oblivion in 1000 years and Stephen Hawking's saying is that his saying and the fact do not have anything to do with each other. It just happened coincidentally, by chance, that Hawking said something and something else happened in the world. There are two events without any causal relation.

This problem of pure chance in prediction and historical events was the problem the German poet, writer, and freemason Gotthold E. Lessing became aware of. In 1777 he wrote an essay *On the Proof of the Spirit and Power* and came to the famous conclusion: "Accidental truths of history can never become the proof of necessary truths of reason. That, then, is the ugly, broad ditch which I cannot get across, however often and however earnestly I have tried to make the leap." (Lessing (a), 53.) He wrote these sentences within the *Fragmentenstreit* (*Fragments from an Unnamed Author*), a number of controversial pamphlets that led to an argument about religion, history, revelation and resurrection between him and the Lutherian priest Johann Melchior Goeze, who insisted to understand the bible as a historical document and the words "revelation" and "resurrection" in it's literal meaning.

Lessing became a victim of censorship by the Duke of Braunschweig, but the Fragments are known as an important step into the historical critique of the Bible. This critique ends up in the understanding that the Bible could not be red as an historical document.

Lessing's realisation, that "accidental truths of history can never become the proof of necessary truths of reason" structured his concept of freemasonry. Because Lessing got aware that the pure mentioning of a historical fact has not at all a binding character. If one says "thou shalt not lie" or "thou shalt not kill" it can only be true, if there is reason in the saying. On the other hand religious people are convinced that the truth of the commandments has its source not in reason but in the believed fact that one has said it on a specific place at a special time. But historical circumstances don't mean anything valuably. That means that if we understand the reason, we do not need to refer to historical fact anymore. Validity of spoken words does only come from reason and not from the fact that someone said them at a specific time on a specific place.

These considerations brought Lessing to the conviction that revelation cannot contain any reasonable truth. It could only be true in an accidental historical way. And concerning the historical truth of revelation, there is a lot of doubt if it ever happened. If Lessing was true, then our moral values have to be founded in a totally new way. The thinkers of enlightenment tried to express this new way in their understanding of "reason." In it's most sophisticated structure the German philosopher Immanuel Kant shaped the reasonableness of moral commandments in his concept of "Vernunft" which leads to the rationality of the categorical imperative.

The difference between the old and the new way of founding morality and it's meaning for a rational concept of freemasonry is widely underestimated. To explain this important difference we can follow a recent publication by Steven Pinker: "How can we tell which theory is preferable? A thought experiment can pit them against each other. What would be the right thing to do if God had commanded people to be selfish and cruel rather than generous and kind? Those who root their values in religion would have to say that we ought to be selfish and cruel. Those who appeal to a moral sense would say that we ought to reject God's command. This shows—I hope—that it is our moral sense that deserves priority." (Pinker, 188)

The thinkers of enlightenment did so too as well. And Lessing defined the relationship between religion and morality in a sense that is a consequence of his understanding of freemasonry, and—as I would say—of his understanding of the former sentence in Anderson's Old Changes. In Lessing's *Education of the Human Race* he draws a line from morality to religion and articulates the idea which Immanuel Kant will point out in detail a couple of decades later in his moral philosophy, with it's categorical imperative.

And remarkably, it is the same meaning of Anderson's opinion. From the acceptance of the moral law opens up a way to religion, not the other way round, as most people think.

First of all Lessing states in § 4 of *Education of the Human Race*: "Education gives man nothing that he could not acquire by himself, but it gives him what he could acquire by himself more quickly and less arduously. Similarly, revelation gives the human race nothing that unaided human reason could not attain by itself; but revelation has bestowed, and still bestows, the most important of these things somewhat sooner."

Lessing calls it "the time of a new eternal Gospel" what will be fulfillment of humanity in the moral sense. "No; it will come, it will surely come, the time of fulfillment, when man, the more convinced his reason is of an ever better future, will nevertheless have no need to borrow motives for his actions from this future; when he will do good because it is good, not because it is tied to arbitrary rewards that were previously intended merely to fix and strengthen his unsteady gaze, so that he recognises the inner, better, rewards of doing good." (Lessing (b), §§ 4, 86, 85)

The roots of morality give reason to be religious. We can deem as the greatest result of enlightenment that reasonable thinking only allows us to begin with the expectation of morality and humanity to find a way to religion. Religion exists because of the need of morality. But pious people always thought it must have been the other way round: because of the religion and because of god we have moral laws. It is, what Kant later in the *Critique of Pure Reason* states: the intent so as to act as if there be a god. Only for moral reasons we refer to god, as he points out: "Thus the transcendental and only determinate conception of God, which is presented to us by speculative reason, is in the strictest sense deistic. In other words, reason does not assure us of the objective validity of the conception; it merely gives us the idea of something, on which the supreme and necessary unity of all experience is based. This something we cannot, following the analogy of a real substance, cogitate otherwise than as the cause of all things operating in accordance with rational laws, if we regard it as an individual object; although we should rest contented with the idea alone as a regulative principle of reason, and make no attempt at completing the sum of the conditions imposed by thought. This attempt is, indeed, inconsistent with the grand aim of complete systematic unity in the sphere of cognition--a unity to which no bounds are set by reason." (Kant, 312)

The small chapter *Concerning GOD and RELIGION* in Anderson *Old Charges* proclaimed in a similar manner to that which Kant would demand at the end of the century: "A Mason is obliged, by his Tenure, to obey the moral Law; and if he rightly understands the Art, he will never be a stupid Atheist, nor an irreligious Libertine." (Anderson) Without having a detailed theory of why that should be, Anderson declared only, the way to religion beginning with the moral law. Those who hold on to the moral concepts of pre- and anti-enlightenment state always the beginning with the existence of god to assure us of moral commandments.

So we can describe the difference between humanitarian freemasonry and religious freemasonry with the difference in these two ways to interpreting Anderson's Constitutions. From the acceptance of the moral law there opens a way to religion of reason, because—as Kant pointed out—we should construct our moral law as if a god has made it, to make it appear valid.

In humanity the concept of god develops into a pure metaphor that does not necessary have to have a literal meaning. We can observe the ceremony in every lodge of freemasons which performs sayings and gestures and state within the act of performing, that everything they say and do only has meaning in a metaphorical sense. In this performance freemasonry shows in a distinct way that it has nothing to do with a church, where the priest and every praying person understands his doing and saying explicit and in a literal meaning.

REFERENCES

Grün, Klaus-Jürgen (b). *Aspects of German Freemasonry: A glimpse into the Humanitarian approach—Two Concepts of Morality and the Masonic Code of Humanity*. In: Transcations of the Manchester Association for Masonic Research, Vol. CIV, 2013, pp. 30-37.

Grün, Klaus-Jürgen (a): *From Ethical Hostility Toward Cooperative Ethics*, in: *Handbook of Moral Motivation. Theories, Models, Applications*, ed. by Karin Heinrichs, Fritz Oser, Terence Lovat, Rotterdam 2013: Sense Publishers, pp. 425 - 444.

Hume, David (). *A Natural History of Religion*. In: *Essays and Treatises on Philosophical Subjects*. Peterborough: Broadview Press, 2013.

James Anderson's Constitutions (1723).

Kant, Immanuel. *The Critique of Pure Reason*, translated by J. M. D. Meiklejohn. Start Publishing LLC: e-book. 2013.

Lessing, Gotthold E. (a), *On the Proof of the Spirit and Power*, in: *Lessing's Theological Writings*, ed. Chadwick. Stanford: Stanford University Press, 1957. 51-55.

Lessing, Gotthold E. (b), *Lessing's Education of the Human Race,* translated by John Dearling Haney. New York: Teachers College Columbia University, 1908.

Pinker, Steven. *The Blank Slate: The Modern Denial of Human Nature.* London: Penguin Books, 2003.

www.theguardian.com/news/reality-check/2015/jun/11/are-naked-backpackers-charged-with-causing-earthquake

VIII

THE MASONIC TEMPLE
BETWEEN UNIVERSAL MODEL AND CULTURAL TROPISMS

FRANÇOIS GRUSON

I will deal with this subject in three parts:

1. The masonic temple as an architectural model;

2. The differentiation of this model by what I call "the tropisms";

3. I will conclude with the danger to see this heritage disappear.

PART ONE: THE MASONIC TEMPLE AS AN ARCHITECTURAL MODEL

Everybody knows the origins of freemasonry in London, in 1717, in the tavern "The Goose and the Gridiron". The interesting thing is the nomadic aspect of the early masonry. Taverns and pubs in London, restaurants and traiteurs in Paris: the place is largely less important that the use of it. However, you an notice the structure of the place itself, which announce the structure of any masonic halls in the world: front room—we call it *parvis* in French—and main room. This nomadic character appears in the illustrations of written divulgations: the taverns and pubs are often replaced by sitting rooms, fitted out to specific ritual activities. This is the case in England, Ireland or France. Philippe Langlet, French historian of freemasonry, made a very interesting study about those pictures. He used to study particularly the bodies and gestures seen in those images. I am more interested myself by the setting and we could ask: where are we, here? in a particular place, perhaps in a chateau somewhere in provincial France, or in hotel particulier in Paris.

Engraving "de Gabanon" – Paris, Ca 1760, Chéreau, d'après Bernigoroth, 1745.

Please notice the carpet on the floor. There is the same, in Abbé Pérau's *Le secret des francs-maçons*, "The Secret of Freemasons". This type of document is often named in French *plan de la loge*, "plan of the lodge". This plan must be understood as a real plan. It is more less like a reproduction of the plan of Solomon's temple in Jerusalem. We can consider it like a real architectural project. It is in the same time the plan of the physical lodge, the place in witch the ritual takes place, and a mental plan that you have to integrate as a programme or mental schedule. Brethren have to learn it, to know it by heart and to able to draw it by themselves. People also can wear it on them, when the plan is drawn on their apron, and can also fetch it with them, on glasses, on plates, on tobacco or pills boxes. Gradually, this plan is leaving the soil and the piece of fabric. It becomes a decorative schedule, and this schedule will gradually reach the wall of the place where ceremonies take place.

Little and little, mental objects of the drawing become real objects in the place: tools, stones, checkerboard on the floor, salomonian columns, etc. A notarial inventory of the lodge "L'union parfaite" in La Rochelle, gives us a very precise list of this ritual equipment, which has not changed during the 18th century or nowadays.

Let's return to Solomon's temple, which is the biblical reference of the masonic temple. Solomon's temple is described in the Kings' Book and in the Judges' Book. During the Renaissance, many authors and architects will attempt to redraw it by the Bible's description. These graphic reconstitutions give the basics of the architectural model of the masonic temple, with its invariants, especially the tripartite division in three different zones: Ulam, outside of the main room, Hekal, the main part of the main room, and Debhir at the east of the temple—actually the west in Jerusalem's—where sits the worshipful master.

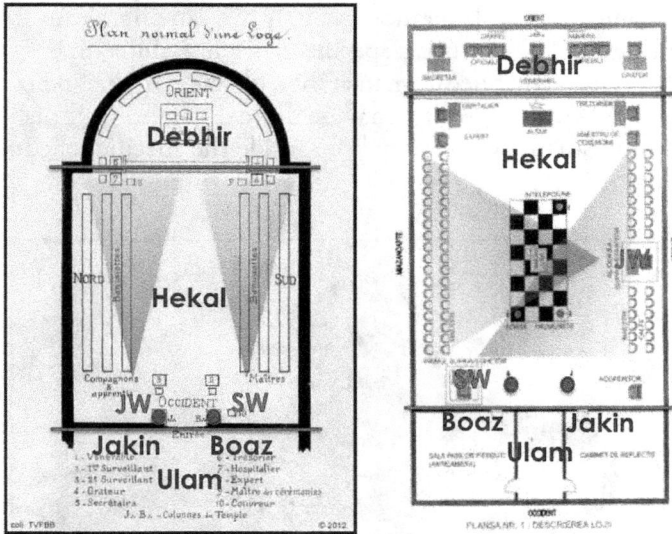

Right: "Modern" schedule in Rite Français—Left: "Ancient" schedule in Scottish Rite.

There are only two variants of this model: the "Modern" one, and the "Ancient" one. You can recognize them by the positions of the two salomonian columns Jakin and Boozand by the positions of the two wardens, senior and junior: in the French Rite—Rite Français Moderne—and in the Scottish Rite—Rite Ecossais Ancien & Accepté. In those two versions, this model it totally globalized: you will find exactly the same schedule, for instance, in Aberdeen, Scotland or in Tokyo, Japan, in Dordrecht, Netherlands, Copenhagen, Denmark or Perigueux, France, or in Bogota, Columbia, La Chaux de Fonds, Switzerland and Kayseslautern, Germany.

PART TWO: THE DIFFERENTIATION OF THE ARCHITECTURAL MODEL BY THE TROPISMS

I borrow this word "tropisms" from biology. I mean, by this word, the ways of adaptation of a model by several aspects: countries, witch means climate, culture, technology or means. With this notion, we can assess the capacity of adaptation of the architectural model witch must stay identifiable.

With their wish of universality, freemasons seek a universal architectural vocabulary. Since the 18th century, Ancient Egyptian style represents their membership of an older tradition than the Judeo-Christian tradition. Inside or outside, Egypt is actually a very easy and recognizable way to express a masonic identity. In France and Italy, we can observe an attempt to create, during the 19th century, a specific masonic architectural style, made with triangles instead of neo-roman arches, like here in Perigueux or there, in Lyon. Worldwide, the reality may be quite different: in India, masonic temples seem Indian, even if they keep inside the specific schedule of the architectural model.

Former masonic temple in Lyon—Destroyed.

We can observe the same phenomena all around the world—unless of course in the countries where freemasonry is forbidden. Sometimes, masonic architecture can borrow to local specific traditions, like Spanish influence in the south of USA, or pre-Columbian style in North-Hollywood, California, or in Cozumel, Mexico. The idea is the same: connect freemasonry to an older local tradition. There is sometimes a form of syncretism in the way to connect freemasonry to local or specific traditions or cultures, like here, in Chinatown in San Francisco. We also must refer to technical tropisms, connected with financial or available means. American pioneers use pioneers' means and local construction materials: wood, brick or timber. In the same way, modern American freemasons use modern materials like concrete, and express a form of modernity in the way they build their new temples.

The most important tropism to consider is probably the local religion. Following countries, the freemasonry is accepted or not following religious conception. The Roman Catholic Church had forbidden freemasonry very soon. In catholic countries, masonic temple are often hidden behind plain and discreet fronts, like in Perugia, Italy, or also here in France, in Besançon, where former churches has been transformed in masonic temples. We can find the same discretion in buildings especially built for a masonic use, like in Angers or Strasbourg. At the contrary, in protestant countries masonic building show themselves as civil institutions, visible and legible in the public space of the city. This is generally the case in Nordic countries, like here in Norway and Denmark, but also in the whole Anglo-Saxon world: Great Britain, USA, Canada, Australia and New-Zealand.

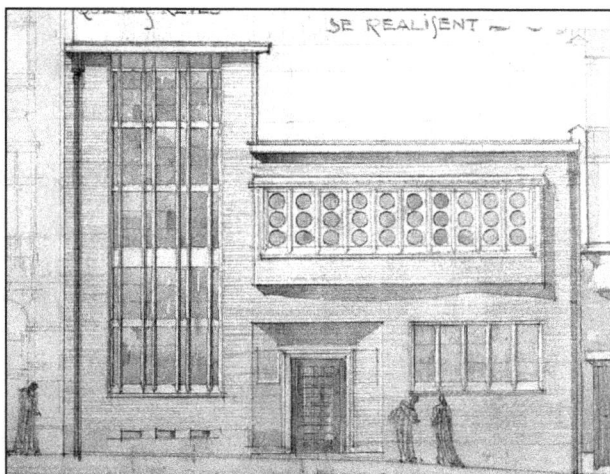

Former masonic temple in Brussels – Fernand Bodson architect.

Conclusion: A Heritage in Danger

I will end this presentation with an alarm call. Masonic architecture is in danger: all around the world, masonic buildings are abandoned, even if they own a real patrimonial value, like in Wilkes Barre, Pennsylvania, or Aurora, Illinois. The main reason is the decline of frequentation of lodges. I found several dozen of examples in the United States of magnificent masonic buildings, abandoned or ruined. In Pakistan, religious intolerance has closed the masonic lodges. Earthquake in Italy, civil war in Liberia: we can check many reasons to find masonic buildings in state of ruins.

Because of a great lack of knowledge about this architecture, we will find the same dereliction all around the word, even in France or in Fiji Islands! Sometimes, despite of civilians' protests, masonic buildings are destroyed, just because people don't know what to do with them. Viollet-le-Duc said that we must accept to transform heritage to avoid loosing it. This is the case in New Orleans, where masonic temple became a luxury hotel or in Portland, Oregon, where masonic temple is now the historic museum of the city. In Brussels, this remarkable masonic temple became the exhibition gallery of the Modern Architecture Archives, thanks to Maurice Culot, who was the first historian of architecture in the word who took care to masonic architectural heritage.

EVOLUTION OF CO-MASONIC ENGLISH-LANGUAGE BLUE LODGE FREEMASONIC RITUAL

KAREN KIDD
Independent Scholar
1 March 2015

The Blue Lodge ritual worked in the Order to which I belong is called "the *Lauderdale*", at times called the "*British Ritual.*" It is a revision of "the *Dharma.*" The *Dharma* was compiled well more than a century ago, mostly from British but also a variety Continental European ritual traditions, with some Theosophical influence that blends well with the pre-existing Judeo-Christian elements.

These are facts but they remain little known, even by most Co-Masons and certainly the vast majority of gender-based Masons. That little knowing creates problems. History loathes a vacuum. When humans don't remember something, they seldom hesitate to make things up. Not lies, exactly. For Masons of any type, "traditional history" equates to 'myth.'

Stories that for generations circulated about Co-Masonic ritual are closer to folklore. As such, these stories are told, retold and become much cherished. Over time, scholars quote these stories, often because it's all they have to go on, and thereby allow themselves to be convinced the stories are true. There's an old movie line that says, "When the legend becomes fact, print the legend."[1] I can tell you from my own experience that there are many who don't want to give up these stories.

I'm not here to retell those stories. I'm here to tell you what really happened—the truth.

1. ROOTS OF CO-MASONIC RITUAL

To find the deepest roots of Co-Masonic ritual, we have to consider the roots of all Freemasonic ritual. And that's not so easy because many of those roots are unknown to us. The history of all Freemasonic ritual cannot be traced in any linear way. That kind of research is ongoing but I am not convinced it ever will be entirely nailed down.

The roots of Co-Masonic ritual grow deep into the Malecraft ritual that came before. And the roots of that are much disputed. We like to say that the roots of our ritual are in the Operative Guilds but that has never been firmly established and there is some research that suggests it isn't true at all.[2] The beginning is somewhere long before the union of the Antients and the Moderns in 1813, sometime in that a murky period Masonically referred to as "time immemorial".

Which is a Masonic euphemism for "we don't know."

We arrive at the dawn of the modern Freemasonic period. It is a cacophony of many rituals and likely little uniformity. "Likely" because, again, this is "time immemorial" and "we don't know." None of this, as yet, is written down. The earliest of modern Freemasonic ritual comes to us only in the exposures and even those represent only a small portion of the rituals being worked at that time. All of these rituals, the unknown and the known - or we think we know or maybe we know a little and what we don't know, we make up - form the tiniest of roots in the tree of English-language Co-Masonic Blue Lodge ritual.

That chaotic pool of ritual was the state of affairs until toward the end of the 18th Century. Slowly, as we move toward the surface, the roots begin to join and thicken as recognizable ritual forms take hold. There amalgamate literally hundreds of types of rituals even within these forms. Though they, in this period, have much in common, there's enough variation that they often have their own names. For *Emulation*-type ritual, there is *Working, Taylors, Logic, Stability, Universal* and more. There is, in fact, much multiplicity in rituals throughout the world but the general forms remain. Freemasons the world over distinguish themselves based on the ritual forms in their locales. This is just as true of Co-Freemasons as any other Freemasons.

2. First Co-Masonic Rituals

The first female Co-Mason was Maria Desraismes, initiated into an otherwise all-Male Lodge "Les Libres Penseurs" (The Freethinkers) at Le Pecq in France. She is initiated into the Craft in a Lodge working some variation of the *French Rite*. In the next decade, she would co-found the world's first

Co-Masonic order, Le Droit Humain, with George Martin, who himself came up through Masonry working a variation of the *French Rite*.[3]

George Martin, sometime before the turn of the 20th Century, created a unique variation of the *French Rite* for use in LDH Lodges, the *Rituel Des Trois Premiers Degrés*. He explained himself in the foreword of the 1905 edition of this ritual, saying, "In a word, I brought over, to the letter, all the ancient rituals with some changes, but without harming the general symbolic spirit in which they had been designed; to simplify or, were necessary, redact them to provide for the broader philosophical spirit of our Obed.·. and the introduction of women into Freemasonry."[4]

George Martin, founder of International Co-Freemasonry, Le Droit Humain, with his wife Maria Georges Martin. George Martin produced the first ritual book, a variation of the *French Rite*, used in LDH Lodges and later would be named for him. An English-language edition was produced for English-language lodges. This image was autographed by the Martins as a gift to LDH-American Federation President Louis Goaziou. Reproduced here with kind permission of the Honorable Order of American Co-Masonry, the American Federation of Human Rights.

This ritual, with its successive revisions over more than a century, is still worked in LDH-French Federation Lodges today. It is not the only ritual being worked in LDH-French Federation Lodges but, for the purposes of this paper, it's the only one I'm going to talk about. This was the ritual worked in LDH in 1902 when the first English-speaking Lodge formed. As such, this ritual helps form the tap root of this tree of English-language Co-Masonic Blue Lodge ritual. We are nearing the surface where the tree will trunk.

At the heart of that first English Lodge and the wider spread of Co-Free-masonry throughout the English-speaking world is Annie Besant. She was a woman of many titles: orator, writer, socialist, women's rights advocate, union organizer, politician, supporter of Irish and Indian self-rule, atheist turned Theosophist, and a great deal more.

Besant and her followers were initiated, passed and raised in Paris into Co-Freemasonry in 1902. It was they who founded the first British Co-Masonic Lodge, Human Duty No 6 in London, consecrated in the autumn of that year. Besant, almost thru sheer force of will, transformed the formerly largely French phenomenon into a worldwide movement that she herself spread throughout the British Empire.[5]

In these very early days, Human Duty used an English translation of LDH's *French Rite* ritual, which continues to be used today under the name *George Martin Ritual*. However, the Brothers of Human Duty decided very early that they didn't like it. And they didn't like it because the French Rite ritual wasn't British. Male members of Human Duty had previous experience with English, Irish and Scottish Malecraft Lodges and understood those ritual forms. The translated French Rite ritual was alien to them. They informed the female members of their Lodge that this ritual was not British, that British rituals were available and, in this way, made total the dissatisfaction with the translated *French Rite* ritual.

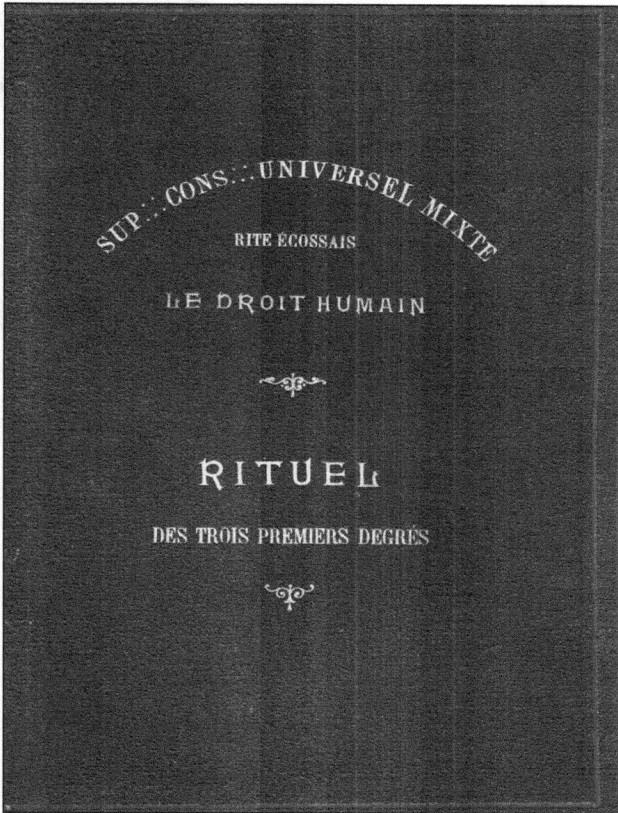

Front cover of the 1905 edition of what later would be called the *George Martin Ritual.*

So the Brothers of Human Duty asked for, and in about mid-1903 got, permission from LDH headquarters in Paris to develop a ritual that they preferred.[6] They were, in fact, given free rein.[7] One of the prevailing myths about the ritual they eventually arrived at is that they stole it. The truth is there was no need for theft. They likely bought the rituals they used from any number of British bookstores. The United Grand Lodge of England did not then—and does not now—authorize any particular ritual for their Lodges to use. For this reason, and as aids to memory, many British Free-masons turned to the many published editions available. These were ba-sically exposures that had been around long enough to become generally accepted.

I've never come across any documentation that spells out exactly which of these rituals were used by these early British Co-Masons but it can be worked backward. The ritual they developed certainly has much in common with the *Text Book of Freemasonry*, of which the latest edition had been released in 1901. I've had marvelous opportunities, for years, to study this topic with ritual scholars who are better at this than am I. The prevailing opinion among us is that this English-language Co-Masonic Blue Lodge ritual has much more in common with *The Perfect Ceremonies of Craft Masonry* and its companion text, *The Lectures of the Three Degrees in Craft Masonry*.

In particular, the earliest Co-Masonic Blue Lodge Tracing Boards in this first ritual's second edition, with a few additions, most closely resemble those in *The Lectures of the Three Degrees in Craft Masonry*. Also, this first ritual's habit of referring to a Candidate as "A.B." could likewise have been borrowed from either or both the *Text Book of Freemasonry* and *The Perfect Ceremonies of Craft Masonry*.[8]

It likely is from these sources that the bulk of *Emulation*-style ritual[9] enters this first English-language Co-Masonic Blue Lodge ritual. There are, however, elements that are not quite so easy to track down but generally look like they come from Irish, Scottish and French traditions. There also is the barest overlay of Theosophical influence that in no way intrudes upon the Judeo-Christian elements present in British ritual forms.

3. ENGLISH-LANGUAGE RITUAL COMPILERS

It is natural to wonder who the editors were. First I'll say who they were not. It wasn't Annie Besant. She never claimed she compiled Co-Masonic Ritual. She most certainly didn't have enough experience to pull off such an editing job in the very short amount of time in which it was done. More critically, she was surrounded by Brethren who did have this experience and it was her habit to delegate jobs like this.

For those who cherish this myth of Besant the ritual editor, I can offer no comfort. There's plenty of evidence that Besant simply did not have the knowledge required. In lectures, speeches and even private letters, Besant habitually confused "Scottish ritual" with the "Ancient and Accepted Scottish Rite", the latter of which isn't Scottish.[10] Whoever produced this first English-language Co-Masonic Blue Lodge ritual not only understood that distinction but also had considerable Masonic ritual experience. This is an error that has too often repeated by modern Masonic scholars who've looked into this history.[11]

As we'll see, Besant's confusion would indirectly lead to the introduction of Scottish ritual into LDH-British Federation.

Two other Brothers I am quite certain were not involved in the initial development of this first ritual were Charles Leadbeater and James Wedgwood. I realize these two are darn near everyone else's favorite suspects but it just isn't possible. Neither man was a Co-Mason in 1903 nor neither had much prior experience in Freemasonry.[12] Wedgwood did not even meet Besant until the following year. Both became Theosophists soon enough but Wedgwood was not initiated into the Craft until 1912 and Leadbeater not until 1915.[13] Both men very likely knew, by association, who the editors actually were and likewise were in a good position to know details about the editing process; but they were not arbiters of that process. Within about ten years, their time as ritual editors certainly would come but neither Leadbeater nor Wedgwood had a hand in compiling this first ritual.

Autographed photo of Charles Leadbeater reproduced here with kind permission of the Honorable Order of American Co-Masonry, the American Federation of Human Rights.

Another "person" who was not a compiler is the Theosophical Master, the Comte St. Germain, with whom Leadbeater said he had been, since 1901, communicating as "Prince Ragozcy."[14] Scholars of Masonry, Co-Masonic and otherwise, very often have claimed involvement of Theosophical Masters in the development of Blue Lodge ritual.[15] I believe the confusion lies in the assumption that Co-Masonic ritual did not evolve so much as burst onto the scene in a sort of "Big Bang". The truth is that Co-Masonic ritual did evolve and the initial process took decades. Just because something was true at one date doesn't make it true in an earlier date. Influence by the "Masters" can be verified for the higher degrees in Co-Freemasonry but not in the Blue Lodge.

In fact, Leadbeater himself found, very late in his career, that he had to explain why there had been no such influence in the development of Co-Masonic Blue Lodge ritual. He explained it by describing a conversation he said he had with Prince Ragozcy in a paper published 17 months before Leadbeater's death 1 March 1934. Leadbeater said he didn't ask Prince Ragozcy about his thoughts on the development of Co-Masonic Blue Lodge ritual until after Leadbeater's Initiation in 1915. By that time, the oldest of Co-Masonic Blue Lodge ritual was about 12 years old and headed into its fourth revision. According to Leadbeater, Prince Ragozcy was satisfied with the way the Blue Lodge ritual had developed without any help from him. Leadbeater quoted the Master as saying:

> "Your new ritual for the Blue Degrees is satisfactory, and should be retained just as it is, except that it would be desirable to shorten some of the Charges[16]. I should recommend you to avoid the uses of specially [sic] Theosophical terms and the introduction of Sanskrit words. I do not wish to be erected into a dogma; there are some of your Lodges which desire openly to recognize Me and to use My portrait. I have no objection to this except that the portrait is a very bad one; I can utilize it and pour force through it. But there may be other Lodges which do not wish to take exactly this line; leave them free to follow their own devices, and do not in any way treat them differently, or slight or look down upon them. We must be all things to all men, as we may by any means save some. For those who desire it and show themselves worthy of it, the Esoteric Masonry should be given in higher degrees, in which the ritual of the lower degrees might be explained."[17]

In addition to having figured out who didn't compile this first ritual, I do indeed have my own suspects for who did. Francesca Arundale, one of the first British Co-Masons and she who introduced Besant to Co-Freemasonry, was herself a ritual expert, as was her nephew, George Arundale. The Arundales both were members of Human Duty. The Arundales also produced the English translation of the French Rite ritual LHD was already using. They also moved to Adyar at the time the new ritual was developed. It seems perfectly logical that the Arundales were up to the task of producing a more British-flavored Co-Masonic ritual.

4. DHARMA

Whoever developed the first English-language Co-Masonic Blue Lodge ritual, it was developed specifically for *Dharma* Lodge in Benares City, in Adyar, India.[18] This is how the ritual got its name, from the name of the Lodge where it first was worked.[19] It soon was in use in Human Duty as well.

Francesca Arundale, one of the first British Co-Masons who, with her nephew George Arundale, may have produced the first English-language Blue Lodge Co-Masonic Ritual, the "*Dharma Workings*". Reproduced with kind permission of the Theological Society in Manila.

The *Dharma* forms the trunk of the tree of Co-Masonic English-language Blue Lodge ritual. From it grows a number of branches, including a few that have been grafted on. Its growth was insured when a general understanding was reached at LDH headquarters in Paris that the *Dharma* would be used in any other English-speaking Co-Masonic lodge founded in the world. However, almost immediately, there was a glaring exception.

Across the Atlantic, in 1903, Antoine Muzzarelli, a French Freemason operating under the direction of George Martin, established Co-Freemasonry in the US.[20] In a whirlwind of chaotic activity, he founded 50 Lodges in the US over the next five years. And he decided very early that the ritual US Masonic Lodges were not going to work was the *Dharma*. He was a French Freemason, familiar with the *French Rite* and, upon seeing the *Dharma* for the first time, announced himself "at a loss to understand" it.[2]

Muzzarelli dealt with that lack of understanding by ignoring the *Dharma*. His successor, Louis Goaziou, continued that policy well into the next decade and struggled to fend it off into the 1930s. Consequently, in this very early period in the history of worldwide Co-Freemasonry, US Lodges turned elsewhere for their rituals. As these lodges worked in multiple languages, including English, Italian and French, it likewise was natural that they worked ritual of different languages. They used the *French Rite*, a translation of the *French Rite* or any ritual they could get their hands on, including US-based *Preston-Webb*-type ritual.

Further, they faced some of the same pressures as did their Brothers in the British Federation of LDH, the desire for a ritual relevant to their own part of the world. This would lead to US Co-Masons developing their own ritual, as we will see, called "the *North American* Ritual".

So with US lodges excepted, the *Dharma* workings were introduced into many English speaking Co-Masonic lodges.

Most of the *Dharma* would have been quite familiar to early Anglo-centric Co-Masons with previous experience in Malecraft Masonry. Rather than create a ritual from out of the ether, the *Dharma* is a compilation of many existing rites, in addition to influence from *Text Book of Freemasonry* and *Perfect Ceremonies of Craft Masonry*. Wedgwood later reported that a total of 52 Craft rituals were consulted for this first compilation[22]. That certainly was a detail he was in a position to know. Francesca Arundale later said that all the rituals consulted were of the Ancient and Accepted Scottish Rite[23], which is rather a broad statement but she, I believe also, was exceptionally placed to know. Mabel Besant-Scott, the daughter of Annie Besant who often acted as her mother's deputy, said "several rituals were used, English, Scottish and French."[24]

My own observation is that the compilation is largely Emulation-type with other British and continental Masonic elements included. The *Dharma* was complete and in use by late 1903, though its official first edition date is 1904.[25]

Producing this ritual had to have been a major challenge and it soon became clear that there were problems with the 1904 edition of the *Dharma*. The ritual itself was very brief and barebones. There were no tracing boards or other illustrations included. More than that, the workings were not arranged in the order in which the ceremonies would be worked, which required quite a lot of flipping back and forth in ritual books. There also was considerable rubric lacking, including instances in which a portion of the ritual was simply announced and then dismissed as "This is done" without any explanation of how it should be done. This would be very confusing for any new Mason. In 1904, there were a considerable lot of new Masons in Co-Masonic Lodges worldwide.

In 1908, the *Dharma*'s second edition was issued with additional rubric, instruction and the first of the Harris-inspired Tracing Boards so similar to those in *The Lectures of the Three Degrees in Craft Masonry*. There also is, on the second edition's title page, an indication of how much the 1901 edition of *Text Book of Freemasonry* may have influenced the *Dharma*. Both list the author as "Compiled by A MEMBER OF THE CRAFT" in the same, or at least very similar, font. The first edition of the *Dharma* did not list an author.[26]

As if to crown this ritual as uniquely Co-Masonic, "the whole [was] adorned by the beautifying hand of The V. Ills. Bro. Annie Besant with 'Mystic Charges'", Arnold Banks later wrote.[27] However, these "Mystic Charges" of Annie Besant in the Blue Lodge, one for each of the three degrees, were not originally so-called. Instead, they appear to have been Besant's impressions of those degrees written specifically for *Dharma* Lodge. In the 1908 edition of the *Dharma* ritual, they were inserted at the end of each degree with the words "It may be read." In later editions, the name "Mystic Charge" was used, likely because they were inserted after the traditional charges.

In 1908, there also appeared another revision of the *Dharma* now known as the *Harrison Ritual*, named after its primary compiler, Frank D. Harrison. Harrison served was Grand Secretary of LDH-British Federation, quite some time after he left the Golden Dawn "because he disliked its Masonic ethos."[28] I have never seen a copy of the *Harrison* nor do I know anyone who has. It could well be that no copies have survived.

5. HARRISON

What recorded contemporary mention remains of the *Harrison* indicates it was very short-lived. Goaziou knew Harrison and he gave as a gift to Harrison a copy of the *North American* ritual[29]. There's every reason to believe Goaziou was familiar with both the *Dharma* and the *Harrison*. In a speech he gave in 1915, Goaziou referred to the *Dharma*'s "confusion at the beginning" and "the *Harrison* ritual that followed the *Dharma* edition differed very much."

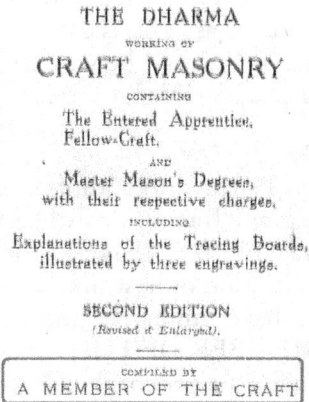

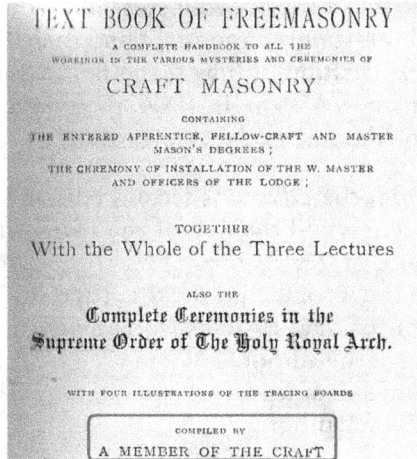

Title pages of the 1908/second edition of the "*Dharma Workings*", left, and the 1901 edition of "Text Book of Freemasonry". There is marked similarity between the two, especially with the compiler listed in both as "A MEMBER OF THE CRAFT" in the same, or at least very similar font. This may indicate how much the latter influenced the former.

Other revisions of the *Dharma* have been far more successful in terms of how much they still are worked. However, a few things the *Dharma* does not have in its 1908 second edition are incense, candle lighting and processions. When they do arrive in the next revision, it won't be because of what often is reported. I find that rank-and-file Freemasons, including Co-Masons, think of these as being Theosophical additions as a matter of course. After all, they ask me, what else could they be?

Well, there were indeed a lot of Theosophists among the early Co-Masons but they weren't all Theosophists. These early Co-Masons also included Male-only Masons and Brothers from other religious and esoteric traditions. Leadbeater and Wedgwood were on the cusp of founding the Liberal Catholic Church. So Theosophy is not the only tradition on the ground at the time.

6. *LAUDERDALE*

It is at this point that Wedgwood enters as a ritual editor. In 1913, Wedgwood was responsible for a revision of the *Dharma* called the *Lauderdale*. Not that it was called *Lauderdale* at the time. When it first was released, it was referred to as the "third" or "1913" revision of the *Dharma*. However, it is with the 1913 revision that another ritual begins to develop and to become something distinct from the original *Dharma*. This distinction would, sometime after 1923, be referred to as *Lauderdale*. That name comes from the LDH-British Federation's Headquarters established in January of that year at 2 *Lauderdale* Road in London.[30]

It seems Wedgwood did not get all the revisions he wanted in his 1913 edition. We don't have a lot of details but Goaziou, almost two decades later, referred to this period as when "Bro Wedgwood began to meddle with the ritual." Goaziou explained that Wedgwood "tried to bring too much of the Church influence into it."[31]

Goaziou made that observation later when Brothers of LDH-American Federation were considering whether to accept the, by then, latest revision of the *Lauderdale* and there was some suspicion there were unwarranted Theosophical elements in Wedgwood's original revision. Goaziou pointed out that it wasn't Wedgwood the Theosophist so much as Wedgwood the former Anglican who, in 1913, was beginning to lay down the ground work of the Liberal Catholic Church. It seems what Wedgwood wanted to add to this 1913 revision involved considerable smells and bells more often associated with church services.

For all his so-called meddling, Wedgwood was allowed to retain in the 1913 revision three elements that actually have their roots in Freemasonry but, pleasantly for him, were very church like. These three elements were processions, incense and candle lighting. Processions and candles can be found in many Masonic orders, sometimes in public and they certainly continue to feature in many continental European Orders.[32] The censing ceremony established in the 1913 revision seems to have been lifted, complete with the same number of thurible swings, from the Malecraft Grand East of the Netherlands.

Most pointedly, these additions are placed not during the ritual itself but just before the Lodge is opened. This was done to avoid any accusations of innovation in the ritual itself, which doesn't begin until the opening of the Lodge.[33]

The notes included in the 1913 edition make reference to consulting "the best of existing rituals and in consultation with experienced Brethren"; and that this revision was intended to "embody some of the best points of these rituals, in addition to the many valuable features peculiar to our own workings." There was additional rubric, made "both necessary and justifiable" by "the rapid growth of our Order in districts where personal instruction is rarely available."

The next revision of the *Lauderdale* followed in 1916, likely by both Wedgwood and Leadbeater, to add Masonic hymns commonly used in Emulation-based English Lodges, in addition to "certain verses from the V.S.L." also used in Emulation-based ritual. It was with this revision that the hymn "Closed is the Solemn Hour" was added as a recessional. Originally written by E. Armine Wodehouse, the hymn also was used for what Wedgwood called "a ceremonial movement named 'The Temple of the Rosy Cross' of which Mrs. Besant, Mrs. Hotchener (then Russak) and I were the principals." The hymn is still part of the Liberal Catholic Church's liturgy, as a retrocessional. It isn't clear why this much "meddling" to bring in an extra-Masonic church hymn was allowed in the 1916 revision when it wasn't allowed in the 1913 revision. However, Wedgwood had picked up much influence in the British Federation in those three years. Also, the hymn is beautiful and comes after the Lodge is closed, so isn't a part of the ritual itself. Perhaps it seemed a very pleasant addition.[34]

The fifth edition of the *Lauderdale*, issued in 1925, provided greater explanation of what, by then, actually was being called the *Lauderdale*, setting it apart from the *Dharma* and other revisions. By this time, Lodges were given a choice among sanctioned rituals with "some preferring the more ornate, others the plainer rituals," the notes of the 1925 edition explained. However, this revision also noted other additions that were making their way into some Co-Masonic Lodge rooms, including "the placing of any picture or pictures on the walls, or of the symbolic chair in the North." These additions, the notes pointed out, "are all non-essential" and that "Lodges should observe towards each other the old rule: 'In things essential, Unity; in non-essentials, Liberty; in all things, Charity.'"

Annie Besant, long time president of the Supreme Council of Worldwide Co-Free-masonry, and just behind her Marie Russak, later Hotchener, in a photo taken as they were leaving the cornerstone laying ceremony at Theosophical Headquarters in London, 29 August 1926. In addition to both being highly influential Co-Masons in Le Droit Humain—British Federation, both also were principals in what James Wedgwood called "a ceremonial movement named 'The Temple of the Rosy Cross.'" This movement made a small contribution, a recessional hymn, to an early edition of what now is known as *Lauderdale Ritual*, a revision of the *Dharma Workings*. Image reproduced here with kind permission of the Honorable Order of American Co-Masonry, the American Federation of Human Rights.

There have been further revisions to the *Lauderdale* over the decades but since 1925 they have mostly involved improved rubric. Co-Masonic ritual was largely set by the mid1920s and the very vast majority of ritual worked in Co-Masonic Lodges today look very much like what developed in the first decades of the 20th Century. Of all of them, the *Lauderdale* is the most commonly worked.

7. OTHER BRITISH CO-MASONIC RITUALS

While the *Lauderdale* is the most successful of revisions of the *Dharma*, it is not the only one. There is the "Verulam Workings", issued in the early 1920s as a sort of compromise between the elaborate *Lauderdale* and plainer English and Scottish workings. There also is the Sydney, produced in 1916, that has much in common with the *Lauderdale* and is so-called because it was printed in Sydney, Australia.

There also are rituals in use in the LDH-British Federation that are not descended from the *Dharma* but, instead, form branches grafted onto the ritual tree. One of these, the Scottish Standard, points out how "the whoops factor" can figure in Ritual acceptance.[35] When the Brothers of Stability Lodge in London were, in 1922, selecting which ritual they would use, the Brothers recalled hearing Annie Besant, in lectures and speeches, for years stating the ritual then in use was "Scottish." The Brothers believed it. More to the point, this particular Lodge was interested in getting back to the origins of Co-Masonic ritual. Their understanding was that this meant real, unadulterated, unedited, unrevised Scottish ritual.

So they paid six shillings each for copies of the Scottish Workings of Craft Masonry.[36] The Lodge also, quite innocently, fully informed Headquarters this was the ritual they intended to use, which should have raised brows at HQ in London but it didn't. It seems Stability's choice of ritual was rubber stamped without question.

Stability Lodge 757's Temple at 27 Hereford Square SW 7 in London was consecrated 10 July 1922. Stability labored several months without issue, quite happily working the Scottish ritual.[37] It couldn't last. The following November, it came to the attention of Headquarters that Stability was working an unsanctioned ritual. They were told to stop. The brethren of Stability made numerous appeals but it finally took the intervention of Francesca Arundale to get Stability Lodge's ritual back. From that date forward, the Scottish Workings of Craft Masonry have been worked in LDH-British Federation.

Another Co-Masonic ritual of LDH-British Federation not descended from the *Dharma* is called the "Irish Ritual."[38] It is unique to LDH-British Federation because of its workings, which are "in the round." It was introduced to the order in the 1950s by a Brother who formerly had been Master of an Irish military lodge. Apparently this particular Irish ritual had been known in the Order except for the secrets, which this IPM agreed to pass on to Glady's Nash-Wortham, who was Most Puissant Grand Commander of the British Federation at the time.

When he did, it apparently sparked a memory for Nash-Wortham. She immediately said to him, "Get busy at once and found a Lodge. There is one typed copy of the ritual in the Library—how it got there no-one knows. I give permission for you to have it."

That first Co-Masonic Lodge working the Irish ritual was Tir N'an Oige, which apparently means "The Land of the Ever Young", or "The Land of Everlasting Youth".

8. *North American*

In all these ways, LDH-British Federation seeded the rest of worldwide English-speaking Co-Freemasonry with ritual developed in that jurisdiction but, as mentioned earlier, it was not universally accepted. In North America, it was an especially hard sell. The Brothers there initially wanted ritual of a North American flavor and for US-based Co-Masons, this was an especially tricky proposition. They were surrounded by a Malecraft Masonry that worked, and still works, a multiplicity of Preston-Webb types.

However, early US Co-Freemasons also were often immigrants who almost as often brought Masonic traditions with them from throughout the world. For them, local was very broad. Muzzarelli and Goaziou certainly rejected the *Dharma* as being too British but they also wanted ritual that would please their heterogeneous brethren.

Both of them left this task to a ritual expert, Alida de Leeuw. Born in Holland in about 1855, she was widowed while still quite young and then decided to enter the education field. A proponent of the Froebel method of Kindergarten, she worked her way to the top of her field. She was among the first Theosophists to become a Co-Mason in North America and she quickly studied her way to ritual perfection.

By 1904, Muzzarelli had soundly—if unilaterally—rejected the *Dharma* and assigned de Leeuw the task of helping him develop a ritual for North

American Lodges. It had largely taken form when Muzzarelli died in the fall of 1908. Goaziou, himself not yet especially expert in ritual, was quite impressed with de Leeuw's work. He gave her "full charge of ritual matters" for the next decade.[39] The ritual she produced is now called "the North American Ritual" but in her day, it was "Ritual of the Symbolic Lodges in America". The earliest editions were printed in Goaziou's own print shop in Charleroi, Pennsylvania.

The ritual de Leeuw produced is rather busy. However, for all of Muzzarelli and Goaziou's decision not to use the *Dharma*, the *North American* has quite a lot in common with the *Dharma*. For instance, the first editions of the *North American* use exactly the same tracing boards as had been introduced in the second edition of the *Dharma*. There also are elements from other traditions, including the barest whiff of Preston Webb and some remarkable elements in the floor work that are reminiscent of European workings.

Alida de Leeuw, an educator, Theosophist and early North American Co-Mason who compiled the "Ritual of the Symbolic Lodges in America", better known as the "North American Ritual". Image reproduced here with kind permission of the Honorable Order of American Co-Masonry, the American Federation of Human Rights.

While the *North American* was, initially, the ritual used in a majority of US Lodges, it was never the only ritual used. It existed alongside the *French Rite* and other foreign language rituals in Lodges where English did not prevail.

It was not until 1934 that the *Lauderdale* was approved for use in North American Lodges.[40] I have no record that the *Lauderdale* ever was so-called by US Co-Masons. Instead, it was called the "English" or "British" ritual. Over the next few decades, this *British Ritual* gained greater acceptance over the *North American*. The British ritual finally assumed totality in the 1990s when the last Lodge of the Order still working the *North American* went dark.

When I was initiated, the ritual was just "the ritual." Very few Brothers called it "the British ritual" or even the *Lauderdale*. Most never knew it ever had those names.

This is how history becomes lost and why myths take hold. But the tree remains for anyone who cares to take a close enough look.

BIBLIOGRAPHY

Anon. "International Co-Freemasonry: Ritual of the Three Craft Degrees Irish Working." Supreme Council of International Co-Freemasonry, 1957.

Anon. "International Co-Freemasonry: Ritual of the Three Craft Degrees (Lauderdale)." Eastern Federation, 1916 Revision issued in 1947.

Anon. "International Co-Freemasonry: the Verulam Workings of Co-Free-masonry." Wm. McLellan & Co. Ltd., 1935

Anon. "The Lectures of the Three Degrees of Craft Masonry." A. Lewis, 1874.

Anon. "The Perfect Ceremonies of Craft Masonry." A. Lewis, 1887.

Anon. "The Perfect Ceremonies of Craft Masonry." A. Lewis, 1907.

Anon. "The Scottish Workings of Craft Masonry, Complete and Accurate" A. Lewis, 1898.

Anon. "The 'Standard' Ritual of Scottish Freemasonry." C.C.& A.T. Gardner, 1927.

Anon. "Universal Co-Masonry, Le Droit Humain: Ritual of the Symbolic Lodges in America." Privately Printed in Charleroi, PA, for the American Federation, before 1914.

Anon. "Universal Co-Masonry: Ritual of the Three Craft Degrees." Privately Printed in Sydney, 1916.

Anon. "Universal Joint Freemasonry: The Dharma Workings." Privately Printed for the Dharma Lodge, Benares City, 1904.

A MEMBER OF THE CRAFT. "The Text Book of Freemasonry." Reeves and Turner, 1874

A MEMBER OF THE CRAFT. "The Text Book of Freemasonry." William Reeves, 1901

A MEMBER OF THE CRAFT. "Universal Co-Masonry: The Dharma Working of Craft Masonry." Marden and Co., 1908.

Bogdan, Henrik, and Snoek, Jan A.M. "Handbook of Freemasonry." Brill, 2014.

Bouchard, Maurice, and Michel, Philippe. "Rit Francais d'origine 1785: Dit Rit Primordial de France." Éditions Dervy, 2014.

Ellwood, Robert S. "Islands of the Dawn: The Story of Alternative Spirituality in New Zealand." University of Hawaii Press, 1993.

Hamill, John, and Gilbert, R.A. "World of Freemasonry: An Illustrated History." Aquarian Press, 1991.

Kidd, Karen. "Haunted Chambers: the Lives of Early Women Freemasons." Cornerstone Book Publishers, 2009.

Kidd, Karen. "On Holy Ground: History of the Honorable Order of American Co-Masonry, the American Federation of Human Rights." Masonic Publishing Company of the US, 2011.

Lawrence, the Rev. J.T. "The Work of the Chaplain and The Director of Ceremonies." A. Lewis, 1920

Leadbeater, Charles. "Ancient Ideals in Modern Masonry: An Address Given to the Sydney Lodge No. 404 in 1915." London Craft Lodge of

Universal Co-Freemasonry, Sydney, 1917.

Leadbeater, Charles. "Hidden Life in Freemasonry." Theosophical Publishing House, second edition, 1926.

Leadbeatr, Charles. "The Science of the Sacraments." St. Alban Press, 1920.

Martin, George. "Rituel Des Trois Premiers Degrés". Supreme Council, Le Droit Humain, 1905.

Mehta, Natverlal. "A Craft Guide: Duties of the Officers and Brethren." Private, 1954.

Paton, Chalmers Izett. "Freemasonry: Its Symbolism, Religious Nature, and Law of Perfection." Reeves and Turner, 1873.

Snoek, Jan A.M., and Heidle, Alexandra. "Women's Agency and rituals in Mixed and Female Masonic Orders." Brill, 2008.

Stewart, Trevor."Freemasonry: Old Records, New Ideas." Australian & New Zeland Masonic Research Council, 2013.

Tillet, Gregory. "The Elder Brother." Routledge & Kegan Paul, 1982.

Wade, John. "'Go and Do Thou Likewise': English Masonic Processions from the 18th to the 20th Centuries : Prestonian Lecture for 2009." United Grand Lodge of England, 2009

Webb, James. "The Occult Underground." Open Court Press, 1976.

NOTES

1   "The Man Who Shot Liberty Valance" (Paramount Pictures, 1962)

2   Examples: Henrik Bogdan and Jan A.M. Snoek's "Handbook of Freemasonry", (Brill, 2014), pages 13–16; and "Chapter 1: Origins and Early Development", particularly pages 9–17, of John Hamill and R.A. Gilbert's "World of Freemasonry: An Illustrated History" (Aquarian Press, 1991).

3   Evelyn Caspersz's article, "The Founders of Le Droit Humain" in the July 1935

edition of *The Morning Star: Journal of the Eastern Federation of the British Empire Order of International Co-Freemasonry*.

4 "En un mot, j'ai apporte a la lettre des anciens Rituels toutes les modifications qui, sans nuire a l'esprit Symbolique general dans lequel ils avaient ete concus; les simplifient ou qui s'imposaient a leur redaction par suite du large esprit philosophique de notre Obed.·. et de l'introduction de la femme dans l'Ordre Mason."

5 "Beginnings of Co-Freemasonry in Britain" pages 64 – 67 of the July 1939 edition of *The Morning Star: Journal of the Eastern Federation of the British Empire Order of International Co-Freemasonry*.

6 A very important document that provides a handy timeline for the evolution of LDH-British Federation Blue Lodge ritual is Arnold Bank's article "Masonic Workings" published in the first quarter 1945 edition of *The Morning Star: Journal of the Eastern Federation of the British Empire Order of International Co-Freemasonry*, pages 14 and 15. By 1945, Banks was Most Puissant Grand Commander of LDH-British Federation and was in a position to know the order of Co-Masonic ritual development. Unless otherwise specified, I am using his timeline.

7 Arnold Banks' article "The Women's Masonic movement in the British Empire", pages 34 – 37 of the April 1937 edition of *The Morning Star: Journal of the Eastern Federation of the British Empire Order of International Co-Freemasonry*.

8 Some Masons unfamiliar with "Text Book of Freemasonry," "The Perfect Ceremonies of Craft Masonry" and many other Malecraft rituals available at the turn of the 20th Century have speculated to me that this use of "A.B.", which continues in modern Co-Masonic ritual, is a reference to Annie Besant. While those are, indeed, her initials, in this case "A.B." is just "A.B."

9 It's important to point out that the Emulation-type ritual these early Co-Masons worked with was Emulation-type as it existed in 1903. In addition to a great deal of variation in all these types that can claim to be "Emulation", the United Grand Lodge of England didn't assign a ritual type at the time. In any case, there have been many revisions in those rituals that Co-Masons have not accepted. And, as we will see, Co-Masons have revised their own ritual and those other Emulation types have not accepted those revisions. For these reasons, it is irrelevant to too-closely compare modern Co-Masonic ritual with modern Emulation-type ritual.

10 As examples, see Besant's 27 February 1908 letter to Ursula M. Bright, written from the Theosophical Society in Adyar, Madras, when she writes, "Ours is the Scottish ritual with a few modifications. ..." British Library, Folder 1 of MS 88999; and "Transactions of the *Dharma* Lodge of the Supreme Council of Universal Co-Masonry, Second edition" issued in 1907 by the Lodge then meeting in Benares, in which Besant describes the *Dharma* as "... the Scottish Craft ritual - properly appertains to the Grand Lodge of Scotland. While differing to some extend from the French ritual, it nevertheless bears a close resemblance to the ritual authorized by the Grand Lodge of England and was adopted, with certain

modifications, as more convenient for the purposes of intercourse with the Orders of Freemasons with which Co-Masonic Lodges in British Dominions would probably come into contact."

11 As an example, see the introduction written by Jan Snoek, specifically page 12, of Snoek and Alexandra Heidle's "Women's Agency and rituals in Mixed and Female Masonic Orders" (Brill, 2008).

12 James Webb's "The Occult Underground" (Open Court Press, 1976), pages 103 and 130; Robert S. Ellwood, "Islands of the Dawn: The Story of Alternative Spirituality in New Zealand" (University of Hawaii Press, 1993), page 132; and "The Collected Works of James I. Wedgwood" (Lulu, 2004), page 245.

13 Gregory Tillet, "The Elder Brother" (Routledge &Kegan Paul, 1982) pages 166-174, 178-184, 215-223, 240 and 255.

14 Charles Leadbeater's "Ancient Ideals in Modern Masonry: An Address Given to the Sydney Lodge No. 404 in 1915" (London Craft Lodge of Universal Co- Freemasonry, Sydney, 1917), pages 6 - 7; and "Hidden Life in Freemasonry" (Theosophical Publishing House, second edition, 1926), page 31.

15 For an example, see Andrew Prescott's "'Builders of the Temple of the New Civilisation': Annie Besant and Freemasonry", specifically page 367, of "Women's Agency and rituals in Mixed and Female Masonic Orders" (Brill, 2008).

16 I have found no evidence this ever was done beyond making parts of the charges optional.

17 October 1932 Adyar Theosophist, Leadbeater's article "The Origins of Modern Masonry", as "recorded by Rt. Rev. C.W. Leadbeater" under the listing "QUESTIONS PLACED BEFORE THE MASTER the Comte de St. Germain."

18 The cover of the first edition reads "Privately Printed for The *Dharma* Lodge, Benares City."

19 First quarter *1945 The Morning Star: Journal of the Eastern Federation of the British Empire Order of International Co-Freemasonry*. By 1945, Banks was Most Puissant Grand Commander of LDH-British Federation and was in a position to know the order of Co-Masonic ritual development.

20 For more details about George Martin's relationship with Antoine Muzzarelli and the establishment of Co-Freemasonry in the US, see Karen Kidd's "On Holy Ground: History of the Honorable Order of American Co-Masonry, the American Federation of Human Rights" (Masonic Publishing Company of the US, 2011).

21 See Muzzarelli's 22 March 1905 letter to Alida de Leeuw, preserved in the archives of the Honorable Order of American Co-Masonry, the American Federation of Human Rights in Larkspur, Colorado.

22 See Third Quarter 1947 edition of *The Morning Star: Journal of the Eastern Federation of the British Empire Order of International Co-Freemasonry*, page 43, the article "The V. Ills. Bro. C.W. Leadbeater, 33°" by Bro Lawrence W. Burt, 32°.

23 Francesca Arundale's report to the Supreme Council 8 October 1923, at the British Library, Folder 3 of MS 88999.

24 Besant-Scott's 7 February 1923 letter to Bro N. Fairclough of Stability Lodge, at the British Library, Folder 3 of MS 88999.

25 See Esther Bright's 12 December 1903 letter to Muzzarelli, preserved in the archives of the Honorable Order of American Co-Masonry, the American Federation of Human Rights in Larkspur, Colorado. Bright states, "The ritual I sent you is exactly what is used in this (Human Duty) Lodge." The ritual Bright sent to Muzzarelli was the *Dharma*, which means the *Dharma* was in use by Human Duty by that date.

26 The printer of the *Dharma* ritual's second edition was Marsden and Company in Manchester while the 1901 edition of "Text Book of Freemasonry" was printed by William Reeves Bookseller in London.

27 Note in Arnold Bank's ritual timeline of Co-Masonic ritual Development published in the first quarter 1945 edition of *The Morning Star: Journal of the Eastern Federation of the British Empire Order of International Co-Freemasonry*.

28 "Freemasonry and the Hermetic Tradition" by R.A. Gilbert, *Gnosis Magazine*, page 6, 1987, formerly accessible at mastermason.com

29 I now own this particular ritual book.

30 Headquarters was established there 2 January 1923. See letter from Besant-Scott to all RWMs 2 Jan 1923, British Library, Folder 5 of MS 88999.

31 Page 9, October 1931 *Circular No 122*, preserved in the archives of the Honorable Order of American Co-Masonry, the American Federation of Human Rights Headquarters Archives in Larkspur, Colorado.

32 As an example for processions, see John Wade's "'Go and Do Thou Likewise': English Masonic Processions from the 18th to the 20th Centuries : Prestonian Lecture for 2009" (United Grand Lodge of England, 2009); and Trevor Stewart's paper, "Scottish Masonic Processions", pages 182 – 209 of his "Freemasonry: Old Records, New Ideas" (Australian & New Zeland Masonic Research Council, 2013). As an example for incense, see page 26 – 27 of the Rev. J.T. Lawrence's "The Work of the Chaplain and The Director of Ceremonies" (A. Lewis, 1920). As an example for candles, see pages 254 and 255 of Chalmers Izett Paton's "Freemasonry: Its Symbolism, Religious Nature, and Law of Perfection", (Reeves and Turner, 1873).

33 Goaziou's *Circular 141* November 1934.

34 Charles Webster Leadbeater, "The Science of the Sacraments" (St. Alban Press, 1920), Page 499; "The Collected Works of James I. Wedgwood" (Lulu, 2004), page 249; and "The Holy Eucharist Shorter Form, Benediction of the Most Holy Sacrament" (Albanus Press, 2004), page 42.

35 The details of the story I'm about to impart here come from letters and other documents preserved at the British Library in Folder 3 of MS 88999.

36 Probably the 1921 edition of "Scottish Workings of Craft Masonry, Complete and Accurate" (A Lewis, London).

37 See April 1924 *The Co-Mason Vol XVI* page 95.

38 For much of what follows about the Irish ritual of LDH-British Federation, see the January 1975 edition of *Australian Co-Mason*, page 3.

39 August 1924 American Co-Mason.

40 Goaziou's *Circular 140* October 1934.

X

FRANCIS PULSZKY'S MASONIC PERIODS

LÁSZLÓ VÁRI

This study presents and analyses the hardly known masonic activity of Francis Pulszky. He was the first Grand Master in Hungary from 1867 to 1888.

Pulszky, Ferenc (Francis, Franz, Francesco) was a respected politician and active participant of the Hungarian revolution. He was one of Louis Kossuth's foreign policy advisors, maybe the most influential, he organized Kossuth's UK, US trip and Italian emigration life. As a real politician, in 1867 Pulszky accepted the compromise with the Austrian monarch and returned from exile. Then he continued his political career as a member of Parliament and started an ambitious scientific career as archaeologist, museum director and organizer of scientific life of Hungary.

FRANCIS (FERENC) PULSZKY (1814-1897)

He was born in a wealthy noble family. He started scholarly career at 15 years of age, his world view is greatly influenced by his uncle, the free-thinker Gabor Fejérváry, passionate archaeologist with whom he made several trips abroad as well.

After the revolution in March of 1848 he became a member of the first Hungarian government deputed to the court of Vienna (in fact the first Hungarian foreign minister).

Escaping after the fall of Hungary's war of independence in 1848–1849, Louis Kossuth appointed him as his personal representative. He organized Kossuth's trip to England and America, and escorted him into USA. (In 1852—during his journey—Kossuth was initiated in Cincinnati as a freemason, preceding Pulszky about 10 years.) Pulszky was the Hungarian emigrants' representative in Torino from 1860, but later turned away from Kossuth and supported Francis Deák. As a result, he returned home at 1866 and supported the Compromise with Vienna.

He was extremely versatile: politician, archaeologist, art collector, a member of the Hungarian Academy of Sciences, Director of the National Museum for 25 years, and not just a grey eminence of the Hungarian scientific and political life.[1] His success was due to his gifts: excellent gift for languages, rapid comprehension, assured sense of reality, good writing skills, added to honesty and ruthless. His opponents however held him pretentious, haughty and cynical person.

His masonic life started in Italy as he was initiated probably in 1862 in the lodge Dante Alighieri and he acceded soon the 33rd grade of Scottish Rite. After his returning home took part in the revival of Hungarian Freemasonry. He became the first Grand Master of the Grand Lodge of St John (1870–1886), then the first Grand Master of the Symbolic Grand Lodge of Hungary (1886–1888). His contribution to the development of Hungarian Freemasonry is exceptional.

Despite these his masonic life is almost totally unknown in Hungarian and international literature.

The well-known William R. Denslow's "10,000 Famous Freemasons"[2] doesn't write anything about Pulszky.

PRE-MASONIC PERIOD

Francis Pulszky's uncle, Dániel Ferdinánd Pulszky of Cselfalva was a freemason, member of lodge "Három koronázott csillaghoz és becsületességhez" (To the three crowned stars and honesty). His maternal uncle was the free thinker Gábor Fejérváry—who moved to his sister, Pulszky's mother—had a great influence on the intellectual development of his nephew. Gábor Fejérváry's father, the art collector Károly (Charles) Fejérváry was a Freemason, whose house was often the place of lodge works. Gábor Fejérváry's old friend, Mihály (Michael) Viczay was freemason as well.

In 1848 Pulszky, as the Secretary of State of the revolutionary government permitted establishing lodge "Kossuth Lajos, a dicső fény hajnalához" (Louis Kossuth, to the dawn of glorious light). He told indeed, that the applicants need no permission at all.[3]

Kossuth's American tour in 1852 was organized by Pulszky. In Cincinnati Kossuth was admitted into Freemasonry together with some fellow emigrants. There was a plan about Pulszky's admission,[4] but then this did not happen. Later, when he was asked about this, he told that the Hungarian emigrants' goal was to enter into both "Johannite" and "Scottish" jurisdictions. This explanation is hard to believe, since he became a member of the Scottish Rite of Freemasonry only 10 years later.

During his emigration to Italy, in 1862 Pulszky took part in Garibaldi's campaign for Rome, in which Garibaldi was wounded in the battle of Aspromonte. It has happened here—also written in Pulszky's memoir—that he (Pulszky) was the only person who noticed that the mayor of a town was freemason and mentioned this to Garibaldi.[5]

1. ITALIAN PERIOD

There are a lot of versions about Pulszky's initiation. He did not report its accurate data. The contemporary Masonic articles wrote 1860 or the beginning of the decade. The name of admissing lodge was "Dante Alighieri" in Turin.

In 1996 Stephen Eördögh's article citing Aldo Mola's book says that on 7 February 1862 the Hungarian emigrants—Francis Pulszky, Stephen Türr, George Klapka—founded together with other participants the lodge Dante Alighieri.[6]

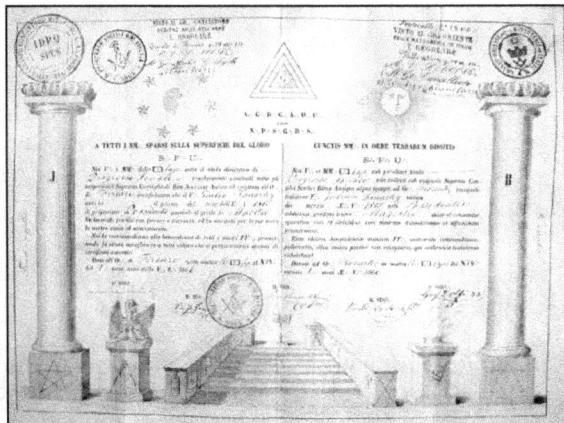

According to Luigi Polo Friz Pulszky was admitted in 1862 into lodge Dante Alighieri, and then he founded the lodge Stella d'Italia.[7]

Philippe A. Autexier in his work "Latomorum Lyra" writes that Pulszky was admitted in 1863 into the lodge

Figli di Campidoglio of Turin.[8]

In January 1864 Pulszky led Bakunin's affiliation ritual in lodge Il Progresso Sociale of Florence.[9] In the same year he initiates Gyula (Julius) Tanárky, tutor of his children. Tanárky was an avid diarist who reported the events of Freemasons. In 1866 Tanárky got the masters degree—on his certificate we can find Pulszky's signature as I. Warden (32. grade).[10]

Apart from the Italians only Pulszky and Bakunin were elected for representatives of the Grand Lodge meeting.

In Italy major part of the emigrant Hungarians joined to one or another Masonic lodge. A separate fund was to support the Masonic lodges' propaganda against the Austrian oppression their (hopeless) uprising plans.

Pulszky was one of the supporters of François de Crouÿ-Chanel pretending to the throne of Hungary.[11] (This was a breaking point with the republican Kossuth.) Crouÿ-Chanel was the head (Sovereign Commander) of the Scottish Rite.

Pulszky gained a lot of political experience in Italy. He stood between the different groups of Hungarian emigrants and the Italian leaders who gave them political and economic support. Meanwhile, as the comrade of WM Ludovico Frapolli (later grandmaster), Pulszky was a partner of the Italian Civil Development and also participated in the struggles, part of which took place within the framework of the Masonic Lodges.

2. PERIOD IN GRAND LODGE OF ST. JOHN (1870-1886)

Pulszky became a member of the first established lodge "Einigkeit in Vaterland" (Unity in homeland) in 1868. Soon he took the leadership from Louis Lewis the founder of the lodge, and then became the leader of Johannite lodges. As the number of Johannite (3-grades) lodges reached 7 in the year of 1870, they established the Grand Lodge of St. John, of which Francis Pulszky was elected as Grand Master. In the same year the number of lodges increased to twenty-two.

Those Hungarian emigrants who were members of the Scottish Rite lodges composed the group led by John Besze and Stephen Türr had the aim to create at home the Scottish Rite. The first "Scottish" lodge, the "Matthias Corvinus, the fair" was founded in 1869, which was soon followed by many others as well. Having failed to reach a fusion with the 3-grade lodges, shortly after the establishment of the Johannite grand lodge "Scottish" lodges founded the Grand Orient of Hungary in 1871. George Joannovics was elected as Grand Master. In 1873 the Grand Orient had 1004 members in 18 lodges.

How could it happen that the Scottish rite 33. degrees Pulszky became the leader of St. John lodges instead of the Scottish rite lodges?

It is likely for two reasons: the first one is probably of sociological nature, the second one is related with Pulszky's individual path of life.

The Johannite lodges social base was the German speaking *citizens* in Hungary, with some Jewish people. Most of the members were politically Deák-party supporters. Members of the Scottish Rite lodges were mainly white collar workers and the rural gentry and some people from the aristocracy. They were politically supporters of the center-left.[12]

Separating from Kossuth in the Italian exile and the center-left party Pulszky became Deák's follower and active supporter. His liberal view of the world caused disengagement from the rural nobility and he became a believer of the bourgeois ideology. All these and perhaps also his personal conflicts with the other emigrants can justify his choice between the two Masonic sides. And another cause could be that being the only 33. degree mason guaranteed his authority and first place among the 3 degrees masons.

So Pulszky' Masonic career refuted the conspiracy theories' conception that a person is defined by Freemasonry in his philosophical and political life. Here we can see just the opposite: Pulszky's Masonic stance was determined by his intellectual and political position.

Pulszky had a great effect on the Hungarian Freemasonry while often using political tools, as we can clearly see in the next cases.

A significant part of the Hungarian Freemasons, especially the Scottish Rite lodges since their founding wanted the fusion union of the two systems. Pulszky successfully resisted them for a long time. First he stated that union cannot be discussed before establishing the Grand Lodge.

When Theodore Csáky, a leader of Scottish side gave a well-elaborated offer for creating a common grand lodge—that could be acceptable for both sides,—Pulszky suddenly established the St. John grand lodge just one day before the planned discussion. Then he insisted on that no negotiation can be about a fusion without a partner Grand Lodge. As an answer the Scottish Rite side established the Grand Orient.[13]

Then Pulszky signed a cooperation agreement between the Grand Lodges. For a long time this agreement was the base to prevent the fusion plans by Pulszky again and again.

However Grand Orient took all efforts for union. Theodore Csaky, Deputy Grand Master for example developed the operational rules of high degrees in order to match the expectations of Johannites. E.g., the new rules strictly separated the first three degrees from the high degrees. In the opposite of the previous habits the chapters and councils prohibited the initiation of candidates.

Pulszky could withstand the pressure for about 10 years but then finally began negotiations about the union of the two Grand Lodges. There were two factors of it. It became obvious that the separately working two grand lodges cannot be as strong—intellectually and financially—as a united one.[14] On the other hand Pulszky's prestige was declined by a case.

Countess Helene Hadik-Barkóczy, a distant relative but a close friend of Pulszky was passionately interested in Freemasonry. She wanted to enter in and therefore took everything for it. She promised financial support for the admission to the lodges and asked Pulszky's intervene as well. The Johannite Grand Master in his own organization didn't dare to do anything, but he involved in the softening a Grand Orient lodge. As a result, the rich aristocratic lady who managed her fortune thanks her "masculinization" regularly was initiated by the lodge of Ungvár. The Grand Orient investigated the incident, qualified it as invalid and punished the participants. The Grand Orient protested at St. John Grand Lodge against Pulszky's intervention, too. For this reason Pulszky did not start on the next grand master election, but his chair remained empty and was re-elected the next year.

Pulszky thus became a weaker negotiating partner, and therefore he changed his strategy, he became main supporter of the fusion, but with Johannite dominance and his leadership of the united grand lodge.

All his calculations fulfilled: the united grand lodge gained unprecedented strength and authority, he became the grand master and some 15 years later the Scottish high degrees virtually died off.

3. PERIOD IN SYMBOLIC GRAND LODGE OF HUNGARY (1886–1894)

In order to reach the fusion of the grand lodges, the Grand Orient admitted Pulszky's primacy, it expressed a number of ways, for example in an article published in their own Masonic journal Hajnal (Dawn). In the "Our Grand Master" series the first one was the article about Pulszky.[15]

21st March in 1886 the Symbolic Grand Lodge of Hungary was founded from the two preceding grand lodges. Francis Pulszky became the Grand Master of the order, Stephen Rakovszky from Grand Orient and Abraham Szontagh from St. John GL were elected as Deputy Grand Masters.

Pulszky was 72 years old, but was working full force as a grand master as well as scientific and political person. His weight in Hungarian society also increased by his children, Augustus Pulszky lawyer, politician, member of the Hungarian Academy of Sciences; Charles Pulszky art historian and corresponding member of the Hungarian Academy of Sciences, director of the National Gallery. The Pulszky family's place in academic, social, artistic field was questioned, many people launched attacks against them. (The embezzlement—false—accusation caused Charles Pulszky's suicide.)

Pulszky was also in the crossfire of attacks and some of them was dealing with his masonic work. One such case was the Liszt affair.[16]

In December 1886 an article appeared in a clerical journal "Magyar Állam" (Hungarian State) against the recently died Liszt, claiming that he in

Hungary was also a lodge member. Pulszky reply states that if Liszt abroad may have admissed into Freemasonry, but all of the communication with him Liszt never signed his masonic membership in any way, so that is out of the question after his inclusion into Franciscan order.[17] The clerical journal after this started a series of articles attacking on Liszt, Pulszky and Freemasonry.

Pulszky stated in his reply that if Liszt might have been initiated into Freemasonry somewhere abroad, he had never manifested his masonic membership in any way. After Liszt entered Franciscan order there was no sense of this question. The clerical journal after this started a series of articles attacking on Liszt, Pulszky and Freemasonry.

Due to the continuous attacks in public life and masonic activities the Grand Lodge preferred to withdraw him from foreground, and therefore he resigned in 1886. The new Grand Master became Stephen Rakovszky. In the beginning of the 1894th year Pulszky leaved the Masonic order, too—perhaps to have nothing to overshadow the celebrations of his 80th birthday.

OVERALL ASSESSMENT

As a young man Pulszky had some family related informations about free-masonry. He was in connection with the Hungarian freemasons in the time of Hungarian revolution (1848–1849) but didn't follow Kossuth when he was initiated in Cincinatti, USA.

His masonic life started in Italy as he was initiated probably in 1862 in the lodge Dante Alighieri and he acceded soon the 33rd grade of Scottish Rite. The lodge's membership also contributed him to widespread deployment of international relations, like with Garibaldi and Bakunyin. He was in close relationship with Lodovico Frapolli, the later Grand Master. He participated in the founding of several lodges to form the Frapolli's Grand Lodge. Pulszky was one of the supporters of François de Crouÿ-Chanel pretending to the throne of Hungary. Pulszky became Deák follower and active supporter of Compromise with Habsburgs, and after his returning home took part in the revival of Hungarian Freemasonry.

In 1868 he became the WM of the lodge "Einigkeit in Vaterland" (Unity in homeland), the mother lodge of English oriented lodges, and later was elected as lifetime honorary WM of the lodge St. Stephen. After the establishment (30th January 1870) of the St. John Grand Lodge of Hungary he became the first Grand Master. When in 1886 the two Grand Lodges

(St. John and Grand Orient) fusioned to the Symbolic Grand Lodge of Hungary he became again the first Grand Master. His primacy and authority in the Hungarian Freemasonry was unquestionable, there was a cult developed around him.[18]

Despite the initiation and reaching 33rd degrees in Scottish Rite, Pulszky after his homecoming became a member, then Grand Master of the 3-stage St. John Grand Lodge. He inhibited the fusion with Grand Orient while it was possible. The causes of that may have been sociological, philosophical and political reasons.

He supported the initiation to the Freemasonry from the background Countess Helena Hadik-Barkóczy. Not into a lodge of his Grand Lodge, but into a lodge of the "competing" Grand Orient. His position shakened because of the above case may have contributed to the fusion of the two grand lodges.

The working period of the united grand lodge is kept the golden age of Hungarian Freemasonry. Social development, intellectual works and charity show the strength of the Grand Lodge. The financial power allowed for building lodge houses in the capital and country as well.

Pulszky practically skipped from this prosperity due to his forced resign two years later caused by political attacks. Before his 80th birthday he leaved the Freemasonry.

NOTES

1 Mikszáth, Kálmán. "Pulszky papa." *Cikkek és karcolatok* Vol. II. Budapest: Mercator, 2005. 1474-1476. http://www.akonyv.hu/klasszikus/mikszath/cikkek_es_karcolatok_2.pdf. Web 16 June 2015.

2 Denslow, William R. *10,000 Famous Freemasons*. Trenton, Mo.: Missouri Lodge of Research, 1957.

3 Abafi, Lajos. *A szabadkőművesség története Magyarországon*. Budapest: Schmidl H. Könyvnyomdája, 1900. reprint. Budapest: Akadémiai. 1993.

4 Berényi, Zsuzsanna Ágnes. „A szabadkőműves Kossuth Lajos. *Kossuth és az egyházak*. Budapest: Luther, 2004. 129. Hajnik,Pál's letter to Nemeskéri Kiss, Miklós; 1852. márc. 5.

5 Pulszky, Ferenc. Életem és korom *Vol. 4. Számkivetés alatt Olaszországban.* Budapest: Ráth Mór, 1882. 122.

6 Eördögh, István. 1996. „Az 1848–49-es szabadságharc bukásának diplomáciai háttere a szentszéki iratok fényében." Aetas 2-3. 189. The cited work: Mola, Aldo A. *Storia della Massoneria italiana dalle origini ai giorni nostri.* Milano: Bompiani, 1992. 66 .

7 Friz, Luigi Polo. La *massoneria italiana nel decennio post unitario: Lodovico Frapolli.* Milano: Franco Angeli, 1998. 55. „Iniziato alla Dante, nel 1862, Pulszky fondò la Stella d'Italia."

8 Autexier, Philippe A. Lyra *Latomorum,* 537. http://www.netzwerk-freimaurerforschung.de/blog/wordpress/wp-content/uploads/2014/03/lyra_gesamt.pdf. Web 16 June 2015.

9 Kun, Miklós. Útban az anarchizmus felé, Mihail Bakunyin politikai pályaképe és eszmei fejlődése az 1860-as évek közepén. Budapest: Akadémiai Kiadó, 1982.

10 Tanárky Gyula naplói, Mol (Hungarian National Archive) R-195.

11 Nyáry, Albert. *Az utolsó magyar trónkövetelő. Különlenyomat a „Századok"-ból* Budapest, 1912.

12 Hass, Ludwik. 1974. "The Socio-professional Composition of Hungarian Freemasonry: (1868 -1920)." Acta Poloniae Historica 30. 79-80.

13 Belányi, Ferencz. 1880. „Jelentés a magyarországi jánosrendi Nagyp∴ első tíz évi működéséről." Kelet, 1 Feb 1880. 9-15.

14 Hass 1974.

15 Hajnal. Journal of Grand Orient of Hungary. Vol. XII. 1. 1885. 1.

16 Autexier 477-479.

17 Pesti Hírlap. 17 Dec. 1886. 2-3.

18 Jászberényi, József. 2004. „Iránta való szeretetünk szilárd és örök", Kelet, A Magyarországi Szimbolikus Nagypáholy lapja, Vol. XLVII. 1. 50-56.

XI

REPORT ON THE SPECIAL COMMITTEE ON THE FRANCKEN DOCUMENTS

BRENT MORRIS

Welcome to the Report on the Special Committee on the Francken Documents. I am Brent Morris, managing editor of *The Scottish Rite Journal.* Before I begin our report, I would like to thank

- Jean-Loup Graton of the Bibliotheque Nationale for supporting and hosting the conference.

- Professor Paul Rich, the obsessive maniac who brought this conference to fruition in less than twelve months (and I describe him thus because only an obsessive maniac could do what he accomplished).

- Pierre Moliere of the Grand Orient Library who has handled so many arrangements, especially those of the Francken Manuscript study group. Pierre Moliere is also very generous. He told our committee that he had chilled a case of Dom Perignon champagne for our refreshments, but when he found out that food and drink could not be present in the same room with some of the manuscripts, he sent the champagne back to the Grand Orient supply room. Maybe next time!

I have been asked to chair this session because I am an amateur—in the basic sense of the word, I am a lover of the subject. For at least 25 years I have been studying and tracking the manuscripts prepared by Henry Andrew Francken. It has been a dream of mine that all known copies of Francken's manuscripts could be brought together to be studied. Pierre Moliere, Librarian of the Grand Orient de France, has taken this dream a step farther by arranging with the Bibliothèque National de France to borrow the "Santo Domingo Manuscript" (Baylot FM^4 15). The Santo Domingo Manuscript is a French collection of rituals that is a near if not direct relative of Francken's manuscripts.

It is somewhat frightening to be thrust into this position. My formal background is in theoretical mathematics and computer algorithms, little connected to reality, and certainly nothing as real as paper, watermarks, ink, handwriting, and so on. Nonetheless, I volunteered and so here we are. (Perhaps more correctly, Paul Rich said to me, "Brent, you've been talking about the Francken Manuscripts for years. Here's your chance to do something other than talk. Put up or shut up!")

I'll begin by giving a brief overview of Francken and what was known about his manuscripts before the World Conference on Fraternalism, Freemasonry, and History. Then we'll talk about our study procedure and what we accomplished.

The largest and most widely dispersed system of high-degree Masonry is the Ancient and Accepted Scottish Rite of thirty-three degrees. It originated in 1801 in Charleston, South Carolina, based upon the Order of the Royal Secret of twenty-five degrees (often called the Rite of Perfection).[1] Unlike some high-degree systems, the Ancient and Accepted Rite has a definite date of birth and well-known founders. Its parent, however, has a more shadowy genealogy. The Order of the Royal Secret seems to have appeared with Estienne Morin when he arrived in Santo Domingo in 1763, but its rituals and ceremonies are well known.

Soon after his arrival Morin set about establishing high-degree bodies and himself as the high-degree authority of the western hemisphere (or at least the Caribbean). Sometime between 1763 and 1767, Morin appointed Henry Andrew Francken, a naturalized British citizen and resident of Jamaica, "Deputy Inspector General of all the Superior Degrees of Free and Accepted Masons in the West Indies."[2] It was Francken who first brought the Order to the British colonies of North America and also appointed other Deputy Inspectors who propagated the rite. He thus prepared the way for the birth of the Scottish Rite.

At least as important as spreading the Royal Secret, Francken preserved its rituals by translating them from French into English and making at least four copies. The Scottish Rite thus has, in addition to a definite birthday and well-known founders, detailed rituals from its origins. There

---

1   The system has most often been called the "Rite of Perfection." Alain Bernheim clearly showed that its proper name is "Order of the Royal Secret."

2   A. R. Hewitt, "Another Francken Manuscript Rediscovered," *Ars Quatuor Coronatorum*, 89 (1976): 208.

have been many subsequent changes and alterations to the rituals of the Scottish Rite by various Supreme Councils, but they all can be measured against those of the Order of the Royal Secret and the foundational work of Henry Andrew Francken.

Much more is known about the life of Francken than that of Morin. Francken was born in 1820 and arrived in Jamaica in February 1857. Just over a year later, on March 2, 1758, he became a naturalized British citizen. A 1762 petition to the Vice-Admiralty Court shows Francken had been an appraiser, a marshal, and sergeant-at-mace in the court.[3] In 1763, Estienne Morin passed through Jamaica on his way to Santo Domingo and had his first opportunity to meet Francken.[4] Francken's wife, Elizabeth, died in 1764, and in 1765 he was appointed interpreter for Dutch and English for the Vice-Admiralty Court. From these linguistic skills, we can infer he was born in Holland[5] or a perhaps a Dutch colony. As a professional translator, it's easy to see how he came to translate and transcribe the rituals of the Order of the Royal Secret.

After being appointed court interpreter in 1765 and with the permission of Lt.-Gov. Moore, Francken traveled to Albany, New York, and New York City, both with Dutch-speaking populations. He married Johanna Low of Newark, New Jersey,[6] and on December 8, 1765, they became the godparents of Johanna Low, daughter of Nicholas and Sarah Low (Johanna's sister).[7] In 1768 he formed Ineffable Lodge of Perfection at Albany, New York, and it opened January 11. The records of the Ineffable Lodge of Perfection indicate that it ceased activity on December 5, 1774.[8] Also in 1768 he made Moses Michael Hays a Deputy Inspector and Knight Kadosh with the power to constitute Grand Chapters of Knights of the Sun and of Kadosh in the West Indies and North America.[9]

Francken was one of two deputies specifically named a founding member of a grand chapter of Princes of the Royal Secret by Stephen Morin in

3 Richardson Wright, "Freemasonry on the Island of Jamaica," *Transactions of the American Lodge of Research*, vol. 3, no. 1 (1938–39): 126–61.

4 A[lain] B[ernheim], "Francken, Henry Andrew," http://www.vrijmetselaarsgilde.eu/Maconnieke%20Encyclopedie/Franc-M/fra-f-02.htm#fransF-14.

5 Wright, "Jamaica,"

6 Wright, "Jamaica,"

7 According to the records of the Dutch Reformed Church, NYC, http://www.wikitree.com/wiki/Francken-12 (accessed 20 May 2015).

8 "Scottish Rite," en.wikipedia.org (accessed 24 May 2015).

9 Bernheim, "Francken."

Kingston, April 30, 1770.[10] In 1771, four to eight years after meeting Morin, he produced his earliest known dated book of constitutions and rituals for the 15°–25°. This manuscript was rediscovered in 1976 and is now in the possession of the Supreme Council for England and Wales. Its spine was marked "Manuscript Ritual of the late Col. Graham of Claverhouse," and a note says the manuscript once belonged to a Captain Graham of Drynie(?) and Claverhouse who, after a period in the West Indies, returned to Scotland.[11] It suffered the indignity of the 25° being cut out shortly after arriving in the Supreme Council, and it suffered near destruction when submerged in water for over six months when the bank vault in which it was stored flooded.

Francken's second wife, Johanna, died in 1777, and in 1782 he was appointed Master of the Revels. This was a largely ceremonial post that "gave him authority over all theatrical performances and the balls and entertainments given by the governor." It also had an annual stipend of 100 guineas.[12] As late as 1783 he was still the official Dutch interpreter for the island,[13] and in that year he was appointed a customs inspector.[14]

Of greater Masonic interest in 1783, Francken prepared another manuscript with rituals 4°–25° for Deputy Inspector David Small.[15] It was forgotten until 1855 when according to a note in the London *Freemasons' Magazine* it came into the possession of an unnamed English Brother. It was purchased the next year by Enoch Terry Carson of Ohio, a prominent American Mason, and subsequently purchased by Samuel Crocker Lawrence of Massachusetts, upon whose death in 1911 it went his library to the Grand Lodge of Massachusetts. This version was rediscovered in 1935 in the archives of the Grand Lodge of Massachusetts and given to the Supreme Council, 33°, NMJ.[16]

Francken prepared at least two other ritual manuscripts, but they do not contain details to let us date them. A third manuscript in Francken's hand with the rituals 4°–25° was found in the archives of the Provincial Grand Lodge of Lancashire in Liverpool around 1984 and is on loan to the UGLE library. "On the verso of the first unnumbered folio is the in-

---

10 Bernheim, "Francken."

11 Hewitt, "Another Francken Manuscript," 208, 209.

12 Wright, "Jamaica,"

13 Wright, "Jamaica,"

14 Bernheim, "Francken."

15 Hewitt, "Another Francken Manuscript," 208.

16 Hewitt, "Another Francken Manuscript," 208.

scription, 'Received from John Caird, Edinburgh—Jas. Caird, Liverpool 30th August 1815.' This is surrounded by a lengthy note by one M. A. Gage recording that on the same date it was given to him by Jas. Caird ... He removed to Liverpool in 181 ... Reference to 1786 in the text provides evidence of an 'earliest possible date.'"[17]

A fourth undated manuscript by Francken with rituals 4°–24° was given by H. J. Whymper to the District Grand Lodge of the Punjab. It is now in the possession of Naveed Ahmed of Lahore, Pakistan. Little has been published about this version. The UGLE Library microfilmed it decades ago and catalogued it as "Rite of Twenty-Five Degrees" but without an author. Thus it remained camouflaged from researchers using the search term "Francken," but it was rediscovered about 2010.

In 1790, Francken lost his post as customs inspector and requested financial aid from the government, having lost his job, been twice widowed, and having house twice destroyed by hurricanes. He was twice given £100.[18] In 1793 he was again appointed Master of the Revels, and in 1794 he was appointed assistant judge of the Court of Common Please for Port Royal and prepared his will. His will contained these instructions: "It is my positive will that my funeral expenses shall not exceed the sum of £20 currency; my coffin to be made of plain deal without any lining on the inside and only blackened outside; to be put into my Coffin in the Cloaths I shall die in and my body not to be washed, and to be carried to the grave without being carried in the Church."[19]

Henry Andrew Francken died May 20, 1795, survived by his son Parker Bennett Francken of St. Kitts, his daughter, Mary Long Goutris, and his granddaughter, Elizabeth Goutris. He was buried May 24 in Kingston Parish Churchyard.[20]

This then is a brief summary of what we knew about Henry Andrew Francken and his manuscripts. What did we hope to discover over the two days we had to study these documents? Perhaps little or perhaps much—it depended on the gods of research. I think I can say that we made progress without being overly effusive.

---

17 John M. Hamill, "A Third *Francken MS* of the Rite of Perfection," *Ars Quatuor Coronatorum,* 97(1984): 200.

18 Bernheim, "Francken."

19 Wright, "Jamaica,"

20 Wright, "Jamaica,"

Let me give you an example of what we looked for when examining the manuscripts. In 1997 while studying the 1783 manuscript at the Library of the Supreme Council, Northern Masonic Jurisdiction, USA, I discovered that several of the pages facing the start of a degree show unusual ghost images from extra pages that were inserted between the pages. These extra inserted pages had drawings of tracing boards and remained undisturbed between the pages long enough for their images to transfer onto the facing page. Alain Marchiset, an antique book dealer who joined in our studies, estimates that it would take at least three to six months for the ink from the tracing boards to burn into the facing pages. In some cases the acid in the paper of the extra pages has caused large rectangular stains. There are at least nine such ghost images of tracing boards, and there may be more, but some technology other than the naked eye and ordinary light are required. As it turned out no ghost images were found in any other version. They are unique to the 1783 Francken.

While I hoped we would find something as dramatic as ghost images, I decided we would be satisfied if we could leave with intelligent questions. It was probably hoping for too much to think we could leave this conference with exciting new discoveries. But sometimes exciting questions are almost as good. Keep in mind that not all attendees agreed with every finding or not as strongly as everyone else. Thus what I will present are consensus results.

1. The 1771 Francken is in a different hand from the other manuscripts. It is also not signed by Henry Andrew Francken. Most thought it was created by a different writer, but there was a strong dissent that it may indeed have been written by Francken but with altered writing, perhaps due to stress or trauma. If it is by a different hand, then it is like the "Jamaica Manuscript," a copy of a Francken by a different writer. (The Jamaica Manuscript is a contemporary ritual manuscript that was reprinted earlier this year by the Scottish Rite Research Society and is available on their page.)

2. The 1783, West Lancashire, and Ahmed manuscripts are the same size with the same number of pages. The 1783 and Ahmed manuscripts have similar bindings. England & Wales was dis-bound as part of the conservation work after it was submerged, but Susan Snell will compare the preserved binding with that of West Lancashire.

3. The watermark on the paper of the Ahmed and West Lan-

cashire manuscripts bear "G R" for "Georgius Rex." Susan Snell believes the watermark and common size and binding indicate these being common United Kingdom record books for use by courts and civil servants. Naveed Ahmed believes the paper and blank books were used by George III for his library. Susan will check the British and Jamaican government libraries for similar books with government records from the period.

4. There is at least one missing intermediate text. The Santo Domingo Manuscript is written in French. As one example, the ritual for the Knight of the Sun is written in the center of the page with dense additions in both margins. The Francken manuscripts have these two pieces of writing smoothly integrated together. There are many small variations in language in the Francken manuscripts that lead Alain Marchiset to conclude that Francken translated each copy from a French mother document that represents the merged texts of the Santo Domingo.

5. In the 22°, Prince of Libanus, each manuscript has a paragraph that begins "This celebrated nation ... " However, the Ahmed manuscript, one of the oldest, was written without the word "celebrated," which was inserted later. This leads us to conclude it is not the English mother for the others, but reinforces out belief there is a French mother.

6. The United States had several lodges of perfection in east coast port cities: Charleston, South Carolina; Philadelphia, Pennsylvania; Newport, Rhode Island; Albany, New York; and others, yet none of them are known to have a copy of the Francken manuscript. It appears that Francken prepared and most likely sold these manuscripts to British Officers, as they all made their way back to Britain with most coming through Scotland; they were not given to the Lodges of Perfection. We know that Francken was in difficult financial straits when he petitioned the Jamaican government for relief in 1790. Perhaps he supplemented his income with his skills as a professional scrivener, using blank books from the Jamaican court's supply cabinet, and selling the fruits of his labors to British officers. This would explain the absence, thus far, in the archives of American Lodges of Perfection and the apparent travels to Great Britain via army officers.

7. All agreed there are most likely other undiscovered copies made by Francken or copies of Francken made by other writers in archives around the world. To support this contention, Paul Ninin wrote to me yesterday afternoon—24 hours ago—to say there are two Francken manuscripts in The Hague in the possession of the Latomia Foundation and the Supreme Council for the Netherlands.[21] Of course we now must compare the handwriting, paper, binding, and text. There will indeed be more to report at the next World Conference!

---

21 Subsequent research indicates the Latomia images are those of the manuscript from the Supreme Council for England and Wales.

XII

Unveiling the Copiale-manuscript:
Layers of Fraternalism, Ritual and Politics
in Eighteenth Century Germany

Andreas Önnerfors
Reader in the History of Sciences and Ideas
University of Gothenburg, Sweden

Abstract

In 2011 data-linguists from Sweden and the US decoded a manuscript written in cipher, the content of which has been unknown for at least the last two centuries (Megyesi). This so-called Copiale-manuscript and the story of its code being broken with methods of new information technology received trans-national media coverage, but its content remains still to be explored thoroughly. What the data-linguists found inside was a ritual written in German for a fraternal order, the Order of Oculists. In its master degree, the Oculists were informed that the secret aim of the order was to divulge the secrets of freemasonry and to undermine its recruitment. Thus, the manuscript thoroughly exposes masonic ritual (in all likelihood) practiced in German territories at the time. What kind of text was it and could it be dated? Is the description of freemasonry in it correct? What does the prevalence of obvious anti-masonry tell us about the context of its origin? These were questions at the beginning of a research process that by no means has reached its completion. In particular, the description of the so-called 'Scottish master's degree', potentially the 'first' higher degree practiced in European freemasonry, has thought-provoking features that augment our knowledge of ritual development. And even more, a clandestine continuation of the degree (the 'Key-lodge') with political overtones provides with fascinating material for further research. The aim of this paper is thus to present the outcomes of preliminary studies of the content and motifs we encounter in the Copiale-manuscript. Factors I will outline below, allow the assumption that it was written somewhere between

1740 and 1754. A more cautious assessment would be, that at least its *content* describes the situation in German fraternalism and freemasonry of the 1740s and that the manuscript possibly is of younger provenance. Not only does the Copiale-manuscript represent an advanced play with ritual secrets, secrecy and transparency as an organizational phenomenon in eighteenth-century German culture, but reveals intriguing layers of religious and political thought, meticulously encoded and now for the first time open for discussion.

Key words: fraternal rituals, eighteenth century Germany, freemasonry, Scottish master's degree, political philosophy, liberation theology

STRUCTURE AND CONTENT OF THE MANUSCRIPT

The 105 octavo-pages of the Copiale-manuscript, de-coded in 2011 by a US-Swedish team of data-linguists, are written in a double substitution cipher, letters of the alphabet are substituted with other letters, logograms or coding elements such as blank spaces. Cryptologic work has been described comprehensively elsewhere and does not constitute the subject of this article (Knight, Megyesi, Schaefer 128-35). Through sequencing of the amount of letters, data-linguists started to pin down the original language of the document and eventually concluded that it must be written in German. An algorithm for transcribing the manuscript produced a more or less 'clear' version, short of the logograms, some of which remain open for interpretation and possibly can mean different things in different contexts. From the German master copy, an automated English translation was produced that however is in need for improvement. One short-term goal is to produce a waterproof German version and once this is done, to translate it manually to English. All translations in this article are my own.

What stands out in comparison to most rituals from the period is a particularly striking feature of the manuscript: its character of a Russian doll or Chinese box, splitting up the text in different layers or dimensions. It can roughly be divided into three main parts: one part (1-27, pagination follows the original document) is devoted to the fraternal order of 'Oculists' ("Hocherleuchte[ter] Oculisten Orden") and its degrees of apprentice, fellow and master. In this third degree the "most secret aim" (25) of the order is revealed, to disclose the secrets of freemasonry and to undermine its dissemination and recruitment. A second part reveals rituals of craft lodges (27-67) as allegedly practiced in Germany at the time and the third part (68-99) the Scottish Master's degree, one of the first higher degrees of freemasonry with both a chivalric and sacerdotal element. Furthermore intriguing is a continuation of the Scottish Master's degree, the 'Key-lodge' (100-04) that clearly demonstrates philosophical awareness of civil and political rights and the need to recover freedom from tyranny by means of violent rebellion. Last but not least alchemical workings (in a 'Lodge of consolation') are also addressed (104-5).

THE RITUALS OF THE 'OCULISTS'

It is obvious that the Order of Oculists (a gender-mixed fraternity) is designed according to a well-established pattern shared with many other fraternal orders and organizations of the period (Henning 1999 68-82). The initiation ceremony has many similarities to freemasonry, with the candidate being introduced to the lodge room by officers with designated tasks. A master of the Oculist lodge questions the candidate who subsequently has to take an oath. The significant element of the initiation ritual is a symbolic eye operation, where optical instruments are displayed. A second oath is taken from which it emerges that there is a context of other fraternal orders, the candidate potentially could be a member of. It is striking that the 'Order of Mopses' is mentioned here, since it was a mixed-gender hoax fraternity the rituals of which were exposed in a seminal 1745 publication, *L'Ordre des Franc-Maçons trahi et le Secret des Mopses revelé* (Pérau), spread across Europe. The Oculist-manuscript makes reference to this particular publication later (61). After initiation follows instruction and education related to the degree: signs and tokens and behavioural rules and modes of reciprocal recognition outside the lodge are explained thoroughly. In the fellow degree the obligation is reiterated; if the candidate meanwhile has joined another secret order, (s)he is immediately expelled. Again, signs, grips and tokens are explained and reference is made (as in freemasonry) to sciences and arts. Also the master degree begins with a renewal of obligation and threat of expulsion. The masterpiece is to be able to read and write the cipher of the order. During the instruction, the master is informed about the origin and secret constitutions of the order as well as instructed in the use of the cipher. He is also presented with a Grand lodge certificate (stipulating that the Order of Oculists consisted of superior and subordinate bodies).

The origin of the Oculists, as told the new master, lies in England. Once upon a time a few friends decided to test the curiosity of the human race by establishing a brotherhood in order to find out how many out of pure inquisitiveness would join a society, the purpose of which was concealed to them, by pretending that there was a big secret. To that end they decided to meet and agree upon randomly chosen signs. And indeed it was thus the 'guild of freemasons' was established. Unfortunately the manuscript is not exactly clear on this point as the sign in the cipher is a big X, a pictogram that either can refer to 'Freemasonry' or 'Order', my reading emerges from the German grammar and context. However, the narrative continues with that one of the friends did miss out to meet the others and later found that "these masons" (direct quote) weren't able to recognize him although he had been a founding member. Moreover "he was particularly unpleased by the fact that the female sex had been entirely excluded" (20: "[...] da es ihm insbesonderheit nicht gefiel dass man das weibliche geschlecht ganz und gar ausgeschlossen hatte [...]") and that the selection of brethren had been so lax. Therefore he decided to establish the Order of Oculists and to entrust the design of freemasonry to this order. The goal was an exposure of masonic secrecy without exposing the Order of Oculists, to disperse the masonic secret and preserve the own. A master was also instructed in the careful selection of new members and as already stated before, in the art of reading and writing the Oculist cipher. Towards apprentices and fellow members of the Order the master was not allowed to mention the secret attention directed towards freemasonry.

Reading the Oculist-rituals, one cannot escape the reflection that they represent an elaborate play with secrecy as a ritualized form of knowledge, not without traits of self-irony. The legend of the Order starts with to explain that humans are born with curiosity and a quest to know something simply because it is secret. A discussion among Englishmen (And why Englishmen? Because England provided the paradigm for enlightenment fraternal sociability?) leads them to explore this condition through what might be labelled a social experiment by constituting a brotherhood that only would reveal its secret purpose to those who join it: "how many would be seduced by their curiosity to join a society without knowing from the outset what they later on would be forced to subscribe to" (21). The experiment goes on with claiming huge secrets and inventing random signs and tokens for mutual recognition. But one of the original creators of the concocted idea did not recognise and was unhappy with the outcome, particularly with the exclusion of women. Hence he established the Order of Oculists, to reclaim the original concept and this, by the nature of the experiment, would of course also include testing the general credulity of mankind and turn the mirror against the candidate joining. As if this then is a self-fulfilment, it is in fact the third layer of the Chinese box that reveals the 'true and initially concealed purpose' of the Oculists, namely to sap freemasonry. It is here the 'double bottom' of the Oculist-rituals manifests, to battle the existence of a secret society by establishing another, following the logic of 'similia similibus solvantur', by creating a Trojan horse or staging a false flag operation. However, the Oculists were not the only order at the time combatting freemasonry. Already during the 1720s the *The Antient Noble Order of Gormogons* was established with an anti-masonic aim. Furthermore the Oculist-order has striking resemblances to the 'Antimasonianske Societet' (AMS), a mixed gender fraternity that was established in the same period in Germany and Denmark in Pietistic circles (Bartholdy 9-39). Already in 1739 this society was established in Hessen, Germany and later on a branch in the Danish monarchy, existing probably for two or so decades. Without going into details, the AMS was formed according to a masonic pattern, but was in its essence intended to combat the spread of freemasonry. In his examination of this fraternity, Bartholdy places the establishment of the AMS within a Pietistic context, reinforced by early anti-masonry, something that probably also applies to the Oculists (Kretschmer 71-212). A further example of such a fraternity is the so-called 'Order of Abelites', *Abeliter-Orden*, revealing its existence in Swedish-Pomerania in 1746. With obvious similarities to freemasonry, the Abelites simultaneously condemned it (Önnerfors1 148-62). Several prominent arguments against freemasonry that already were prevalent in Britain during the late 1720s, such as the exclusion of women, the attraction or rather distraction by pretended secrets or taking 'unnecessary oaths' are mentioned by the Oculists.

'TRADITIONAL' FREEMASONRY

From 1730 onwards, a considerable output of exposures of freemasonry were published, the most prominent and influential among them arguably represented by Samuel Prichard's *Masonry Dissected*. These exposures were also treated in the press of the time. The Oculist-manuscript makes reference to exposures and their German translations, but they are not copied straight away. There are elements in the description of masonic ritual and organisational praxis that appear to be based on experience or oral accounts and the section on freemasonry is hence titled 'Trustworthy older news on freemasonry, however augmented with new observations'. One is inclined to ask who provided with these 'new observations'. The account (27-68) starts with a paragraph on the age of freemasonry, the design of a lodge room and finally initiation rituals for apprentice, fellow and master. A long passage is devoted to signs and tokens of freemasonry and how to behave inside and outside the lodge. The section 'On the so-called arrangements or new features' (61) mentions explicitly that the occurrence of imposters and the German translation of *L'Ordre* (see above) had prompted the lodges to adopt their own signs and passwords. These are given for Berlin, Frankfurt and Marburg (passwords in order: "Tecton", "Archimedes", "Solon"), cities that all appear on Dotzauer's map (1989) of early German masonic lodges established previous to 1750. In Berlin the right index finger is placed against the lips to signify "eternal secrecy", which allows the assumption that the compiler of the manuscript had access to information through direct contacts or experiences with German freemasonry at the time. The account of freemasonry in the first three degrees is completed with a description of table lodges, general rules and regulations and how to summon to lodge meetings. In relation to known exposures of the time (such as printed and discussed by Carr) there are a number of markers with the help of which it would be possible to identify the Copiale-version with accuracy and thus establishing what has been taken from which potential written sources and what has been added from others. One of the more challenging problems is for instance that the description of the first degree tracing board (35-7) not is in accordance to any of the known exposures. By method of exclusion it is possible to say that later German tracing boards (for instance of the 'Strict Observance' or 'Swedish' rite for that part) *not* are similar to this, although there are some similarities with the "Drawing for the Apprentice-Fellow's Lodge" (as reproduced in Carr 441).

German freemasonry (having in mind that in the times before 1871 and definitely before 1815 it is very difficult to make a clear cut definition of what 'Germany' is or 'German' refers to) started at the latest in the second half of the 1730s by an English establishment in Hamburg. But at the same time, German territories also were exposed to French influence. It would certainly be possible to compare and place the manuscript exposure within a certain family of degrees and future research is definitely needed to carry out this task diligently. Apart from the 'traditional' elements of masonic degrees, there are some distinctive markers that could help to identify the exposure properly. In the introduction to the ritual (27) it is for instance mentioned that masonic fraternities already were in existence during the reign of Elisabeth I and Charles II (Carr 35). Furthermore it is claimed that a tract was published in 1710 treating these societies. The exposure is said to describe freemasonry after 1723. The lodge interior is described as having four separate rooms, which is in concordance with the 1746/7 exposure "Le Franc-Maçons Ecrases" (Carr 295). A peculiarity is the existence of a winding staircase on the tracing board with seven steps and that the four corners of the world are marked with English abbreviations (E S W N). These both factors speak for an English master copy, at least for this part of the exposure. The ritual of initiation has no obvious or self-evident peculiarities (however a specialist of eighteenth century rituals would possibly come to another conclusion), apart from the fact that the oath is spelled "as in Masonry dissected" (42: "wie sie in dem zergliederten freymäurer wort zu wort vorsagt").

Samuel Prichards exposure *Masonry Dissected* was originally published in 1730 and contained a brief prologue and extensive descriptions of masonic degrees in the form of catechisms for each. *Masonry Dissected* appeared for the first time in a German translation, "Die zergliederte Freymaurerei" in 1741, as an appendix to the German translation of the second edition of Andersons *Constitutions* (1738), *Neues Constitutionenbuch der Frey-Maurer*, Frankfurt 1741, pages 323-46. The German translation was reprinted three years later in a work titled *Der sich selbst vertheidigende Freymäurer* ("Self-defence of a freemason"), Frankfurt and Leipzig 1744 (52-73). A reference to "Die zergliederte Freymaurerei" (which reoccurs a couple of times, for instance also on 55) suggests that the rituals of the Oculists were written close to the publication date of the German translations. Another element that speaks for an English master copy is that the Oculist-manuscript makes references to that the Order of Freemasons is older than the Order of the Garter and the imperial Order of the Golden Fleece and that a toast is raised to the English Grandmaster. Furthermore, the third degree speaks of 'Hiram' as the architect of Solomon's temple, whereas French ritual families stick to 'Adoniram' (Snoek 11-53). Moreover, the wardens of the lodge are called (39) "jüngerer" (junior) and "älterer" (senior), which is similar to the English expressions. However the French term "surveillants" also occurs in the Oculist-manuscript. On page 61, reference is made to *L'Ordre*, a prominent exposure that, as already mentioned, was disseminated in original and translation and that was reviewed in the press across Europe. *L' Ordre* was also used as the inspiration for the first visual exposure of freemasonry, a collection of engravings originating in France and reprinted in Germany in 1745 (Bernigeroth). In the Oculist-manuscript a song is quoted that we find in its original in *L'Ordre* (68). Summing up the findings so far, the impression is that *Masonry dissected* is one of the main sources to the exposure in the Oculist-manuscript and that inspiration also is drawn from *L'Ordre* since French expressions (such as 'tres venerable') occur. Certainly the person who compiled the exposure must have had personal experience from freemasonry, either directly or indirectly. Hence it appears as if the description of masonic degrees is authentic and provides with a still of the dynamic ritual praxis worked in German lodges of the period, exposed to both French and English influences.

THE SCOTTISH MASTER'S DEGREE

Far more surprising, if not spectacular is the content of pages 68-99, since it in detail describes different rituals and practices of the "maitre ecossois", the "Scottish master [...] a completely new innovation [...]" (69: "der grad eines Schottischen Meisters ist eine gantz neue Erfindung [...]").

Without touching upon the extremely complex developmental history of masonic higher degrees in Europe (a history that unfortunately not has been worked upon yet in an academically satisfying manner), new source material has surfaced after 1990 that provides with evidence that masonic lodges working in the so-called 'Scottish Masters Degree' were in existence in Prussia and other German territories since 1742 (Mollier1 74-88; Mollier2 24-8; Bettag and Snoek and 61-96). Only few, short and inaccurate printed exposures from the early period of this degree are preserved (Carr 157-200 and 307-24). Any exposures in manuscript such as the one in Copiale are extremely rare; the related manuscripts I have consulted so far were obviously written for use in the lodges and not with the aim of exposing masonic rituals. This degree is an independent continuation of the third degree and has more religious, outspoken Christian and chivalric references. During the later development of masonic degree systems (documentary evidence suggests at the latest in 1748, if not earlier), another combined (Scottish) apprentice-fellow degree was inserted in between the third and the fourth (later on sixth) degree (Önnerfors2 13-26). But in the Oculist-manuscript only the Scottish master's degree is described, which speaks for that the exposure was produced indeed shortly after its first appearance. A fourth degree of freemasonry was/is known in English freemasonry as the 'Royal Arch', from the beginning of the 1740s and onwards and a further source of inspiration might be the degree-complex of the Royal Order of Scotland, Heredom Kilwinning, also originating in the same period.

The Oculist-manuscript goes on to outline two main varieties of rituals, "In the French lodge" (73-5), in the "Lodges common in Germany" (75-86) and more specifically "The Scottish lodges in Brunswick [Braunschweig] and Berlin" (86-99). It is striking that, whereas the description of the three first degrees is full of references to contemporary exposures, the content of the Scottish degrees appears to be entirely related by first-hand or second-hand experience/accounts; which of course begs the question of who possibly could have provided such inside knowledge. The 'French' lodge referred to might be *L'Union*, established 30 November 1742 in Berlin, recruiting a huge number of prominent members and active in constituting new lodges, for instance in Frankfurt/Main and Copenhagen. The ritual working language of *L'Union* was most certainly French, the preserved minute book is also written in French. But back to the manuscript. The tracing board of the French lodge is described as follows:

In the centre a glittering star with an 'I' is displayed, sun and moon, a skull and a coffin, the Sanctum Sanctorum, Noah's Ark, Ark of Covenant, Acacia twig, Brazen Sea, Babylonian Tower and the like. The lodge is opened with 3 times 27, the initiate is told to walk in to the Sanctum Sanctorum to be purified like a Levite (a priest). The apron has yellow, red, blue and white elements and a red sash with a golden triangle (compare with Exodus 39 where the priest's garment are described). The password of the degree is 'Gabanon' or 'Iaquinet', the master's word 'Jehovah'. In the catechism, the candidate is supposed to say that he was admitted in the Sanctum Sanctorum beneath the Acacia. He was purified as a Levite. The sign of the master represents the epiphany of God in a cloud. Q: "Why is the glittering star so highly adored in the Order?" A: "Because it was through its glaze venerable master Hiram was recovered, when the freshly dug earth was located." This appears to be an important piece of information, since according to Snoek the first mentioning of this peculiar light occurred in the Scottish Rectified Rite after 1782. It is obvious that the new dignity of the master brings with it to be admitted to the Sanctum Sanctorum and that Hiram is likened to a (high) priest. Q: "Why do you in particular revere the Acacia?" A: "Since Hiram's grave, the venerable priests', was marked with an Acacia."

The general description of the 'German' Scottish lodges is far more comprehensive (75-99). Scottish lodges in Germany are said to have fixed membership numbers (between twelve to sixteen), which certainly not is the case for the later development, particularly after 1760. It is also possible to read in a membership rule of 'past-rank', in the ideal case Scottish masons have a long-standing experience, preferably as officers in a lodge. The later development in the Swedish rite would make the Scottish master's degree a prerequisite for becoming W. M. of a blue lodge and would embrace elements of a Installed Master's ritual (however significantly different from Emulation, but still placed in the immediate continuation of the three craft degrees). The Oculists learned that there were strict rules of admission in place and how the interior of a lodge was designed. In the East a square altar with a green cloth was placed on top of which four candles, a vase with oil and herbs, a bible and a (presumably massive) 'battle sword' (the German has 'Schlachtschwert'). The square tracing board contains characteristic features: the setting is the destroyed temple of Jerusalem, "four circles and four squares alternately drawn around each other and on top of which are drawn four broken columns, in the form of an St Andrew's Cross". We find also the Ark of the Covenant, Noah's Ark, mount Sinai and the Brazen Sea. The candidate carries a cord around his neck and is (as in the French ritual) purified by water. An oath is taken on the Book of Genesis. The token of the Scottish master (97) has striking similarities with the one used later in the Swedish rite, displaying the crucified St. Andrew, who also is the patron saint of the order and accordingly celebrated on the 30 November (Rudbeck 156). The motto of the

Scottish master is given as "Dulcia post amara" ("Sweet after the Bitter") and the passwords as 'Adonai' and 'Jehova'. A remarkable ceremony is that of masonic knighthood, described on pages 83, 88 and 93. The Scottish master is also referred to as a Knight of St. Andrew. In the catechism it is asked: Q: "Are you a Scottish Master?" A: "No one prevents me from walking into the Sanctum Sanctorum whenever I wish to." Q: "Where were you admitted?" A: "In the Sanctum Sanctorum beneath the Acacia." In comparison to the 'French' lodge there are significant overlaps, such as the mentioning of Levite purification and that mastery provides with admittance into the Sanctum Sanctorum, with other words, that it brings a sacerdotal privilege. Both accolade and anointment are practiced, which begs the question whether the degree is to be seen as a double degree with a sacerdotal and a chivalric component.

In the subsequent section, the manuscript speaks explicitly of customs practiced in the Scottish lodges in Berlin and Braunschweig, which fits with the spread of the early Scottish degrees in Germany in so far that the first Scottish lodge was established in Berlin in 1742. A lodge was founded in Braunschweig in 1744 and it is probable that some freemasons went further to work in Scottish degrees thereafter. As in the French ritual the Scottish masters degree continues the Hiramic legend, the replacement of the master-word after the violent murder of the architect and the re-discovery of the lost word (99), "we have found what since centuries has been lost", "[...] wir haben wiederfunden was seit so vielen iahrhunderten verloren gewesen [...]". Furthermore it is described that the freemasons united themselves with the Order of St. John during the time of the crusades and that they together were cleaning up the site of the temple of Jerusalem ahead of its reconstruction. During this work the adytum (Sanctum Sanctorum) was rediscovered and in its centre four cubic and four circular stones (96): "The chevaliers maçons were amazed to find the word 'Jehovah' on the last of the stones" ("[...] die chevaliers macons erstauneten für verwunderung als sie auf dem letzten dieser steine das wort jehova gewahr worden [...]". This expression of 'freemasons-knights' is remarkable as it forms the backdrop to the momentous chivalric complex of motifs within freemasonry, flourishing particularly during the period 1760-1782. Whoever compiled this part of the Copiale-manuscript must have possessed direct insight into the structure and workings of Scottish master degree lodges in Germany and France at the time. Since no accurate printed exposures are known and even handwritten copies of the ritual for the early period are extremely rare, it is very likely that this account was produced from one or several oral sources and/or from personal experience, limiting the circle of those who potentially were able to communicate this information.

There are substantial overlaps in content between the description in Copiale and the manuscript "Ecossais de Prusse ou Le Chevalier de St. André,"
dated to around 1750 and supposedly originating from *L'Union* in Berlin
(Bettag and Snoek 137-42). A brother Dall or Dahle from Copenhagen in
1747 obtained the right to establish a lodge in Copenhagen and his sketch
of a tracing board resembles the design as outlined here. Yet another Scottish lodge was established in Denmark in 1748 and here the similarities of
the tracing board are greater with the lodges in Berlin and Braunschweig
(Bettag and Snoek 130 and 132). The rituals of "Le Parfait Maçon" in
Carr (157-200) have also many similarities to the symbols described in
the Oculist-manuscript. Snoek has characterized this family of rituals as
the third, 'Harodim'-tradition to which he also counts the Royal Order of
Scotland. It is obvious that the Copiale-manuscript provides yet another
piece in the advanced jigsaw that we slowly are able to place concerning
the evolution of the Scottish and higher degrees in European freemasonry.

THE KEY LODGE

The rituals, symbols and ideas of the "so-called Key lodge" ("die so genan-
nte Schlüssel loge") described on pages 100-4 are not to be found elsewhere. To the best of my knowledge, no other ritual connected to freemasonry displays such an outright condemnation of tyranny and abuse
of power and none promotes political ideas related to natural liberty and
the right to (armed) resistance so clearly. Mainstream masonic rituals and
normative texts like orations or charges rarely touch upon any obvious
political issues or political ideas for that matter which although doesn't
make them un-political per se. However, the themes addressed in the Key-
lodge, such as peace, rebellion, natural freedom, the necessity to form a
corps of armed resistance, a three-headed monster that represents violent
government, tyranny and the like place the workings of the lodge in a
political setting.

On the tracing board of the lodge seven symbols are displayed (100): (1)
an olive branch as the sign of peace, (2) a drum which calls for a general
rebellion, (3) the goddess Fama (Fame) with her trumpet, "calling the
freemasons [or the 'Order', depending how to dissolve the pictogram of the
big X, here I choose the grammatically most likely reading] to regain their
natural freedom" ("die 'big X' wieder zusammen ihre natürliche freyheit
wieder zu erlangen"), (4) a three-headed monster (conventionally this is
Cerberus, the dog guarding the entrance to the underworld) representing
a government that "by force of violence and stratagems has bereaved
man of his natural freedom, enjoyment of timely matters and what man

depends upon" ("[...] welche durch gewalt und list den menschen um seine natürliche freyheit und den genuss der zeitlichen dinge und was wir menschen benötiget sind gebracht [...]", (5) an exalted mountain, "symbolizing tyranny with which we are suppressed in our current slavery" ("[...] tiranney womit wir in unserere jetzigen sclaverey gedrucket werden [...]"], (6) three snakes (a triple caduceus?) symbolizing the positive values nature, justice and fortitude and (7) spears, pistols and banners "are the weapons of freemasons [most likely reading of the pictogram] in order to recuperate their lost liberty ("[...] sind waffen der 'big X' ihre verlorne freyheit wieder zu recuperieren [...]"). Some of these symbols, such as the drum and Fame, are in fact mentioned in the part of "Les Francs-Maçons Ecrasés" that treats the architects/Scottish masons (Carr 307-14).This strong rhetoric is repeated on a number of occasions throughout the text.

If this not is thrilling enough, the philosophy of liberation is reinforced by religious references. In the catechism of the degree its purpose is emphasized as "to kill the three-headed beast" and the intriguing exchange of questions and answers continues:

> Q: *Where is this monster to be found?*
>
> A: On a mighty mountain.
>
> Q: *Does anyone know how strong the beast is?*
>
> A: Tyranny, pride, injustice and ignorance. [...]
>
> Q: *Why does the beloved brother want to do this project?*
>
> A: For the almighty God who is the origin of everything.
>
> Q: *From where has the brother received the secret of this project?*
>
> A: Through a secret revelation.
>
> Q: *When and at what time has the brother received this revelation?*
>
> A: On a Sunday.
>
> Q: *At which place has the brother received this revelation?*
>
> A: In the house of the supreme God. [Asked what he saw there, he describes the tracing board.] He promises "rather to die for my natural freedom or to regain it".
>
> Q: *How were you initiated/accepted* into the Key-lodge?*

A: I am born out of the body of a mother [a womb?], which is: free, no one's subject and not subjected to any human law, only subjected and responding to God alone.

* = the German has "auf- und angenommen", where "aufgenommen" rather implies to be initiated and "angenommen" accepted, possibly pointing at these two practices in freemasonry.

Since the degree clearly is a continuation of the motifs in the Scottish Master (same passwords, access is granted to the Sanctum Sanctorum "whenever it pleases" the candidate), one can ask what the Key-lodge stipulates here, somewhat enigmatically. The revelation to carry out the project of regaining (natural) liberty was obviously received in a church, but initiation is likened to birth out of a womb. The conclusion though is quite surprising, since the individual thus is free by birth and hence not subjected to any fellow human (why?) and not to any man-made law (which might refer to pre-political/religious foundations of natural rights, distrusting the capacity of man-made political law to secure essential rights) and last but not least, only responding to a supreme divine authority. The question is who represents these qualities? Are they even attainable by a human being? Or does the Key-lodge identify the candidate with Christ, born of the Virgin Mary, the only human (theologically interpreted) subjected "God alone"? More research is needed to clarify this issue.

According to the person who compiled the Oculist-manuscript the Key-lodge was invented by "unsettled idlers" and has "most certainly to the largest extent disappeared". But in the context of masonry such a strong emphasis on the fight against usurpation and tyranny, natural freedom and free will is very unusual. Particularly striking is the call for a general rebellion and the question is of course, against whom? Considering the possible origin of the manuscript around the middle of the 1740s, there is a potential answer, the Jacobite rebellion of 1745. Without too much over-interpretation, would it be possible to assume that the Key-lodge calls freemasonry or the Order of St. Andrew to the weapons, as a tool to gather support for the Jacobite cause (Mollier3 59-73)? The programmatic message of the Key-lodge would speak for such a reading and points forward to concepts of liberty, right of resistance and independence as subsequently realised during the 1776 and 1789 revolutions in the US and France. Let us though not forget that the only piece of evidence of a link between freemasonry and the political philosophy of liberty and violent struggle for liberation (intensified by religious overtones that point in the direction of some form of liberation theology) is the Copiale-manuscript itself, an exposure with a clear anti-masonic bias. Furthermore the manuscript states that the ritual has become obsolete. But still it was incorporated into the enumeration of contemporary masonic praxis. Since the documentation of it in the parts that relate to craft and Scottish degrees does not appear implausible, why would suddenly the account relating to the Key-lodge slip over to fiction or hearsay and falsify ritual praxis at the time? In any case, the motifs of the Key lodge are worth exploring further.

ALCHEMY

In the very final paragraphs of the Copiale-manuscript (104-5) a 'Consolation-lodge' is mentioned. This "society of alchemists" has its own tracing board, ceremonies and symbols; "their work aims primarily at to fixate Mercury". This lodge is said to be in existence in Halle. However the author of the manuscript tells us that "this new association" probably not will last long and hence not is qualified for further investigation. What is worth noticing is however that the Copiale-manuscript is another proof for the association of freemasonry with alchemy; purely alchemical degrees of freemasonry were developed during the 1760s and the manuscript points at their prefiguration two decades earlier.

DATING OF THE MANUSCRIPT AND CONCLUDING REMARKS

Based upon several factors I have come to the conclusion that the most likely dating of the Copiale-manuscript, or at least its content, is the middle or end of the 1740s. First of all, the time for the establishment of the Oculist Order as such speaks for this interpretation. Henning (510) claims that the order was founded in 1742 and in existence for two decades. A printed book of constitutions was published around 1745. In the period yet two other mixed-gender fraternities with a similar program as the Oculists were established in German territories and in a Pietistic context, the "Anti-masonic Society" and the "Order of Abelites". The manuscript refers to the mixed gender fraternity of Mopses, which was exposed in 1745 in *L'Ordre*, a work that not only is directly mentioned in the manuscript, but from which at least a song, if not other elements, is quoted. Furthermore another exposure, "Die zergliederte Freymäurerei" is referred to, a pamphlet that circulated in a German translation since 1741/1744. As I have suggested above, the potential master copy for the Copiale-exposure is an English ritual, potentially supplemented with French sources. Masonic ceremonies described are quiet simple and not as elaborate as later ritual in German masonic lodges and definitely not of the advanced degree systems in place between 1760 and 1782. When it comes to the exposure of the Scottish master's degree, the ritual speaks of a "completely new innovation", which makes sense if we take 1742 as the starting date of the dissemination of such degrees in German territories. Furthermore only one degree is described, at the latest for 1748 further preparatory Scottish degrees are known at least in France and the Austrian Netherlands. The degree in the Oculist-manuscript has parallels to another source that is dated to 1747 and 1748. Again, the Scottish master's degree as practiced in German territories between 1754 and 1782 is far more elaborated, however some striking similarities do also exist. If the 'Key-lodge' indeed covertly seeks support for the Jacobite cause under the veil of a continuation of the Scottish master's degree, then dating the manuscript around 1745 makes sense and after 1746 (Culloden) it makes further sense that the compiler claims it has disappeared. References to a lodge working with alchemical symbolism previous to 1760 are highly interesting. After 1760, alchemical imagination within freemasonry peaked. Considering that a 1738 exposure (or rather apology) of freemasonry claimed that alchemical knowledge existed in the lodges, the existence of such a society in Halle adds to our understanding of the prevalence of alchemy within an early masonic context. In fact, none of the arguments listed above speak for that the (content of the) Oculist-manuscript was originally composed later than 1750, rather the contrary. The impression is overwhelming that the author used all available sources around 1745, printed exposures as much as oral accounts or potentially personal experience.

Concerning the Oculists, their organizational form, ideas and praxis were enacted within a well-established pattern of fraternal orders in Europe. We find rituals for initiation, conferring of further degrees and different practices for concealment of internally communicated arcane knowledge. At the same time the normative standards are high, the ennoblement of truth is an outspoken aim. Vision turns into a general metaphor of enlightenment per se, the ritual eye operation serves the purpose to open the eyes for those who naively believed to find something within secrecy. The aim of an enhanced capacity of vision is to undermine the alleged abuse of secrecy for destructive and overly esoteric purposes, by freemasonry.

Last but not least it is important to stress the fact that the Oculist-manuscript proves that it does make little sense to research freemasonry without considering the wider frame of fraternal orders and associations. As the manuscript forcefully demonstrates, freemasonry and fraternalism, their performances, practices and expressions represent interwoven phenomena of enlightenment sociability.

WORKS CITED

[Bernigeroth, Johann Martin (Ed.)]. *Le Cotumes des Francs-Maçons dans leurs assemblees principalement pour la reception des apperentifs et des maitres, tout nouvellement et sincerement decouvertes.* Leipzig: Berniger-oth, 1745. Print.

Bartholdy, Nils G. "'Det Antimasonianske Societet' – antifrimureri eller pietistisk loge?" *Acta Masonica Scandinavica* 12 (2009): 9-39. Print.

Bettag, Klaus and Snoek, Jan. *Quellen der Eckleff'schen Andreas-Akten.* Flensburg: Freimaurerische Forschungsvereinigung Frederik: 2012. Print.

Carr, Henry. *The Early French Exposures.* London: QC, 1971. Print.

Dotzauer, Winfried. "Sozialstruktur der Freimaurer in Deutschland." *Aufklärung und Geheimgesellschaften.* Ed. Helmut Reinalter. München: Oldenbourg, 1989. 110-125. Print.

Henning, Alois. "Eine frühe Loge des 18. Jahrhunderts: Die 'Hocher-leuchtete Oculisten-Gesellschaft' in Wolfenbüttel". *Festschrift für Günter Mühlpfordt.* Ed. Erich Donnert. Vol. 5. Weimar, Köln, Wien: Böhlau, 1999. 65-82. Print.

Knight, Kevin, Megyesi, Beata, and Schaefer, Christiane. "The Secrets of the Copiale Cipher". *Journal for Research into Freemasonry and Frater-nalism* (2012), 128-35. Print.

Kretschmer, Ernst Paul. "Die Antimassonische Sozietät und die Lo-gen Heinrichs XII. zugleich ein Beitrag zur Geschichte des Pietis-mus". *Quellen zur Geschichte der Freimaurerei.* Vol. 2. Leipzig: Zechel 1918/19. 71-212. Print.

Megyesi, Bea. Uppsala University, Sweden. "The Copiale Project", Uppsala University, 2011. Web 22 June 2015 <http://stp.lingfil.uu.se/~bea/copiale/>. Online.

Mollier, Pierre. (1) "L' 'Ordre Écossais' à Berlin de 1742 à 1751", *Renais-sance Traditionelle,* 131-132 (2002). 74-88. Print.

—. (2) "Le 'Maître écossais': sur la piste du plus ancien haut grade" i *Franc-Maçonnerie* 37 (2015). 24-8. Print.

—. (3) "Les Stuarts et la Franc-Maçonnerie: le dernier épisode", i *Renaissance Traditionelle* 177-178, 2015. Print.

Önnerfors, Andreas. (1) *Svenska Pommern: kulturmöten och identifikation.* Lund: Minerva 2003. Print.

—. (2) "The Establishment of the Swedish Scottish Degrees". *Kilwinning* (3) 2011. 83-94. Print.

[Pérau, Gabriel Louis Calabre]. *L'Ordre des Franc-Maçons trahi et les Secrets des Mopses revelée.* Amsterdam: NN 1745. Print.

Rudbeck, Johannes. *Kanslirådet Karl Friedrich Eckleff – det svenska frimuraresystemets fader.* Stockholm: Norstedts 1930. Print.

Snoek, Jan A.M. . "The Evolution of the Hiramic Legend in England and France", *Heredom* 11 (2003). 11-53. Print.

Uppsala University, Sweden. "Transcription of Copiale document", Uppsala University, 2011. Web 22 June 2015 <http://stp.lingfil.uu.se/~bea/copiale/copiale-deciphered.pdf>. Online.

XIII

PRAIRIE CHARITY:
MASONIC BENEVOLENCE IN
LATE NINETEENTH CENTURY MANITOBA

BRIAN ROUNTREE
Librarian, Grand Lodge of Manitoba
2015

INTRODUCTION

The early teachings that a Freemason receives explain how the Craft patiently ministers "to the relief of want and sorrow," and that it calls upon its members to "exercise that virtue" which Freemasons "profess to admire," that is to say, Charity. Freemasonry also instructs its members to extend "charity and consolation to their fellow creatures in the hour of their affliction."

As a result, Freemasons have been providing assistance to those less fortunate than themselves for many years. It is recorded that the Freemasons of Dublin, Ireland, in 1688, presented a "well-stuffed" purse of charity to a destitute brother (MacLeod 2).

The first recorded case of Masonic benevolence of the modern Grand Lodge system appears to be that of Antony Sayer, Gentleman, who was elected as the first Grand Master of the Grand Lodge in June 1717. Sayer later had some financial difficulties and several times he petitioned the Grand Lodge for charity which he received (Antony Sayer).

The children of Masons were not neglected. The Royal Masonic School for Girls and The Royal Masonic School for Boys were established to educate the children of Freemasons who were unable, through death, illness or disability, to support their families (Royal Masonic School ...)

CHARITY

In his address to the Annual Communication of the Grand Lodge of Manitoba, Grand Master William G. Scott said:

> Social gatherings are by no means to be overlooked, but as Masons the great and blessed principle of charity has a paramount claim upon our sympathies and our finances. (Proceedings 1906)

While there are many examples of charity to be found around the world, let me tell you of one. The Winter 2012 issue of *Beacon* from the Grand Lodge of Ohio tells an interesting story about its Masonic home. For a few years beginning in 1935 young James Ziegler and his siblings were cared for at the Ohio Masonic Home in Springfield. In 2000, James and his wife arrived at the Masonic Home, now refurbished into seniors' apartments ("Coming full circle").

EARLY MANITOBA

Manitoba is in the centre of Canada, and its capital city of Winnipeg is sometimes is called the heart of the North American continent.

European explorers and settlers travelled in the area for decades. The Red River Colony was organized by Thomas Douglas, 5th Earl of Selkirk, beginning in 1811. The settlers were given a large tract of the country for their colony and eventually they built at the forks of the Red and Assiniboine Rivers, the location of present-day Winnipeg.

One newcomer, Mr. A. P. Stevenson, describes the Manitoba countryside in 1874.

> About that time things were pretty much in the raw, or just about as nature left them ... Nearly two-thirds of (our route) was through swamps with water two or three feet deep. The ox and cart were mired three or four times, and what a delightful time we greenhorns had up to the waist in water with millions of mosquitoes adding their cheerful note (and bite) to the proceedings ... The following morning we found our ox had broken loose ... The distance we had to travel was 30 miles, a dead level plain, without a tree, shrub or twig, no house of any description, not a drop of water to drink. So we had to

start on foot for the same place ... walking with blistered feet on a hot day in the month of June, 1874. (Hambley 22)

Stevenson settled at the growing town of Nelson which had, by 1881, a population of 1,000. Nelson was an important place being the site of the land registry office for the district as well as having courthouse, one hotel, three churches, stores and other services, including three doctors. Nelson was on a regular stagecoach route to Miami, Carman, and other points to the north and east.

Those stagecoaches brought copies of local and distant newspapers and in 1881 the people of Nelson could have been reading the *Winnipeg Daily Sun, The Portage la Prairie Weekly,* or even *The Globe* from Toronto, Ontario in addition to local newspapers.

Overland road travel, or even river travel, worked well; however, as they read the newspapers, some of the area residents began to recognize the benefits of a railroad, and, especially, of having that railroad go through their town.

THE RAILWAY

There was a rail line through southern Manitoba at this time. Completed in 1878, that line ran south from St. Boniface to the international boundary at Emerson and was a way of connecting Manitoba to eastern Canada by rail through the United States.

By 1883, the year when the people of Nelson were holding meetings to decide "How Can Nelsonville Get a Railroad?" there were a number of small towns in the area.

Back in 1874 Alvey Baker Morden brought his wife and children to Manitoba from Ontario. (Morden 23) They arrived in Fort Garry (now part of Winnipeg) where a friend mentioned the available land to the south. Alvey and his two eldest sons checked it out and returned to fetch the rest of the family to settle down on property that was 100 km south-west of Winnipeg and just 25 km north of the border with the United States.

By the 1880s the focus of the residents was on the Canadian Pacific Railroad as it built a cross-Canada railroad line. In 1882 the management decided to by-pass established settlements such as Nelson in favour of a nearby creek because it provided water for their steam locomotives. The CPR built a water tower, and a small station that was named Cheval, and soon people wanted to build nearby (Morden, Mort Cheval 5). The company purchased the land around the station which had belonged to Alvey Morden: as a result, it was not long before the growing community was renamed Morden.

HEALTH CARE

Health care in those early days was limited. The pioneers might learn healing from the local Aboriginal peoples, and they might have some family cures, but doctors and nurses were few and far between. Nelson, Manitoba was fortunate to have the services of three doctors who would serve the community from their offices, make house calls, and travel long distances to reach people in need.

Every community's cemetery would give mute testimony to the effects of serious illnesses when it was seen how many had died due to tuberculosis, smallpox, typhoid or scarlet fever. No one was immune but infants and young mothers were quite susceptible to these diseases. As one pioneer recalls:

> Typhoid fever struck our family when I, the youngest, was only nine or ten months old. All the family except me was struck down by this dread disease ... Mother was the last to be stricken, and, after nursing the rest of the family, her resistance was gone. She died on Christmas Day, 1893, and was buried in the little cemetery at Nelson, where her second oldest child, a baby, was also buried. (Mann)

Rural doctors did not always have the expertise or the facilities to treat serious cases, or be able to provide long term care. The patient could be sent to the closest hospital, Winnipeg, but that was over 100 km away and a very difficult journey even for healthy people.

Elsewhere, in 1859 in England, cottage hospitals began to appear across the country. The movement started because the Reverend J. H. Sapter, Rector of Cranley, had observed a local doctor and his assistants treating an accident victim. Since the patient could not travel, they realized there was a need for some local facility where people could receive urgent care. It was not long before Mr. Sapter "made a cottage available, rent-free, which after being whitewashed and simply furnished opened after a few weeks as the first cottage hospital" (Cottage Hospitals).

Having a local hospital meant that long journeys to city hospitals were not always necessary. It also meant that they had facilities to deal more immediately with emergencies and that physicians knew their patients and the treatments they needed. Also, no matter how long a patient was in the hospital, it meant that family and friends were able to visit so that the patient would not feel isolated and cut off from them.

A New Idea in Southern Manitoba

Belmont Lodge, No. 13, A.F. & A.M., under the Grand Lodge of Manitoba, was established in Nelson, Manitoba in 1880 and moved to Morden in 1885. It was locally called the Morden Lodge although the name did not officially change until 1942.

At the November 20, 1890 meeting of Belmont Lodge, the Worshipful Master, Corbet Locke, presented a scheme to erect a Cottage Hospital in their town of Morden, resulting in the following 18 motion:

> Moved by Bro, Hansen, seconded by Bro. McConnell, that the sum of $100.00 of the funds of this Lodge be voted towards establishing a fund for the erection of a Hospital in the town of Morden, the said amount to be deposited in the Commercial Bank here to the credit of a Committee to be appointed by the W. M. (Belmont Lodge, Minute Book 1)

The Lodge then sent a letter out to all the lodges in Manitoba about their plan.

> The Officers and Members of Morden Lodge, being mindful of the duties imposed upon them by their obligations and in the exhortations and charges in the several degrees of craft Masonry, and feeling that they should not be drones in this world's hive, ... have resolved to make a united effort to do a lasting good to the community, by erecting a hospital to be known as "The Freemason's Hospital", at Morden ... to be open to the sick and languishing no matter whence they come, so long as we have beds to lay them on. (Robertson 4)

An article in the *Manitoba Daily Free Press* for September 10, 1891 records an appeal to the wider public for funds to build the hospital. It mentions that "The building we are anxious to erect is designed after one declared by experts to be the best cottage hospital yet erected." The hope was to have the "foundation stone laid by the Grand Master of the province, with full Masonic ceremonial" in October 1891 (The Morden Hospital).

The cornerstone was actually laid on 1 July 1892. At this Special Communication of the Grand Lodge mention was made by

> R. W. Bro. D J. Goggin ... on behalf of the M. W. Grand Master, ... congratulating the brethren of Morden on the commendable Masonic spirit and the enterprise shown in commencing the erection of such a useful building, and expressing the hope that success would crown their efforts. (Proceedings 1893)

The first Annual Meeting of the Freemasons' Hospital Committee was held in Dufferin Hall in Morden on April 19th, 1893. At a Directors' meeting that followed immediately, Corbet Locke (a local judge and a Freemason) was elected President.

Corbet Locke, speaking in his 1897 Address, as the Most Worshipful the Grand Master of the Grand Lodge of Manitoba, gave a review of the Freemasons' Hospital up to that time.

> I doubt not that I will be expected to refer to the Hospital and I gladly embrace this opportunity to let you know something of what has been done, of what property has been acquired, and of the position of the hospital financially. I am also glad to refer to the work in the hope that the *veritus* of what has been done in this sparsely populated jurisdiction to furnish means of relief to the sick, may be a spur to other jurisdictions of the same so exactly, in my view, in accord with the tenets of our order.
>
> ... When the work was taken in hand many expressed the fear that though the erection of the building might be accomplished that it could not be maintained, and that the maintenance of it would be a constant drag on the Craft—such however has not been the event. (Proceedings 1897)

It is important to note that the only money available to the Hospital for maintenance and operations, other than from revenue, was the Hospital Committee membership fees: even these were at the will of the donors, and therefore varied from year to year. During the years of the Hospital's existence it became a common practice for Directors and supporters to be out canvassing for members during the few days before the Annual Meeting, in order to be assured of enough members to fill the Board of Directors.

No limitation was placed on membership of the Hospital Committee as long as individuals or corporations made annual donations. The Board of Directors consisted of 17 men elected annually. Provision was made, however, to increase this Board by allowing the town councils of Morden and nearby Stanley to each appoint a Director in any year that they made a donation toward the maintenance of the Hospital. Reeves of other Municipalities were permitted to become *ex-officio* Directors under the same conditions. The Worshipful Master of Belmont Lodge No. 13 was an additional Director, by virtue of his office.

No yearly grants were available from Municipal and Government sources in the earlier years of the Hospital's operation. It was therefore dependent upon generous donations from the residents of Southern Manitoba, from the Grand Lodge, and from fundraising activities as well as sales of such items as paperweights and china bowls.

Paperweight in the collection of B. Rapson. Image used by permission.

China bowl in the Manitoba Masonic Archives. Image used by permission.

From almost the beginning there was a Women's Hospital Aid Society, as well as a Nurses' Home Aid Society, that did some fundraising. There were also a variety of events held where the collections or donations were passed on to the hospital. Examples include concerts, Celtic Balls, sermons at a Divine Service attended by Masons, and talks such as

The World's Fair for a Quarter

Rev. Alfred Andrews will give his lecture on the World's Fair in Minnedosa on Thursday, Oct. 19th. After the lecture he will present a dozen fine magic lantern views of the principal objects of interest.

Minnedosa Tribune
12 October 1893

One of the problems faced by rural physician was collecting fees. Many people sickened and died without medical care because they could not pay for it. Often, medical care was provided but the doctor was not paid.

Sometimes the doctor was paid in kind rather than cash. In December 1935 a girl was born at home in Crandall, Manitoba and the cost of the nursing care was $32.00. Over a four-month period, the bill was paid by the following (Twells 13):

2 loads of wood	$ 4.50
Chickens and 2 doz. eggs	$ 0.80
1 load of ice	$ 1.00
1 load of wood	$ 2.00
Chickens	$ 0.45
½ wood, 1 ice, 1 wood	$ 4.25
4 months milk @$2.20	$ 8.80

Sometimes even the hospital had to wait for payment. In 1920 the Directors' minutes make a special note: "Mr. H. Williams, a patient in the hospital in 1901, who was unable to pay his hospital bill, felt that he was now in a position to do so, sent his cheque for the sum of one hundred dollars as a donation" (Board of Directors 1920:153).

These are only a few examples that demonstrate the credit that is due to those who loyally supported the Freemasons' Hospital in many ways to maintain a service so important to the people.

THE HOSPITAL

Postcard in the author's collection.

The Freemasons' Hospital in Morden was a reality. The new 22-bed hospital was officially opened on March 10, 1893. There were two public wards (male and female) and four private wards—accommodation for twenty-two patients, though as many as twenty-six have been in the building at one time. This Freemasons' Hospital was also a unique venture in all of Canada.

> Upwards of twenty-five thousand days of treatment have been had by over fifteen hundred patients, with an annual death rate of a small fraction over three per cent, which is said to be the best showing of any hospital in Canada ... It is understood that this is the only hospital built exclusively by the craft on this continent. ("Mason's Silver Celebration")

No doubt the recurring outbreaks of typhoid fever and other dangerous diseases are what led to the construction of a separate isolation ward for the care of those patients. A motion to build the ward was passed at the 1903 annual meeting of the Board of Directors because the local residents were "fully alive to the necessity of the existence of such an adjunct to the Hospital." As with any building project, there were complications and delays but the isolation ward was built by the end of the year.

Modern improvements were always added to the hospital building. Examples include lighting, telephone, kitchen equipment, and sanitary facilities. Sometimes they involved a lot of exercise. In a recent play about the town of Morden, the newly-installed elevator was described in these terms:

> There was great excitement when the elevator was installed in the hospital. One of the Masons reported he had gone for a ride. He said the elevator was going to make life easier for the nurses and doctors. Instead of carrying their patients up the twenty steps from the operating room to the ward, they could use the elevator.

> There was enough room for the patient on the stretcher and the nurse. She put on the gloves supplied and then hauled away on the ropes. Away you went as slick as anything up to the next floor! (Evenson *Morden is 120*)

To meet the demands made upon the hospital, a new wing was added and opened in 1928. It was named "The Locke Wing" in honour of Judge Corbet Locke to recognize his long and valuable services to the institution. He was annually elected the president of the Board of Directors from 1893 to 1926 when he retired and left the community.

THE NURSING PROGRAM

Soon after the Hospital opened a Nursing School was developed and the Nurses' Home built in 1898.

The Lady Superintendent, assisted by local doctors, was in charge of the lectures given to the student nurses over a two-year, and later a three-year, training period.

The nursing students received a salary during their period of training, set by the Board of Directors, at $8.00 per month for the first year, $9.00 for the second year, and $10 for the third year. In 1920 these salaries were raised to $12.00, $14.00 and $16.00.

Similar to other nursing programs, the graduate nurses had their own distinctive cap possibly inspired by the Shrine's fez ("Symbol of a Profession").

Symbol of a Profession
One Hundred Years of Nurses' Caps

Freemasons Hospital School of
Nursing, Morden, Manitoba
Evelyn (Hainsworth) Witt,
graduated 1939
1999.267.64

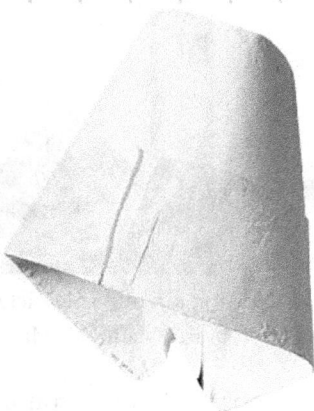

There was also a certificate and a distinctive sterling silver lapel pin.

Nursing pin of Mary Winram, graduated 1914.
From the collection of the Manitoba Masonic Archives. Used with permission.

Early in the 1930s the Board of Directors arranged for a new style of pin to be given to the graduating nurses.

Nursing pin of Annie Tickner, graduated 1933.
From the collection of the Manitoba Masonic Archives. Used with permission.

The training of registered nurses continued until the end of 1942, when provincial regulations became so stringent that the Board found it impossible to secure and pay the necessary instructors. From 1946 the hospital took on the training of practical nurses but it all ended with the closure of the hospital in 1952.

END OF AN ERA

> [Belmont Lodge] has given proof of Masonic earnestness in the erection of a hospital and nurses' home, which exemplify in a marked degree the benefits of that cardinal Masonic virtue – charity.
>
> R. W. Bro. John Campbell
> (Proceedings 1899)

The Freemasons' Hospital was kept up-to-date over the years but it was beginning to show its age in in the 1940s. Changes were made in the provincial regional health organization that provided for the construction of a new hospital and nurses' residence to be financed through the issue of municipal debentures.

When the new hospital was completed, and officially opened on July 4, 1952, the *Winnipeg Free Press* report mentioned that "Present on the platform were Donald Buchanan, an old-timer of the Morden area, who witnessed the cornerstone laying of the Freemasons' hospital here July 1, 1892." ("Schultz ...")

In 1951 the Freemasons' Hospital of Morden was purchased by Tabor Home Inc. and converted into a 32-bed personal care home, opening in October 1952. The building was demolished in 1969 with the result that the cornerstone, along with those items laid with it in 1892, returned to Morden Lodge No. 13. Some items stayed with the Lodge records and are now in the Grand Lodge Archives. In 2001, the Freemasons' Hospital cornerstone went to a brand new hospital, the third one in that area of the province.

EMERGENT COMMUNICATION
An Emergent Meeting of the Grand Lodge of Manitoba was convened at the Boundary Trails Hospital on Saturday, July 14, 2001 for the purpose of dedicating the cornerstone. This cornerstone is the same cornerstone that was laid at the original Morden Hospital that served the community for many years. (Proceedings 2001)

CONCLUSION

In 1986 a Manitoba Past Grand Master wrote:

> "Masonry in Manitoba has always been in the forefront of community endeavours ... " (Robertson 4)

The Freemasons' Hospital may have closed in 1952, but the Masons of Manitoba have not been lacking in projects since then.

The Grand Lodge of Manitoba supports two initiatives with the Canadian Cancer Society: (1) *Masons Care* which has provided drivers and vans to take patients to and from their treatments since 1983; and, more recently, (2) a fundraiser called *Relay for Life*. The Grand Lodge also supports a program of the Canadian Blood Services called *Partners for Life*.

The *Masonic Foundation of Manitoba, Inc.* is a separate charitable entity to which anyone can contribute.

Individual Lodges have their own chosen organizations to which they contribute for the benefit of the community.

In 1901, M. W. Bro. Corbet Locke could proclaim proudly that since the hospital opened in 1893 "treatment has been given to upwards of two thousand sick, that many capable lives have been saved, and that the Masons of Manitoba thereby became in time universally serviceable to mankind" (Locke 3).

Over one hundred years later, Manitoba Masons demonstrate in a variety of ways that Charity is important and remains a key concept in the Masonic Way of Life. Our conclusion is that we can return, with a slight alteration, to the beginning of our story—*Prairie Charity: Masonic Benevolence **Continues** in 21st Century Manitoba.*

WORKS CITED

Belmont Lodge, No. 13, A.F & A.M. Minute Books: 1888-1999. Winnipeg, Man. Archives of the Grand Lodge of Manitoba.

"Coming full circle: a childhood resident returns to Springfield." *The Beacon.* 19: 1 (2012): 1. Print.

Cottage Hospitals. Web. 4 February 2015. <http://en.m.wikipedia.org/wiki/Cottage_hospital>

Evenson, Catherine. "Re: Freemason's Hospital." Message to the author. 29 January 2015. E-mail.

Evenson, Catherine. *Morden is 120.* N.p., 2002.

Hambley, George H. *Trails of the Pioneers.* Basswood, Man.: The Author, 1956.

Locke, Corbet. "The Brother in Distress. *Western Mason.* May, 1901: 3. Print.

Mann, Jessie._Pioneering in Southern Manitoba. *Manitoba Pageant.* (17: 1) Autumn 1971. Web. 15 August 2014. <http://www.mhs.mb.ca/docs/pageant/17/pioneering.shtml>

MacLeod, Wallace. *For the Cause of Good.* Toronto: The Masonic Foundation of Ontario, 1990.

"Mason's Silver Celebration." *Manitoba Morning Free Press.* Winnipeg, June 13, 1900, page 10.

Morden Centennial Souvenir Booklet and Program July 5-11th. Morden, Man, 1982.

Morden, Mort Cheval, Pinancewaywinning, Lake Agassiz. Morden, Man.: Morden Centennial Committee, 1981.

"The Morden Hospital." *Manitoba Daily Free Press.* 10 September 1891, page 5.

Proceedings. Grand Lodge of Manitoba. Winnipeg, 1875-

Red River Colony. Web. 4 February 2015. <http://en.wikipedia.org/wiki/Red_River_Colony>

Robertson, Fred. "The Freemason's Hospital." *Masonry in Manitoba.* 41:13 (1986): 4. Print.

Royal Masonic School for Girls. Web. 2 February 2015. <http://www.royalmasonic.herts.sch.uk/History_of_RMS/index.php>

Royal Masonic School for Boys. Web. 2 February 2015. <http://en.wikipedia.org/wiki/Royal_Masonic_School_for_Boys>

"Schultz Terms 56-Bed Hospital 'Equal To Any'." *Winnipeg Free Press*, July 5, 1952, page 8.

"Symbol of a Profession: One Hundred Years of the Nurse's Cap." Web. 15 February 2015. <http://www.historymuseum.ca/cmc/exhibitions/hist/infirm/inevo05e.shtml>

The Freemason's Hospital, Morden, Minute Books: 1893-1952. Winnipeg, Man. Archives of the Grand Lodge of Manitoba.

Twells, Maxine. "Using Your Initiative." The Leaf of the Branch. Brandon, Man.: Manitoba Genealogical Society, South West Branch. 15: 2 (2003): 13. Print.

XIV

SANTA ANNA, THE MASON

CASEY D. STANISLAW, M.A.
Lee Lockwood Scottish Rite Library and Museum
Waco, Texas

In the collective imagination of Texans, the dark visage of General Antonio López de Santa Anna looms large as a villain, a rogue, a manipulator, a womanizer, and a ruthless tyrant. Ironically, a masonic legend has persisted for many years that Santa Anna's life was spared from the wrath of vengeful Texans at Battle of San Jacinto and the months afterward due to his masonic membership, a proposition put forth by William Denslow in 1957 in his book, *10,000 Famous Freemasons*, which can be regarded as largely speculative and without supporting evidence. Although suggestions as to his membership-by-association have been noted by many historians and biographers, Santa Anna's masonry was not definitively confirmed until 2008, when his 1825 Scottish Rite patent was discovered in a closet in the Chancellor Livingston Masonic Library and Museum in New York City.

To date, a detailed treatment of the patent and of Santa Anna's masonic history has not been published in English. As an introduction to the topic, a review will be given of historical research done before 2008 concerning Santa Anna's masonic membership. The details of the patent and a translation will then be presented, along with considerations as to the regularity of the masonic body which issued it. Secondly, a review of Santa Anna's history and the status of masonry in Mexico during the time period will be discussed, and suggestions will be made as to how Santa Anna came to be made a mason in 1825. Thirdly, data will be presented concerning the patent's authenticity, and two discrepancies in the patent will be noted which suggest that Santa Anna was a mason for political purposes and in name only, and that he utilized his masonic membership only to further his career. In conclusion, the patent's historical impact will be considered, along with suggestions for further study.

As a prelude to the study of this unique primary source document is worthwhile to review the statements of historians prior to this time, who wrote without the conclusive information contained in the patent. These historians can be roughly divided into two groups, those writing before 1990, and modern scholars writing from 1990 to present. In the first group we find the previously mentioned Denslow, who notes that Santa Anna gave the masonic sign of distress at San Jacinto to several soldiers, including Sam Houston, and that he owed his life during captivity to the masons assigned to guard him, and later, as a sign of appreciation, presented a masonic apron to John Stiles, one of his guards. Denslow notes that he was an *escocés*, or Scottish Rite mason, who later became a *yorkino*, or York Rite mason (Denslow, Vol IV, 96-97). Charles Stuart is another oft-cited writer, who reported in his book *Masonic Soldiers of Fortune* (1928) that Santa Anna was a "renegade mason" due to his reconciliation with the clergy and the abolishment of the York Rite College in Oaxaca in 1833 (Stuart 256-276). Dr. James Carter, in his seminal work *Masonry in Texas* (1958), quotes a first-hand account stating that Santa Anna "filled the air" with masonic signs after his capture (Carter 284-285). Carter also recognizes Santa Anna's masonic membership through a reference to a classic work written in Mexico in 1884, *Historia de la Masonería en* México *desde 1806 hasta 1884* by José María Mateos, who states flatly, "*Santa Anna era masón escocés*" ("Santa Anna was a Scottish Rite mason.") (Mateos 62). Besides that of Mateos, two other volumes written in Spanish serve as obligatory starting points for any Mexican masonic research projects: *Una contribución a la historia masónica de México* (1899) by Richard Chism; and the two-volume set, *Apuntes para la historia de la masonería en* México (1950) by Luis J. Zalce y Rodríguez, both of whom affirm Santa Anna's masonic membership (Chism 36, de los Reyes Heredia 63). In addition to these masonic historians, others have also made passing references to Santa Anna's *escocés* membership, including Lucás Alamán in *Historia de México, Vol V* (1885); and Wilfred Henry Callcott, in *Santa Anna: The Story of an Enigma that one was Mexico* (1936) (Várgas Márquez, 49-57).

What has been generally lacking from these earlier historians is a more detailed treatment of Santa Anna's masonic activity, the particulars of which are beginning to come to light through the work of the second group, a new generation of twenty-first century researchers, who have begun sketching the activity of masons in Mexico during the time period through the research of newspapers, fliers, letters, and previously unavailable archives. Historian Will Fowler, in his 2007 biography, *Santa Anna of Mexico*, portrays an up-and-coming Santa Anna who was identified politically as a *yorkino* at the beginning of his political career, despite being enmeshed in political maneuverings between centralists and federalists in the mid-1820s and having close allies in the Veracruz region who were *escoceses*. Mexican researcher María Vázquez Semadeni also affirms Santa Anna's masonic associations through his *yorkino* political activities, although noting that (excluding the patent) there are no elements that positively confirm his masonic membership (*La formación*, 172, n. 121).

Let us now turn to the newly discovered Scottish Rite patent, presently housed at the Livingston Masonic Library and Museum in New York City, under the care of curator Catherine Walter. The artifact, dated December 12, 1825, was discovered in 2008 by Walter as she was going through a box of items donated in 1960 by the Master of Americus Lodge #535, then located in Whitestone (Queens), New York. In its time period, a patent of this type would have been carried by the bearer folded in a leather pouch, which would have been presented to verify one's Scottish Rite membership, certified by his *ne varietur* (signature) in the left margin. The patent was found folded, and although damaged and missing the portion where Santa Anna's *ne varietur* would have been, the patent clearly states that Antonio López de Santa Anna was certified and recognized as a Master of the Royal Secret (See Appendix 1). The certificate itself is paper, attached to a vellum backing, with handwritten text in Spanish and Latin, two woven ribbons, two stamped seals and a red wax seal. In the upper left corner appears the iconic double-headed eagle of the Scottish Rite, with the Latin phrase "Universi terrarium Orbis." In the upper center an angel flies upward with the words "Evolat Ad Immortalitatem." On the right side of the document are images which reference Scottish Rite degrees, the Ladder of Kadosh, and a representation of a Knight Templar, which is meant to be Jaques de Molay. Above the knight and next to the ladder is an urn with a sword through it, on top of a three-headed serpent with crowns on each of the heads. The serpent is a unique feature of the patent and will be discussed below.

The preliminary research on this document was done by Mexican scholar Carlos Martínez Moreno, in his Master's Thesis for the Universidad Nacional Autónoma de México in 2011 (*Tesis*, 276-89, 794-95). The principal text of the document is handwritten abbreviated script, and some of the text is unreadable or missing, but a substantial portion of it remains, and a complete transcription as reconstructed by Martínez Moreno is provided in Appendix 2, along with an English translation. A summary of the text follows:

- Issued by the Grand Territorial Consistory of Yucatán (Ancient and Accepted Scottish Rite of Freemasonry), established to the Orient of the Paraclete, which is properly

and legitimately constituted in the Sovereign Grand
Consistory of the 32nd Degree.

- Confirms that "we have duly examined our Illustrious
  Brother António López de Santa Anna, born in Jalapa, State
  of Veracruz, of 29 years of age ... various degrees that he has
  legitimately received, and to his special petition."

- Certifies, recognizes and proclaims Santa Anna to be "very
  expert," a Past Master of Symbolic Lodges, and lists his
  Scottish Rite degrees, beginning with "Secret Master" and
  ending with "Sublime and Illustrious Prince of the Royal
  Secret," and member of the Sovereign Grand Territorial
  Consistory of Yucatan.

- Authorizes Santa Anna to inspect all Chapter College Lodges
  of the Royal and Military order, according to the grand
  constitution and the regulations of the Consistory.

- Orders all Knight Prince Brothers and Sublime Masons to
  admit and receive him as a 32nd degree mason.

- Signed and sealed, given in the Consistorial Chamber near
  the Orient of Arcadia, "beneath the celestial vault," 12
  December, 1825.

What is definitively known is that the certificate was issued to Antonio
López de Santa Anna on December 12, 1825, and clearly recognizes him
as having received the degrees entitling him to represent himself as a Master of the Royal Secret of the Ancient and Accepted Scottish Rite.

Martinez Moreno provides detailed data on the regularity of Mexican
lodges and establishes that masonry first became established on the coast
through Spanish military lodges, later becoming annexed by the Grand
Lodge of Louisiana under the York Rite. On July 12, 1817, *Reunión de
la Virtud No. 9* in Campeche was annexed, followed by *Aurera de ****
No. 18* in Yucatán, Cuba (Mérida) on July 12, 1820. As will be discussed
below, the Yucatán, and especially Mérida, maintained a strong Spanish
sentiment after independence due to their close relationship with Cuba.

In 1821 the *Gran Oriente Territorial Español-Americano* (Spanish-American Grand Territorial Orient) was organized under the Scottish Rite in Cuba, followed by the Consistory of the Sublime Princes of the Royal Secret 32° in Veracruz, the latter of which reclaimed their authority over the symbolic degrees, and over the lodge *Arquitectura Moral* in Mexico City. A document dated 1823 suggests that the Grand Consistory of the Yucatán separated itself from Havana and united with the Grand Consistory of Veracruz, which would have still had jurisdiction over it in 1825 at the time of the issue of the Santa Anna's patent. This Scottish Rite Consistory most likely corresponded with *Logia Aurora Yucateca* in Mérida. (Martínez Moreno, *Tésis* 274).

In 1825 a faction of *escoceses* in Mexico City, through U.S. Plenipotentiary Joel Poinsett, received charters for York Rite lodges from the Grand Lodge of New York, and formed *La Gran Logia Nacional Mexicana del Rito York* (National Mexican Grand Lodge of the York Rite), with Vicente Guerrero, José María Alpuche Infante, and Lorenzo de Zavala among its first grand officers. In the following years many Scottish Rite lodges would convert to become York Rite lodges, and these two groups would come to define political parties and shape the debate in the coming years, with the *yorkino* faction representing a more inclusive and progressive group with strong federalist tendencies and an anti-Spanish agenda; and the *escoceses* maintaining a more aristocratic group, in favor of more gradual reform and sustaining loyalties to aristocrats and politicians of Spanish heritage who remained in Mexico after independence. As shall be shown, in 1825 Santa Anna would have been caught in the middle of the *escocés/yorkino* debate (Fowler 96).

Compelling evidence suggests that Santa Anna's Scottish Rite patent is authentic and not a forgery, but before considering these points it is worthwhile to place the artifact within its proper context by reviewing Mexican history during the early 1820s, and situating Santa Anna within this milieu. After the overthrow of Emperor Augustín I in 1823, Santa Anna was appointed military commander of far-away Yucatán (which at that time included with it the present-day states of Campeche and Quintana Roo), a remote province that had independence tendencies of its own. His first assignment was to mediate a dispute between the region's two largest cities, Mérida, the capital on the north shore and heavily dependent on maritime trade with Spanish Cuba, and the centralist-leaning Campeche, located a little further south and closer to Mexico City. The region was on the verge of civil war, and in February of 1824 the political class in Campeche sent 2000 troops to Mérida to force the state legislature to obey the mandate from the central government to cut off all trade with the Spanish. Santa Anna arrived, portraying himself to the *yucatecos* as "the friend of Liberty," expounding upon the virtues of a political system that was federal, republican and liberal; and urging them to settle their differences peacefully. Civil war was averted, but Yucatán still remained divided, as Campeche was commercially dependent on Mexico and trade with Veracruz and New Orleans, while Mérida remained economically loyal to Spanish Havana. Santa Anna drafted a resolution to Congress recommending that the implementation of the Spanish trade ban be postponed for Mérida, an action which won him local political clout but did not solve the problem. Always the soldier, he came up with a solution that could please both the federal government and those of the people of Yucatán: liberate Cuba from the Spanish. In the summer and fall of 1824 he prepared troops for the expedition and urged Congress for its adoption, which was backed by President Guadalupe Victoria but in the end was rejected (Fowler 79-85).

It is in this scenario that Santa Anna is first associated with masons and masonic organizations. Back in his hometown of Xalapa, in Veracruz province, a secret masonic society known as *La Gran Legión del* Águila *Negra* (Grand Legion of the Black Eagle) had been established with the purpose of promoting and bringing about Cuban independence, along with being a political alternative to the *escoceses*. Given that Guadalupe Victoria was the founder and *varón fuerte* ("strong male") of the organization, and that Victoria had backed Santa Anna's plan despite strong opposition from the capital, Santa Anna's ties with Victoria and the Veracruz region suggests that there may have also been a masonic association. The *Gran Legión*, though it remained an independent organization and a clandestine masonic lodge, bore similarities with the York Rite in its practices and rituals. Considering our knowledge of Santa Anna, it would appear that his philosophy matched well with the stance of the *Gran Legión del* Águila *Negra,* an organization with the specific purpose of combating the Spanish and not embroiled in the finger-pointing between *yorkinos* and *escoceses* (Vázquez Semadeni, *La formación,* 101-105; "La Gran Legión", 153; Fowler 84).

Frustrated and unable to complete his mission in the Yucatán, Santa Anna wrote four lengthy letters requesting permission to leave between July 1824 and February 1825. He was recalled in April of 1825 and appointed director of engineers in the capital, a post he declined. He returned home to the economically strategic region of Veracruz, which served as the port of call for commerce going to and from Mexico City, where he declared that he was retiring from politics, got married, and bought his country estate of *Manga de Clavo.* From 1825 to 1827 he channeled his energy into looking after his young wife, running his hacienda, purchasing and acquiring most of the land between Xalapa and Veracruz, and solidifying his power as the local *caudillo* from his strategically placed *hacienda* on the road to Mexico City. Santa Anna was a social animal who very much enjoyed the cockfight, so it is natural to believe that during this leisurely time period that he might have become associated with a group of masons, but unlike many of his compatriots, his name is not found in the leadership or on the roles of any masonic group, nor have any historians strongly linked him to any group by association, neither *yorkino, escocés,* nor *novenario,* another quasi-masonic political group formed in 1827. By all indications, Santa Anna was a mason of convenience and for political purposes only (Fowler 86-90).

Although removed from the volatile Yucatán Santa Anna found himself divided between his nationalistic loyalties in Mexico City and his economic interests in Veracruz. After the ratification of the new constitution in 1824 and the formal establishment of the York Rite in 1825, political loyalties in Mexico would divide along *escocés / yorkino* lines, which put Santa Anna in the middle between his *yorkino* allies in the capital, and his *escocés* associates and family in Veracruz. Santa Anna's legal representative in Mexico City, Jose María Tornel y Mendívil, President Guadalupe Victoria, and *veracruzano* minister of finance José Ignacio Esteva all became *yorkinos,* along with Vicente Guerrero. The region of Veracruz maintained a strong *escocés* base, and Santa Anna's brother, Manuel López de Santa Anna, was one of the editors of the *escocés* newspaper *El Veracruzano Libre* ("The Free Veracruzan"). Fowler, writing without the benefit of the recently discovered Scottish Rite patent, makes a strong case for Santa Anna being a *yorkino.* In 1825 he bought the Veracruzan *yorkino* newspaper *El Mercurio,* and identified strongly with the federalist *yorkino* associates in the capital. Fowler states:

> The unsubstantiated accusation that Santa Anna was an *escocés* in 1827 is consequently difficult to believe. At a national level, he was a *yorkino* both in ideological terms and in terms of his personal allegiances. It was at a regional level that the profession of his political faith became difficult to express (98).

In 1825 many *escoceses* were converting to become *yorkinos,* so why did Santa Anna become an *escocés* in December of 1825? Santa Anna's strong alliances with Guadalupe Victoria are well-known, as well as his desire to lead an expedition to Cuba. His close proximity to the meetings of the *Legión del* Águila *Negra* in Xalapa also suggests a desire to participate in that group, and, as it was a quasi-masonic organization, his "ticket" to gain admission might have been provided by membership in the Scottish Rite. Martínez Moreno supports this theory by noting that this was common among *escoceses* of the era:

> [E]l documento ... es consistente con la tesis que sostengo sobre las diferentes posturas políticas que asumieron los escoceses en la primera mitad del siglo XIX, que no se derivan necesariamente de la filiación al rito masónico, sino de las redes de intereses, la coyuntura y el cálculo político. (*Tesis*, 228)

> [The document is consistent with the thesis that I maintain over the different political postures that the *escoceses* assumed in the first half of the nineteenth century, which were not necessarily derived from affiliation to the masonic rite, but to the networks of interest, the situation, and political calculation.]

Let us now consider the question of the patent's authenticity. The first and most obvious question that must be answered is, how did it get to New York? Santa Anna had a very long career and was head of the Mexican state nine times, stepping down for the last time in June of 1855, at the age of 61. Vilified by his country, he went into exile with his family to Colombia, and later to St Thomas in the Caribbean, where in 1861 he would go on record supporting the establishment of a constitutional monarchy in Mexico under Archduke Ferdinand Maximilian. In February 1864, hoping to play a part in the unfolding events which would place Maximilian on the throne of Mexico, he returned briefly to Veracruz, but before disembarking his transport ship in Veracruz harbor he was asked to sign a document in French in which he pledged his support for the French monarchy and promised "to abstain from all political demonstration and to do nothing, be it written or verbal, that would make my return to my country be other than a simple citizen" (Fowler 324). The latter pledge earned him further banishment a few weeks later by the French authorities in power when he was accused of violating it. He returned to St. Thomas, where he was paid a courtesy visit in January 1866 by US Secretary of State William Seward, after which he convinced himself that the U.S. was inviting him to intervene in overthrowing Maximilian's reign and heroically return as the Restorer of the Republic. In May 1866, at age 72, persuaded by false documents and proposals from several con men, he invested most of his savings and property in the sale of war bonds (See Appendix 3) and relocated to Elizabethport, New Jersey, where he believed that US aid for his venture would be forthcoming. Back in Mexico, support for deposed president Benito Juárez was gaining momentum, and Juarez' representatives in the US set about to discredit Santa Anna. News of Santa Anna's presence in New York was not well-received by The Juarista Club in New York, who published a statement in May of 1866 declaring Santa Anna an "odious tyrant", a traitor, and one who has always betrayed his country (Fowler 326-7). It is not known whether the Juarista Club in New York City had any masonic affiliations, but regardless of Santa Anna's connection with this club, it is surmised that during his stay in New Jersey, and later Staten Island, that Santa Anna proffered his Scottish Rite patent to bolster his credibility, perhaps to connect with masons there, and left it in the care of a lodge. Notes from Catherine Walter at the Livingston Museum indicate that the document was donated to the museum's collection in the 1960 by Gustavo Ferrer, then Worshipful Master of Americus Lodge No. 535 in Whitestone (Queens), New York. To date this lodge's records have not been examined to ascertain if Santa Anna had any association with this lodge or its members.

The question also arises as to whether the document could have been forged in its time period. Martínez Moreno points out a critical detail which supports the patent's authenticity: the triple-headed serpent with royal hats on each head, one of which is a papal tiara. The inclusion of this heretical detail in 1825 supports the claim that the document is genuine:

> Si se tratara de un documento falsificado es difícil comprender la razón por la que no hay noticia de que haya sido difundido un documento masónico del año 1825 de Antonio López de Santa Anna ... ; porque, reitero, el diploma cuenta con una imagen de una víbora tricéfala con una tiara papal en una de sus cabezas, y en el contexto del imaginario de la época, habría sido un recurso político invaluable para usarlo en su contra.
>
> De haberse difundido en el siglo XIX mexicano, tan caracterizado por la superstición y el fanatismo religioso, se habría acompañado de un escándalo y habría dado elementos a los que calificaban a los grupos masónicos de satánicos.
>
> ...
>
> Reitero que el símbolo de la víbora tricéfala con una tiara en una de sus testas, como el del diploma de Santa Anna, habría tenido un impacto muy fuerte en el imaginario de la época de haberse difundido para usarlo en su contra (*Tesis*, 285-287).

[If we are dealing with a falsified document it is difficult to understand the reason that there is no notice that there had been made known a masonic document from the year 1825 of Antonio López de Santa Anna ... ; because, I reiterate, the diploma contains an image of a three-headed serpent with a papal tiara on one of its heads, and in the context of the imagination of the era, it would have been an invaluable political resource to use against him.

To have been made known in the 19th century in Mexico, so characterized by superstition and religious fanaticism, it would have been accompanied by scandal and would have given elements to those that characterize masonic groups as Satanists.

...

I reiterate that the symbol of the three-headed serpent with a tiara on one of its heads, such as that on the diploma of Santa Anna, would have had a very strong impact on the imagination of the era to have been made known to use against him.]

In spite of the relative certainty of the patent's authenticity, two historical discrepancies are noted in the patent. The first, pointed out by Martínez Moreno, is the age of Santa Anna, which is incorrectly specified on the document, stating that he was 29 years old, when in fact he was 31 at the time. This can be put down to clerical error, but another more circumstantial discrepancy arises through a parallel study of Santa Anna's biography, for which Fowler provides ample evidence: Santa Anna did not live in the Yucatán at the time of the issuance of the certificate. Neither is there biographical evidence to suggest that he traveled there during the time period, given his strong propensity to come home only months earlier, and the trip between Veracruz and Mérida necessitating travel by ship. He was also preoccupied with local responsibilities and the care of his *hacienda*. Also noteworthy is that the patent states that it was awarded under a "special petition" ("*pedimiento espcecial*") and not in normal circumstances. It is therefore proposed that Santa Anna received his Scottish Rite masonic degrees *en absentia*. Since he was not present, it is little wonder that his age was incorrectly recorded. As previously mentioned, Santa Anna may have needed to provide proof of his masonic membership in order to gain entry into the *Gran Legión del Águila Negra,* and it is hypothesized that he called upon some old friends in Yucatán to provide this evidence in the form of a Scottish Rite patent. In conclusion, let us consider what has been learned and what questions merit further study. At the very least, we have learned that Santa Anna's Scottish Rite patent is a unique surviving artifact from the era, and that the detail of the three-headed serpent has not been observed on any other similar patents. It remains to be seen whether the investigations in masonic archives in Mexico and other parts of Latin America will yield similar documents, or if there are any parallels between the three-headed serpent and the *Gran Legión* At the very least the document confirms the regularity of a Scottish Rite Consistory in Mérida in 1825.

From a Texan standpoint, it can now be definitely confirmed that the generals of both armies at the Battle of San Jacinto were masons; whether or not they recognized and received each other as such is a subject for another paper. This possibility actually begs a bigger question: given that there were masons on both sides in the Texas War for Independence, did they share masonic fellowship in the years leading up to 1836, during the *empresario* period in Texas? Many signs point to "yes," but the looming figure of Santa Anna has clouded the investigation, as Mexican masons who were allies to the Texan cause tend to be dismissed along with Santa Anna. Now that we have a better picture of Santa Anna's masonic legacy, the time is ripe for further investigation into this fertile field of history.

APPENDIX 1

Item C45-102, 1825 Scottish Rite Certificate of Antonio López de Santa Anna

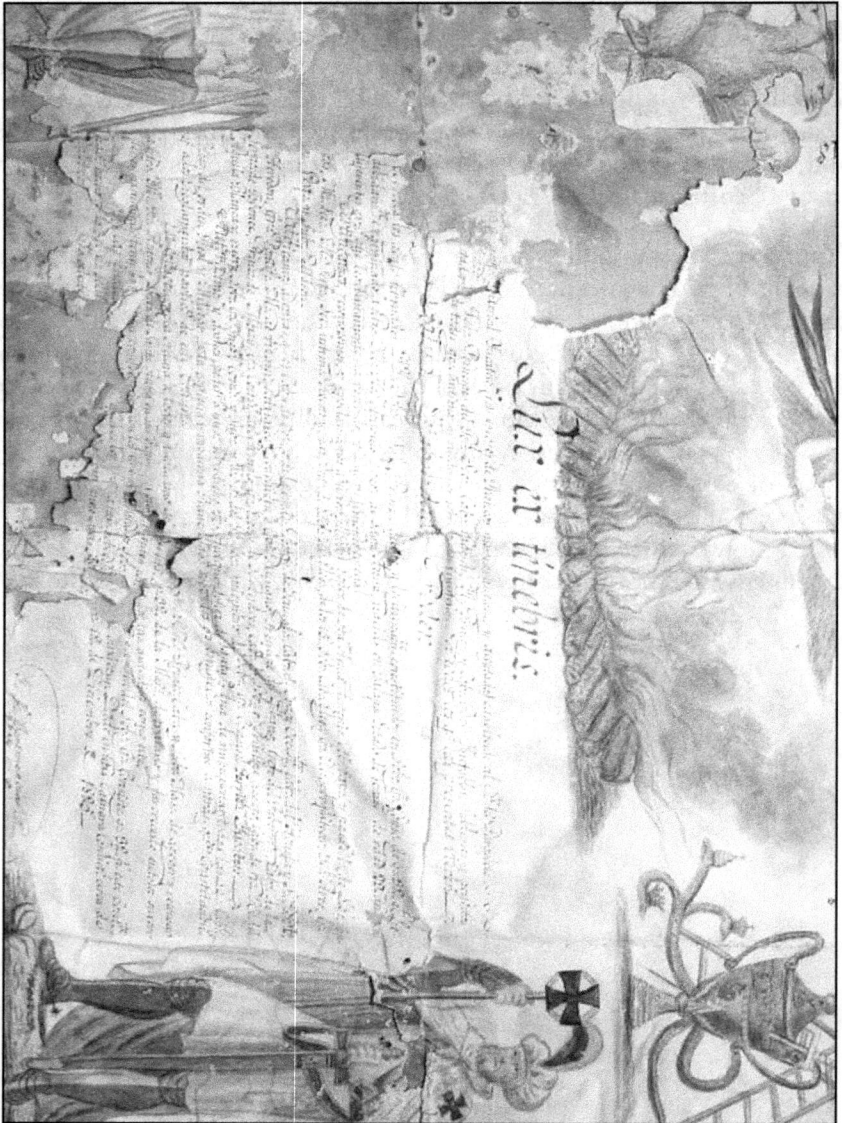

APPENDIX 2

Transcription and Translation of the 1825 Santa Anna Patent

Transcription of the Santa Anna Patent, with line numbers.
Sources:

- Primary source information from notes compiled by Catherine Walter, Curator of Chancellor Robert Livingston Masonic Library and Museum, New York, New York.

- Supplementary information by Carlos Martínez Moreno, Master's Thesis, 2011.

- English translation by Casey D. Stanislaw.

Notation:

- *[Square brackets] denote an abbreviation in the document which has been expanded.*
  For example: "Cab :. " = "Cab[alleros].

- *<Angle brackets> denote a best guess at missing or damaged text. Example: Line 6: <S> A L U D*

1. Universi terrarum Orbis Evolat ad Immortalitatem Architectoris Gloria ab Ingentis

2. Lux ex ténebris

3. G[ran] C<ons>ist[orio] T<err>itorial Yucateco (rito escoses de Francos masones antiguos y aceptados) establecido al O[rien]te del Paracleto

4. ... < A los S>ob[éranos] y Val[ientes] Principes del R[ea]l Sec[reto], Cab[alleros] Kadosch, Yl[ustres] Princ[ipes] y Cab[alleros] G[ran]des Ynefables, Sublimes y perfectos

5.   ... tados < ... >de todos gg[rados] antiguos y modernos sobre
     <los> dos Emisferios. A todos los q[ue] las presentes vieren.

6.   < S >A L U D   E S T A B I L I D A D   P O D E R

7.   < ... > los abajo firmados YY[lustres] Sob[éranos] y
     Val[ientes] Princ[ipes] deb<ida> y y legitimam[en]te
     constituidos en Sob[erano] G[ran] Cons[istorio] de g[rado]
     32 q[u]e he-<mos>

8.   debidam[en]te examinado a n[ues]tro Yl[ustre] H[ermano]
     Antonio Lopez de Santa Anna, nacido en Jalapa Estado de
     Verac[ru]z de edad 29 año<s>.

9.   < ... > diferentes gr[ado]s que legítimamente ha recibido, y a
     su pedimento especial

10. Certificamos, reconocemos, y proclamos a n[ues]tro
     Yl[ustre] H[ermano] Lopez de S[an]ta Anna Antonio M[uy]
     Exp[erto] y pasa[d]o M[aestro] de LL[ogias] sim-

11. <boli>cas, M[aestro] Sec[reto], M[aestro] Perf[ecto],
     Sec[retario] Intim[o], Prevost[e] y Juez, Ynt[endente] de
     Edif[icios], M[aestro] Eleg[ido], de los 15, Sob[erano]
     Cab[allero] Eleg[ido,] G[ran] M[aestro] Arquitecto, R[ea]l
     Arco, G[ran]

12. <Eleg[ido]> Perf[ecto] y Sub[lime] Mason.

13. Certificamos además, q[ue] es Cab[allero] de Or[iente],
     o de la espad[a,] Pont[ífice] de Jerusal[em], Cab[allero]
     de Or[iente] y Occid[en]te, Cab[allero] del Aguila, y
     S[oberano] P[rincipe] R[osa] {symbol} [Cruz],

14. < ... > Heredon, Gr[an] Pontif[ice], M[aestro] ad vitam,

Patriarca Noachita o C<a>b[allero] Prusiano, Principe del
Libano, Gefe del Tabern[ácul]o, Cab[allero] de la

15. Serp[iente] de Bronce, Princ[ipe] de Mercy G[ran]
Com[endad]or del Templo, G[ran] Esc[os]<é>[s] de S[an]
Andres, Cab[aller]o del Sob[erano] o Princ[ipe] acepto (sic.),
Cab[allero] de K[adosh] H[ermano] del

16. Aguila Blanca y negra, Sob[erano] G[ran] Ynq[uisid]or,
Com[endad]or y Sub[lime] y Y[lustre] P[rincipe] del R<ea>l
Sec[reto], miembro del Sob[erano] G[ran] Consis[torio]
Territ[orial] Yucateco.

17. Autorizamos y damos poder a n[ues]tro sobredicho
H[ermano] Antonio Lopez de Santa Ana (sic.) de
inspeccionar todas las LL[ogias] Cap[ítulo]s

18. Coleg[io] del orden Real y Militar de la antigua y moderna
Frac Mas[onerí]a sob[r]e los Emisferios conforme a n[ues]
tras g[ran]des Constitucion[es]

19. y a los Reglamentos partic[ular]es de este Consist[orio]

20. En consecuencia ordena a todos y a cada uno de <los>
HH[ermanos] Princ[ipes] Cab[alleros] y Sub[limes]
Mas[ones] de acoger y reconocer

21. a n[ues]tro Yl[ustre] H[ermano] Antonio Lopez de Santa
Anna en sus diferen<t>es cua< ... >es lita< ... > <g>[rado] 32
de la Mas[onerí]a, de tratarlo y favorecerlo en todos sus em-

22. peños, prometiendo tener la < ... > a e ... sido ... ... rio ... con
los que se < ... > enten con <ti>tulos tan autenticos como
este.

23. <C>on las cuales < ... > Nos los ba<jo fir>mados Sob[éranos]
< ... ... > del Sob[erano] G[ran Consist[orio] g[rado]
32 p[rime]r -en- este Cont[inen]te,

24. Hav[ien]do hecho p[or] la (¿?) el G[ran] sello < ... > a n[ues]
tro sobre <d ... ... n>e varietur. Dado en n[ues]tra Camara
Consist[oria]l cerca de

25. O[riente] ... A<rcadia> ba<jo la bóv>eda celeste < ... > 12. de
Diciembre de 1825.

26. (Firmes ilegibles)

English Translation

Line 1: To the whole world Flying to immortality All Glory to
the Architect

Line 2: Light from Darkness

Line 3: Grand Territorial Consistory of the Yucatán (Ancient
and Accepted Scottish Rite of Freemasonry), established to
the Orient of the Paraclete.

Line 4: To the Sovereign and Valiant Princes of the Royal Secret,
Knights of Kadosh, Illustrious Princes and Grand Ineffable
Knights, Sublime and Perfect

Line 5: (Accepted) ... of all ancient and modern degrees over two
Hemispheres. To all who are present may see:

Line 6: HEALTH – STABILITY – POWER

Line 7-8: ... The below signed Illustrious Sovereign and Valliant
Princes properly and legitimately constituted in the Sovereign Grand Consistory of the 32nd Degree, that we have duly
examined our Illustrious Brother António López de Santa
Anna, born

in Jalapa, State of Veracruz, of 29 years of age.

Line 9: ... various degrees that he has legitimately received, and to his special petition

Line 10-12: We certify, recognize and proclaim our Illustrious Brother López de Santa Anna Antonio an Extreme Expert and Past Master of symbolic Lodges, Secret Master, Perfect Master, Intimate Secretary, Provost and Judge, Intendant of Buildings, Elected Master, of the 15, Sovereign Knight Elected, Grand Master Architect, Royal Arch, Grand Elected Perfect and Sublime Mason.

Line 13: We certify furthermore, that he is Knight of the East, or of the Sword, Pontiff of Jerusalem, Knight of the East and West, Knight of the Eagle, and Sovereign Prince of Rose Cross, < ... >

Line 14-16: < ... > Heredom, Grand Pontificate, Master *ad vitam* (for life), Noachite Patriarch or Prussian Knight, Prince of Libanus, Chief of the Tabernacle, Knight of the Bronze Serpent, Prince of Mercy Grand Commander of the Temple, Grand Scot (Scottish Knight) of St. Andrews Sovereign Knight or Accepted Prince, Knight of Kadosh Brother of the Black and White Eagle, Sovereign Grand Inquisitor, Knight Commander and Sublime and Illustrious Prince of the Royal Secret, member of the Sovereign Grand Territorial Consistory of the Yucatan.

Line 17-19: We authorize and give power to our said Brother Antonio Lopez de Santa Ana (sic.) to inspect all of the Chapter (Capitular?) College Lodges of the Royal and Military order of ancient and modern Freemasonry over the Hemispheres conforming to our grand Constitution and to the particular regulations of this Consistory.

Line 20: Consequently it is ordered to all and each one of the Knight Prince Brothers and Sublime Masons to admit and recognize

Line 21-22: our Brother Antonio Lopez de Santa Anna in his various (??) 32nd degree of Masonry, to treat and favor him in all of his efforts, promising to have ... been ... with those that (have been invested) with such authentic titles such as this.

Line 23: With which ... we have signed below Sovereign < ... > of the Sovereign Grand Consistory of the 32nd Degree, first on this Continent,

Line 24-25: Having made for the ... the Grand Seal ... to our *ne varietur* (signature) Given in our Consistorial Chamber near the Orient of Arcadia (?), under the celestial vault, 12 December, 1825.

Line 26: (Signatures illegible.)

Appendix 3

Detailed Image of Angel

APPENDIX 4

Detail of Knight of Kadosh

Appendix 5

Detail of Urn, Ladder of Kadosh, and Three-Headed Serpent

APPENDIX 6

Magnified Detail of Section Containing Biographical Information

BIBLIOGRAPHY

Primary Source Document

Gran Consistorio Territorial Yucateco Rito Escosés de Francos Masones Antiguos y Aceptados, Diploma de Sublime Príncipe del Real Secreto grado 32°, issued for Antonio López de Santa Anna, December 12, 1825. Chancellor Robert R. Livingston Masonic Library of the Most Worshipful Grand Lodge of the State of New York, F&AM, Tom Savini, Director. Images, Data, and Research Notes Courtesy of Catherine Walter, Curator and Photographer.

Secondary Sources

Carter, James D. *Masonry in Texas: Background, History, and Influence to 1846.* 2nd Ed. Waco: Committee on Masonic Education and Service for the Grand Lodge of Texas, 1958.

Chism, Richard E. *Una contribución a la historia masónica de México.* Nueva ed., copia exacta de la publicada en 1899. México D.F.: Editorial Herbasa, 1993.

de Hoyos, Arturo, and Alain Bernheim. *Freemasonry's Royal Secret: The Jamaican "Francken Manuscript" of the High Degrees.* Washington, D.C.: The Scottish Rite Research Society, 2014.

de Hoyos, Arturo. *The Scottish Rite Ritual Monitor and Guide.* 3rd. ed. Washington, D.C.: The Supreme Council, 33°, Southern Jurisdiction, 2010.

de los Reyes Heredia, Guillermo. *Herencias secretas: Masonería, política y sociedad en México.* Universidad Autónoma de Puebla, 2010.

Denslow, William R, Freemasons, and Missouri Lodge of Research. *10,000 Famous Freemasons.* [N.p]: Board of Publication, 1957. Print.

Fowler, Will. *Santa Anna of Mexico.* Lincoln: University of Nebraska Press, 2007.

Martínez Moreno, Carlos Francisco. *El establecimiento de las masonerías en México en el siglo XIX.* Master's Thesis in History, Universidad Nacional Autónoma de México, 2011.

_____. "La Sociedad de los Yorkinos Federalistas, 1834. Una propuesta hermenéutica de sus estatutos y reglamentos generales a la luz de la historia de la Masonería." Revista de Estudios Históricos de la Masonería Latinoamericana y Caribeña (REHMLAC) (Vol 1., No. 1), 2009.

Mateos, José María. *Historia de la masonería en México, desde 1806 hasta 1884.* México: 1884. Primary Source Edition, facsimile published under public domain laws, Lavergne, TN: (n/p) 2015. See http://icgtesting.com/.

Morrow, Ortho C. "Why Did Sam Houston Spare the Life of Santa Anna at San Jacinto?" Texas Mason Magazine (Vol. XVII, Issue 2) Spring, 2008, p. 6-7. http://www.grandlodgeoftexas.org/texas_mason/2008-spring.pdf. Accessed June 17, 2014.

Reichstein, Andreas V. *Rise of the Lone Star: The Making of Texas.* Trans. J. R. Wilson. College Station: Texas A&M University Press, 1989.

Reséndez, Andrés. *Changing National Identities at the Frontier: Texas and New Mexico, 1800-1850.* New York: Cambridge University Press, 2005.

Rich, P. J. "Freemasonry and Fratricide in the Early Mexican Republic - A Reappraisal of Joel R. Poinsett." Transactions of the Texas Lodge of Research, XXX (1995-1996) 72-85.

Stuart, William M., R..W.. *Masonic Soldiers of Fortune.* Macoy Publishing and Masonic Supply Company, New York, 1928.

Thompson, E. N. "Antonio Lopez de Santa Anna. Part I." Transactions of the Texas Lodge of Research, XXII (1986) 74-83.

_____. "Antonio Lopez de Santa Anna. Part II." Transactions of the Texas Lodge of Research, XXII (1986) 120-134.

_____. "Mexico's Masonic War (Brothers Divided)." Transactions of the Texas Lodge of Research, XIX (1983) 37-44.

Vargas Márquez, Wenceslao. *La masonería en la Presidencia de México.* Mexico: (self-published), 2010.

Vázquez Semadeni, María Eugenia. *La formación de una cultura política republicana: el debate público sobre la masonería : México, 1821-1830.* México, D.F.; Zamora: Universidad Nacional Autónoma de México ; Colegio de Michoacán, 2010.

_____. "La Gran Legión del Águila Negra, documentos sobre su función, estatutos y objetivos." Relaciones, Estudios de Historia y Sociedad, (111, Vol. XXVIII), Verano 2007, 143-166.

_____. "La masonería en México, entre las sociedades secretas y patrióticas, 1813-1830." Revista de Estudios Históricos de la Masonería Latinoamericana y Caribeña (REHMLAC) (Vol 2., No. 2), 2011.

XV

A Masonic Pretender to the Hungarian Throne: François Claude Auguste De Crouy-Chanel

Demetrio Xoccato

The biography of marquis François Claude Auguste de Crouy-Chanel is an affair with many and complex implications. He was a character who monopolised the chronicles of that time and as a protagonist crossed more than a half a century, meeting some of the most important men and impacting (positively or negatively) many social realities.

1. A Restless Youth

Born in Duisburg (Prussia) on 31 December 1793, the son of marquis Claude François de Croy-Chanel [sic] and Marie Charlotte Bagel d'Urfé, thanks to the French Revolution he spent his childhood in exile. After Napoleon Bonaparte's takeover, the nobles who had emigrated had the chance to return home and the boy's parents took the opportunity to come back to their home, in Grenoble ("Empire Français"). Before long the family succeeded in retrieving all the lost influence and, for this reason, his father was appointed as first Justice of the Peace in their home city and then keeper of water and forest in Laon (Picardy). Thanks to this peace of mind, Crouy-Chanel could finish his upbringing beside Abbe Raillane, a renowned tutor (he was, also, Stendhal's teacher).

Having completed his school education, in 1813 he became one of Napoleon's pageboys. After the Emperor's defeat and his exile on the island of Elba, thanks to his father's connections he managed to be assigned as an army officer under king Louis XVIII. On 1 January 1814 the 20-year-old boy was put into service of the royal guards with the rank of colonel.

Since this career didn't suit his purposes and ambitions—he needed "a

215

wider theatre" (Saint-Edme and Sarrut, "Biographie de M. A. De Crouy-Chanel" 357)—, Crouy-Chanel decided to resign and in 1817 he started to go on a long pilgrimage across Europe. While he was undertaking the *Grand Tour,* he had to deal with an unpleasant legal vicissitude which implicated his family.

His brother, count Nicolas Henri Jean François de Crouy-Chanel, born in 1799, had sued duke Joseph Anne Auguste Maximilien Croÿ d'Havré for the exclusiveness in using the coat of arms of the Arpad royal house of Hungary, from which the Crouy-Chanel family claimed to descend. The latter not only rejected the demand but he made a counter-attack, asserting that the count couldn't use the Crouy surname because it was owned by his lineage. Finally, on 12 May 1821, the Court reached a Solomon-like verdict: the tribunal arranged that Croÿ d'Havré had no right to the coat of arms of Hungary but, at the same time, Nicolas de Crouy-Chanel should have given up half of his surname (Villeneuve and Carette 486).

In June of such a tumultuous year the marquis showed his first public stance. The Greek revolt was challenging the political order established by the Restoration. In addition to the popular participation of shopkeepers, farmers and orthodox clergy—something new compared with all the previous rebellions—, there was also the new Romantic feeling which was very sympathetic with the Greek cause. Crouy-Chanel sent to Armand Emmanuel duke of Richelieu, at that time Prime Minister, a letter where he underlined the profits France could gain from the international crisis. Especially, he wrote that Greece had the right to retract from Turkish domination because the Sultan's power was based not on legitimacy but on brute force. Such a message, which suggested destroying the recent and precarious European balance, couldn't be accepted. Without government support, Crouy-Chanel engaged himself in the fight, supporting economically all the subscriptions for the insurgents (Saint-Edme and Sarrut, "Crouy-Chanel de Hongrie" 358–59).

2. A Plotter in the Iberian Peninsula

In 1823 the marquis started his conspiratorial career. After the liberal unrest of biennium 1820-21, a constitutional regime had developed in Spain, but king Ferdinand VII was fiercely against it. Indeed, he had tried in every possible way to re-stablish his full sovereignty, invoking the Saint Alliance's help. Within the confusing Hispanic situation, where moderates and radicals were now confronting each other, in 1822 a government held by Bourbonist loyalists (the so-called Regency of Urgel) had been created in Catalonia. From the beginning the counter-revolutionary movement had made contact with all European cabinets searching economic and military aid against the Bourbons' enemies and, in spring 1823, a contingent made up of French soldiers had arrived.

At this juncture the marquis stepped out on the stage: he, thanks to his connections inside the financial world, was involved by count and journalist Achilles de Jouffroy d'Abbans in an unofficial diplomatic action. In order to support the war effort without depending on the authoritarian French expeditionary force, Urgel's Finance Minister, Juan Bautista de Erro, had aired to the editor-in-chief of *Gazette de France* his will to get into debt. Crouy-Chanel's brokerage led bankers Guebhard and Pictet to offer their assistance. To sign the agreement, the two men left for Spain (Saint-Edme and Sarrut, "Crouy-Chanel de Hongrie" 359).

Acquainted with the plot, French Prime Minister Joseph de Villèle asked the police to put under arrest Jouffroy. It was a move dictated on the one hand by the need of firmly maintaining the ministerial leadership in the war and on the other hand by the will to force the Spanish administration to accept the loan established by France and the Rothschilds. Having lost his fellow in Burgos, the marquis, not being cited in the orders, could continue his journey. Finally, in early July he arrived in Madrid, causing great consternation from viscount Jean-Baptiste de Martignac, Villèle's correspondent. The offer he made to Erro consisted in 200 million of reals (the Spanish coin) with an interest rate of 50% (Martignac 194, 206). Even though it was an offer economically inadmissible, a genuine usury, the Regency agreed. Therefore, in less than three days the agreement was stipulated, but for a lower sum (50 million with a higher flat-rate, 55%)(Ouvrard 123). This choice would have been a financial burden which would have loaded on the country for decades. Crouy-Chanel got 999.000 francs as reward ("Crouy-Chanel" 33).

The stay in Spain gave him the opportunity to try an economic initiative, apparently a successful one. Thanks to minister Erro, he managed to obtain the concession of the Royal production of textiles (founded by Charles III), whose head office was in Guadalajara (Castile). Once he got the license, he came back home and he established a company for managing the business in Paris.

In June 1824 a now wealthy Crouy-Chanel grabbed the chance to start, together with his brother and 16 others partners, a commercial bank, called Delacodre and with 50 million francs as corporate assets. As well as the usual cash and lending operations were also scheduled gold and silver transactions. The marquis pre-eminence was clear: that's why he was chosen as Vice-President (*Banque Commerciale et Foncière, Sous La Raison Delacodre et Compagnie. Prospectus et Statuts* 24).

Soon hotel Vendôme, his residence, became a meeting place for diplomats, civil servants, and deputies, all interested in this "neutral field" where they could talk ("without compromising oneself") about issues not yet in the public domain (Saint-Edme and Sarrut, "Crouy-Chanel de Hongrie" 360). Villèle himself, having acknowledged Crouy-Chanel's cleverness, thought to co-opt him for a new confidential initiative.

Faced with the Spanish colonies' reluctance to come back under Ferdinand VII's control, the French Prime Minister believed, as the only way out, Mexicans would have had their own king, Francisco de Paula. In fact, Ferdinand VII's younger brother was a fair compromise between the republican choice made by the rebels and the will to maintain under Bourbons' control the American colonies. According to USA secret services, in September 1825 there were interviews between the Mexican and French representatives, in search of an agreement (Poinsett 1632-33). Given the monarch's opposition, in 1826 Villèle opted to step over his power, sending the marquis in Madrid to meet the infant of Spain.

The choice of Francisco de Paula seemed right: for a long time, he and his wife Luisa Carlotta of Naples were intolerant towards the other members of the dynasty. The secret negotiations bore fruit and Crouy-Chanel got the job to meet the Mexican government and South American monarchists and to arrange a transition as smoothly as possible. The infant of Spain gave his word on the one hand to keep the actual provisions made by the administration and the hired officials, on the other hand to promulgate a general amnesty and a Constitution (Moral Roncal 159).

Appointed plenipotentiary (he was also able to confer titles), the marquis returned to Paris to discuss with Villèle and to plan a one million pounds loan, needed for this conspiracy.

However, the French Prime Minister hadn't warned his king and when he learned about this intrigue he stated his opposition. For him this solution would have been the same as accepting the Duke of Orleans to become sovereign over French colonies (Saint-Edme and Sarrut, "Crouy-Chanel de Hongrie" 362). In the face of Charles X's firm opposition, the French government withdrew, leaving Crouy-Chanel alone, but he decided to continue the operation.

For the future imperial administration of Mexico, he got in touch with several prominent figures, identifying the following men: state adviser Alexandre de Talleyrand-Périgord, tenant general and peer of France Edmond duke of Dino, lieutenant general Antoine de La Roche-Aymon and sea captain Alexandre Gallois. All these people gave their agreement to become ministers in a future government (Hidalgo y Esnaurrízar 25).

After he got these positive replies, in spring 1827 Crouy-Chanel went to London to negotiate the money for the enterprise. Unfortunately, the diplomatic functions with prime minister George Canning couldn't take place because he should have explained the plot and the conspirators. Fearing to compromise the machination, he decided to keep silent, so losing every chance to obtain the sum (Saint-Edme and Sarrut, "Crouy-Chanel de Hongrie" 362).

The sad return to Madrid took place in a situation which was now completely hostile. The Spanish government, well-informed of the infant yearnings, had issued Francisco de Paula to stop immediately the plot and he had promptly obeyed. Ignoring the facts, Crouy-Chanel had a meeting with the prince, during which he was reconfirmed. The infant's ambiguous attitude lasted for quite some time until he sent an emissary to Paris for revoking all the marquis' powers.

The adventure's inglorious end had a series of consequences in the economic sphere. First of all banker Martin Louis Goupy and Nicolas Henri de Crouy-Chanel had paid out a great sum for support and grants (Saint-Edme and Sarrut, "Crouy-Chanel de Hongrie" 363). Despite the commitments made in December 1828, Francisco de Paula two years later had not yet paid a dime. So they entrusted Letoust, a former judge, to go to Spain and to finally get the money back. At the end of 1830 he arrived in the country but he was immediately stopped by the police in Burgos and forced back. Francisco de Paula didn't want to talk with conspirators any-more: Spain was now off-limits.

The financial problems were not limited to the money spent for the infant's cause because, while Crouy-Chanel was engaged in this reckless political action, the company for managing the production of textiles in Guadalajara had taken such a major hit that the marquis's wealth was heavily damaged. In addition to the unsuccessful sale of shares in the Paris stock exchange, there had been a crash in London where the marquis had raised 600.000 pounds (equivalent to 15 million francs). At the end the company had run out of business (Saint-Edme and Sarrut, "Biographie de M. A. De Crouy-Chanel" 364).

Nonetheless, in 1828 Crouy-Chanel was already arranging a new and bold plan, this time focused on Portugal, a country only just under Miguel of Braganza's control. He had returned from exile on 22 February 1828, expressly for becoming regent on behalf of his under-age niece, in reality to overthrow the girl. Pressing the 26-year-old man towards this solution was his mother Carlota Joaquina of Bourbon, a staunch supporter of absolutism. Even if the prince had sworn to maintain the parliamentary institutions, he firstly dismissed from office the upper echelons of the army and then on 14 march the Cortès offered him the crown. Actually, the mastermind behind all events was his mother, the dominus of the new regime. The royal court rapidly became a magnet for adventures and spies, coming from the Iberian peninsula as well as from the Habsburg empire (Correspondance politique, Portugal). These were the circumstances in which Crouy-Chanel operated. Fortunately he could count on his good relations with Manuel da Silveira Pinto (whom he probably met in Spain), marquis of Chaves and Carlota's faithful follower, and on Luzuriaga, representative of the Spanish papal party (legitimist formation at the origin of the Carlist movement) (Rousseau 80).

The warm welcome he received from the new king and especially from the Queen Mother led the marquis to win their favour. After thinking of how to take advantage of a regime established recently (and, for that reason, weak) he decided to follow the usual action: to offer his financial brokering. Since the Portuguese government needed money, he worked with some Parisian stockbrokers to obtain a loan. Despite the failure in the transaction, his relationship of trust didn't break: he was able to save the life of some Portuguese dissidents, including colonel Manuel Bernardo Chabi—a brother Freemason (Oliveira Marques 333)—, and he set about trying to gain Charles X's recognition of Miguel I. In the light of all these failures and of his worsening condition caused by his many trips, he decided to leave the Iberian peninsula and to go to Italy, to Rome. The pope and papal court's benevolence allowed him to make Felicité de Lamennais and Father Gioacchino Ventura's acquaintance (Andreu).

As he returned briefly to Paris, Crouy-Chanel plotted a new plan which promptly submitted to the pontiff. He was persuaded that Papal States needed a reform focused on the poors' relief and the way to follow was to renew the bureaucratic machinery. This new project, who could count on his prelate friends, seemed to be ready to start when a scandal, which implicated the marquis, broke out.

The revolution of 1830 had risen to power Louis-Philip but since the government hadn't reached enough strength, the police had started an iron control over all the backers of the past regime. During this overseeing, in

1831 he was arrested and charged with having put on the market counterfeit money; a heavy charge because if found guilty, Crouy-Chanel could have been sentenced to death. After awaiting trial for nine months, on 5 September 1832 the judge acknowledged his innocence, and he was freed (*Le National; Journal des Débats*).

3. CROUY-CHANEL AND LOUIS NAPOLEON

Becoming close to Bonapartists, in September 1838 Crouy-Chanel reached Arenberg and talked to Louis Napoleon. During the dialogue the marquis explained his political vision, meeting with the approval of the exiled prince. In fact, he had put forward a plan summed up with the phrase "alliance of democratic principles to the Napoleonic sentiment" (Saint-Edme and Sarrut, "Biographie de M. A. De Crouy-Chanel" 373). Right after the meeting, the marquis started his new political career as the prince's supporter. Several months later, during a journey to London, he had another meeting with Louis Napoleon, and they decided to set up a newspaper whose aim would have been to gather democrats and Bonapartists and also to push French public opinion towards a series of reforms, the most important one to repatriate the exiled prince.

The first number of *Le Capitole* was published on 15 June 1839 and the marquis was appointed director and acted as owner (Glikman 52). This newspaper wasn't the only one on the French political scene openly Bonapartist because there were also the *Journal de Francfort*, guided by Charles Durand, and Mocquard and Manguin's *Le Commerce*. Louis Napoleon's new strategy was to collect together all the hostile forces, adding another means to the usual informal meetings and clubs. From September a series of debates about the line of conduct started inside the editorial staff and consequently Crouy-Chanel resigned. Since the prince had used his own money for this operation, the marquis had to give reasons for the management and so he organized all the papers and the journey to London. However, the police, knowing the deed, made a move and on 27 November arrested him again. The charge against Crouy-Chanel was conspiracy against the state (Saint-Edme and Sarrut, "Biographie de M. A. De Crouy-Chanel" 374).

His arrest gave the opportunity for a day of reckoning inside the world of Louis's followers and the newspapers, instead of pressing for his freedom, launched a campaign against him.

The trial caused so much uproar in France that the Russian Empire was also accused of bing involved in the plot and so the French Premier had an explanatory meeting with the Russian ambassador.

After five months in jail, on 7 march 1840 Crouy-Chanel was finally freed because the proofs of guilt weren't enough (Chélard 27). Apparently this trial, which had undermined also Louis Napoleon's prestige, was a blow to their friendship and, even if the marquis tried several times to meet the prince, his request was always rejected.

When he retrieved his freedom, initially Crouy-Chanel seemed to have completely dropped his political/conspirative activities, retiring to private life. In those years he focused on studying the railway system, along with his old friend Jouffroy. They were especially interested in improving this system still at down, where the accidents were everyday occurrences. His serenity was destroyed in February 1846 by his son's death and, according to his nephew Henry Gerothwohl de Croÿ-Chanel [sic] this sad event encouraged the marquis to go back in action (Gerothwohl de Croÿ-Chanel 217).

In 1847 he was already in the Royal court accredited to Louis-Philip's sister as delegate of Papal interests. In fact, thanks to de Lamennais and Ventura's intermediation, he had re-established the relations with the Vatican lost in the 1820s. So in 1848 he was in Rome, once again as broker for a financial transaction. The business was a 14 million scudi loan disbursed by De Llaud bank to Vatican State (*L'Alba*).

While he was taking up in this sensitive operation with the Roman Finance minister, he received the first provision of information about the February revolution and the contemporaneous repatriation of Louis Napoleon. The fall of Louis-Philip lay open the path for Paris. Initially elected as member of the constituent Assembly, the nephew of the famous emperor was appointed President of the Second Republic within a few months. The 1852 referendum completed his seize of power. With the proclamation of Louis Napoleon as emperor, the marquis' life witnessed a radical change. The transition to an authoritarian regime, urged Napoleon III to dramatically revise the French foreign policy: from now on the French state would be the guardian of oppressed peoples against Austria. This also explains why the new emperor was so interested by the Italian situation.

If in 1858 Napoleon III reached an agreement with Camillo Benso count of Cavour to unify Italy he was searching a way to gain the support of Hungarian emigration. Actually, when the Revolution of 1848 had failed, many Hungarians, worried about the Austrian repression, had left their home, going all over Europe and also reaching the USA. One of the leaders, Lajos Kossuth, had tried to include the most important States in this issue, bringing himself near to Piedmont. So, Turin, the capital city, had become the coordination centre of all refugees (Furlani).

Since Kossuth wasn't particularly loved by the French, Napoleon III thought it could be a great idea to use his old companion in order to gather all the exiles under his rule. So, in 1859 the old adventurer (Crouy-Chanel was 66 years-old) reached Turin (Kovalovszky 380).

4. THE ITALIAN FREEMASONRY AND THE HUNGARIAN EMIGRATION

His arrival immediately raised great concern because the promises made by the Savoy government had been so far a mere paper exercise. There was a gloomy climate, which encouraged a massive distrust towards the Hungarian leaders.

The marquis' first decision was to meet Kossuth. During the meeting he tried, without success, to impress the former Finance minister of Hungary, claiming the powerful support he could bring to Hungarian emigration. Kossuth's answer was emblematical: "only the nation could dispose of the crown" (Kovalovszky 380). It clearly appears that the latter regarded with a fair amount of suspicion the whole project for a series of reasons, such as the danger to decrease his own prestige in favour of the newcomer. However, the main problem was purely political: despite his republican faith he had become convinced that a constitutional monarchy was the best solution but he was thinking about another candidate. During that year he offered the crown to prince Napoleon-Jérome who, to avoid alarming all European kings, declined.

Since the meeting was a failure, Crouy-Chanel returned to Paris where there was another Hungarian leader waiting to talk to him, general Gyorgy Klapka. Officially, the latter, member of the Hungarian National Committee, welcomed the marquis and agreed that a centre for propaganda would have to be created in Turin. One of the operating base's first acts was publishing a proclamation where it was emphasized Klapka's endorsement.

Things weren't exactly this way: since the situation was basically blocked, the general opted to wait and see the real purposes of Crouy-Chanel, even if this could be in reality an "adventure" driven by "private interest" (*Il Diritto*).

Having got this first, even if cautious, backing, he rapidly got in touch with several of the exiles' best-known exponents and he particularly befriended baron and genealogist Albert Nyáry. A correct use of his own re-sources, used to relieve the poor Hungarians, vastly increased the marquis' authority.

In 1861 was printed the first of a long series of pamphlets, *Les fils d'Arpad* (Sarrut). Germain Sarrut's work was yet another advertising operation, aimed at supporting the marquis but, taking a closer look, it also showed that ambiguity which would have undermined the exploit. In fact, Crouy-Chanel didn't present himself to the public opinion as a pretender to the throne, but as a man who simply wanted the recognition of his Hungarian origins. Obviously, if the Hungarians had opted with a referendum to acknowledge him as king, he would have done his duty.

The foreign press grasped the duplicity of this statement and questioned the marquis' moral integrity, causing his harsh response. On 16 October, following the article from *L'Indépendance belge*, he sent an amendment where he reaffirmed his position: he "never" felt like the heir of a king-dom, because only the Hungarian people could dispose of this crown (F. C. A. de Crouy-Chanel).

On 10 November the marquis launched a new message, directly address-ing the Austrian ambassador in Paris and the king, Franz Josef I. The gen-eral tone was imperative: either Hungary should be set free or he would spearhead a revolution (Gerothwohl de Croÿ-Chanel 227–229). Thanks to the money spent to convince the newspapers, the letter was widely reported through all over Europe. According to Nicolas Kovalovszky, in addition to this challenge, Crouy-Chanel, without regard to its cost, even hired a composer, Lagarde, in order to write a "song of the Hungarian re-vival": by this time the marquis was on everyone's lips (Kovalovszky 381).

He also organised a series of pamphlets, written in German, French and Hungarian which would have circulated under the counter all over the Austrian Empire.

All this feverish activity lasted for a brief morning. The Hapsburgs' defeat and the proclamation of the kingdom of Italy (March 1861) decreased Napoleon III's interest towards this project. The emperor's eyes were al-ready focused on greener pastures (quickly thereafter, in December 1861, would begin the Second Franco-Mexican War).

In addition to having lost the French emperor's support, the quarrel be-tween the marquis and Kossuth was reaching its peak. In fact, until then he had refused to recognise Crouy-Chanel's claims and the situation was so tight that before long he would have stopped every contact with the latter's followers.

The crisis inside the Hungarian emigration had significant repercussions also on the Italian Masonic situation. In opposition to James Anderson's teachings, the choices of political nature, instead of staying outside the Lodge, came in and torn the masonic world.

Italian Freemasonry was reborn into a new life only recently, in the winter of 1859. That December the Italian Grand Orient had been established in Turin. The subalpine chief town had rapidly become a point of reference for all the freemasons scattered all over Italy, but the following year a hostile Supreme Council had already been founded in Palermo. Indeed, the Grand Orient was openly in favour of the government and so Giuseppe Mazzini and Giuseppe Garibaldi's followers (all republicans) had decided to shift to this alternative pole. However, the latter hadn't been authoritative enough and quite a few Historical Left's representatives had entered the moderate obedience.

So, in 1862 the Grand Orient hosted, on different positions, all the protagonists, Crouy-Chanel included. If Kossuth and István Türr acknowledged themselves in the moderate party, Klapka and Ferenc Pulszky were members of Dante Alighieri lodge, which was immediately quarrelsome and independent. As we will see, this history of this Atelier, established on 7 February 1862, will run in parallel with what will happen inside the profane world. Analysing the data, we can see how important the Hungarian democrats were: from 1862 to 1864, 33 well-known exiles were lodge members (Polo Friz, *1866. Una Missione Segreta Di Lodovico Frapolli a Berlino. L'emigrazione Ungherese* 17–18).

Having the 33rd degree since distant 1818, Crouy-Chanel had a sort of moral supremacy over the young Italian Freemasons. He was one of the earliest members of Dante Alighieri lodge, soon becoming a leading figure.

After Filippo Cordova, esteemed Cavour's advisor, was elected as Grand Master of the Italian Grand Orient, the Torinese lodge on 4 March started a battle against him, reporting irregularities and lobbying. In all of this, they created a committee of inquiry in a completely autonomous way. It was a genuine indictment of the masonic management.

The moderates faced this act of lawlessness firmly and forced the closing of the lodge, which, as a reply, left the Grand Orient and put itself under the Supreme Council of Palermo (Novarino, *All'Oriente Di Torino. La Rinascita Della Massoneria Italiana Tra Moderatismo Cavouriano E Rivoluzionarismo Garibaldino* 124).

This explains why suddenly the conflicts among Crouy-Chanel's backers and opponents increased. The spark that triggered everything was the decision to offer the refugees command to Klapka, who at the time lived in London and was in the dark. In April 1862 a manifesto was published in which the general was stated as the only Hungarian leader. The need to give all the power in the hands of one person, was a wish felt by many but it was also a way to drive out Kossuth.

Within a month 70 Hungarian general staff officers had signed up the manifesto, demonstrating how the pro-Savoy faction was growing weaker by the second (Kovalovszky 382).

The balance of power inside the emigration had completely changed and Klapka had to take a hard decision: if on the one hand he had been one of the earliest to look closely at Crouy-Chanel, on the other hand this appointment could compromise his reputation, connecting his fortune to the marquis. For this reason he decided to give up the task, saying that he had nothing to do with these controversies (*L'Alleanza*).

In an effort to settle this sudden setback, in May the marquis went to London to meet with Klapka in person. The reply was of a provisional nature: the general should go to the royal court in Paris, in a bid to increase his understanding of the situation. Since the information he got didn't change his mind, from this moment on he stopped publicly supporting the initiatives in favour of Crouy-Chanel. Klapka's action was really dubious because if in the profane world he disappeared next to the marquis, in the masonic sphere their activity was always joint.

Despite the fact that Kossuth had been temporarily silenced, Crouy-Chanel couldn't celebrate because, as the Klpaka affair showed, the exiles' support wasn't as expected. Indeed, the support was linked to the dissatisfaction towards their leaders rather than a deep trust in Crouy-Chanel's abilities and so this was an extremely volatile situation.

For this reason, the propaganda committee printed, that June, a new pamphlet by Nyáry, entitled *Les droits des Arpad*: it was a way to rally the troops (Nyáry).

Meanwhile, the state in the Craft was increasingly complex and muddled. The Dante Alighieri lodge, now under the Supreme Council, had realised that this obedience was disorganised, a myth more than a reality, where personalism dominated. So, on 5 July, the lodge decided to become independent from everything and everyone. However, this phase didn't last long and on 7 October it was already back in the Italian Grand Orient.

Since the whole affair had vastly weakened the moderates, they decided, to calm things down, to appoint Lodivico Frapolli, a dear friend of Crouy-Chanel and future Grand Master (1867-1870), honorary member of the executive council. That way, apparently, the tear was mended (Patrucco 36).

Meanwhile, to keep up his pre-eminence among the Hungarians Crouy-Chanel had to relaunch his candidature again and again and to pay out in order to avoid that the project collapsed. In December 1862 he carried out a new striking action, that is filing lawsuit against Francis V d'Este. In accordance with the marquis, since he was a direct descendant from Etienne II (king of Hungary) and Beatrice d'Este, the former duke of Modena had not rights on the titles and properties of this house.

That same month, a series of Brothers, led by Worshipful Master Frapolli, Francesco De Luca (who was to be the next Grand Master) and Crouy-Chanel, established a Scottish Rite Concistory, a first solid step towards the founding of a Supreme Council. Dante Alighieri lodge, just returned under the Grand Orient, was already attacking the moderate management (Polo Friz, "Ludovico Frapolli E L'emigrazione Ungherese Nel Risorgimento Italiano" 276).

The split couldn't be passed over in silence and it was immediately demanded to close the lodge. In response on 20 March 1863 the Supreme Council became a reality. With that move, all Freemasons who were against the moderates now had a Masonic body based in Turin, alternative to the Grand Orient. The difference was also profound from the point of view of rituals: if the democrats belonged to the Ancient and Accepted Scottish Rite, the majority of the moderates followed the Italian Symbolic Rite (with three degrees). Besides the marquis, among the founders there were Klapka e Nyáry (*Gran Bolla di fondazione del G ∴ Concistoro*). During the founding meeting the organisation chart was decided and since Crouy-Chanel was the most respected one, he was elected Sovereign Grand Commander. He would maintain the assignment until 1864.

The moderate's reply was a well-thought-out coup de theatre: on 27 March the Grand Orient announced the birth of a Hungarian Grand Orient, under its tutelage. Kossuth was Honorary Grand Master, while Türr Active Grand Master (Polo Friz, "Ludovico Frapolli E L'emigrazione Ungherese Nel Risorgimento Italiano" 276).

In May, the Dante Alighieri Brothers were pretty sure victory was close at hand. They were so self-confident that they drafted guidelines for when they would have controlled the Grand Orient. For example, in order to avoid further disagreements Frapolli, along with Crouy-Chanel, Klapka, count Théodore Csàky and Gyòrgy Komàromy, arranged the principle of freedom of Rites (Frapolli).

In the meantime in the non-Masonic world, Crouy-Chanel was still keeping on his campaign, every-time reaffirming that he wasn't aiming at the crown but he was simply offering his help to the Hungarian cause. For this purpose, on 18 September he sent a mail to the Italian Foreign Office, in which, after briefly reminding his lineage and the common grounds between Italy and Hungary, he suggested to Victor Emmanuel to select among his house the most suited person to become king of the future independent state. Looking closer, this was not a concrete offer but a call for greater commitment in the Hungarian question, instead (Ministero degli affari Esteri. Commissione per la pubblicazione dei documenti diplomatici 194–195).

The marquis' position was extremely tricky: if in civil society he needed the Historical Right endorsement, inside the Masonic world he was one of their opponents.

Meanwhile, the faithful Nyáry from 1862 had been spending a lot of time to find the historical evidences showing the truth of the accusation against Francis V and, once procured all the documents, in early October the marquis went to Modena to closely monitor the judicial process. So, on 12 October 1863 the trial started in the local court. It was an unprecedented event which made a great fuss. At first (and understandably) this sensation was limited to the local public opinion: two days after the beginning of the trial *Il Panaro*, a liberal and anticlerical newspaper, openly supported Crouy-Chanel, resulting in a reaction by the Catholics, directed by professor Bartolomeo Veratti (Furlani 617).

After a while, the national newspapers took sides, creating two opposite camps where, if the *Journal des Nationalités* supported the marquis, *Il Difensore* defended Francis' cause.

In addition to the printing press, Crouy-Chanel recruited the finest and the most prestigious Italian lawyers (who were also parliamentarians), such as Giovanni Battista Cassinis, Pasquale Stanislao Mancini and Sebastiano Tecchio. This was a careful but expensive decision: that way he would have rallied both the Left and the Right to his party, as *L'Unità Cattolica* promptly underlined (*L'Unità Cattolica*).

In November 1863, in an effort to gain a fraction of the money spent, Crouy-Chanel started a new financial undertaking. As agreed with Frapolli and banker Leonce Piguerre de la Boulaye, he, along with Bro. Antonio Mordini, entered the Supervisory Board of a new bank, the Cassa mobiliare di credito provinciale e comunale of Turin. It was a wicked choice once again, because this initiative would have increased his deficit rather than diminish it. After having lost its capital, the bank started several daring transactions, gambling on the extraction of sulphur in Sicily (Cassa mobiliare credito provinciale e comunale; Polsi 76).

At the end of 1863 Crouy-Chanel's fortune was slowly fading. Napoleon III and Victor Emmanuel II had no more interest in supporting this political project and so, at the beginning of such a difficult legal battle, the marquis found himself suddenly alone. Not seeing how the international context had changed, he stubbornly stated the need of a "holy Alliance" of oppressed peoples against Austria (*Il Diritto*. 28 Nov.).

5. THE FALL

The year 1864 was the divide. In May all the knotty problems were solved in one way or another.

First of all the proceeding against Francis V got its first instance. During the sitting of 9 May the court sanctioned its incompetence in this matter and so rejected the petition. He didn't lose heart and decided to continue: on 25 August, with a new group of lawyers led by Mancini, a trial carried on. All of this would have definitely ended on 25 August 1866 at the Supreme Court of Turin with the final defeat. His claim towards the house of Modena was completely dismissed.

The Masonic General Assembly held in Florence from 21 to 24 May was definitely more propitious. During this meeting, the democratic tendency, managed by Frapolli, outclassed the moderate one. These crushing elections saw a complete change in the Italian Grand Orient (now called Grand Orient of Italy): Garibaldi was appointed Honorary Grand Master, while De Luca Active Grand Master. That way the crisis started in 1862 was finally reassembled (Novarino, *Grande Oriente d'Italia. Due Secoli Di Presenza Liberomuratoria* 31–32).

Having aided the winning party, Crouy-Chanel underestimated the setback in the legal field. Since now he could count on a unified and cohesive freemasonry the defeat seemed smaller. In reality the situation was rapidly deteriorating.

The biggest problem came from the European context where the relations between Prussian Kingdom and Austrian Empire were increasingly worsening. Being sure there would have been a war, on 3 July 1865 Crouy-Chanel published a new manifesto inciting to rebellion the Hungarian nation. As in the past he stated that he wasn't driven by hunger for power but by his desire to die in his ancestral land (Kovalovszky 383).

This was his last appeal since the public opinion would have basically ignored him some time later. The Third Italian War of Independence of 1866 would have definitely destroyed his last dreams of glory: the alliance formed between Italy and Prussia against Austria would have created a new European set up where the Hungarian exiles were more a nuisance than a weapon to use.

The Hapsburg dynasty itself radically changed its approach towards the Hungarians. In Spring 1867 the Austro-Hungarian Compromise was signed. The establishment of two crowns and two Parliaments (in Vienna and in Buda) would have assured the survival of the Empire for another 50 years. In the short term many refugees decided to come back home, severely damaging Crouy-Chanel.

Meanwhile, Napoleon III had decided to call him back to Paris and so he returned to France, hoping to find new economic and political support. Since the emperor still refused to back up this initiative, the marquis had to deal with all the debts he had contracted. In a desperate attempt to repay his creditors he tried several paths and one of which became a new and big scandal. An unfaithful receiver, working for the French railways reserve fund, had taken 3.293.000 francs and the marquis had received a part of this amount ("Crouy-Chanel" 33).

Therefore, in 1866, besides seeing his appeal against Francis d'Este rejected, on the other side of the Alps he was sentenced to hard labour by default as well. Returning to Paris the following year, he tried with all his power to bring an appeal against the decision which, in practice, ratified the end.

While he was fighting this new battle, he held contacts with his Italian Brothers, acting as an intermediary with the Supreme Council of France. On 19 April 1867 he wrote one last letter to Frapolli where he claimed to have met several times the people in charge of the Ancient and Accepted Scottish Rite, Sovereign Grand Commander Jean-Pons-Guillaume Viennet and Lieutenant Georges-Maurice Guiffrey. The goal was to establish official relations especially with the Supreme Councils of the USA (Polo Friz, "Lodovico Frapolli, La Loggia Massonica Dante Alighieri E L'emigrazione Ungherese" 111).

However, on 10 May the final court judgement arrived. In a complete lack of interest on the part of the general public, who only a few years ago was so interested in the marquis, the tribunal found him guilty but it commuted the penalty to 3 years in prison and to pay 10.000 francs (*Supplemento al Giornale di Padova*).

Everything was over: old and by that time left alone, he spent his last remaining years with his wife in Paris. Even if retired from public life, the French government, most likely on Napoleon III's orders, guaranteed him a pension of 3.000 francs (Chélard 28).

His death occurred on 1 September 1873 and it was reserved and modest: the funeral cortège which followed the coffin from church of Notre-Dame-des-Champs to the graveyard consisted of no more than 20 people (*L'Impartial Dauphinois*). So ended the life of one of the most controversial figure of the XIXth century.

CONCLUSIONS

As a closing remark we can say, with some degree of certainty, that Crouy-Chanel was an unprejudiced person who, even if he believed in a constitutional monarchy, had absolutely no problems plotting with the most convinced supporters of absolutism in the Iberian peninsula. It's not easy to understand if he was a player or a pawn in the game of politics: surely, he was a factor several governments had to take into account.

Alongside his love for intrigue, he had a passion for reckless financial transactions, whose results were always unfavourable.

With regard to the Italian context, we can state his action rather than disturbing was revealing of how weak the balances were. On the Hungarian emigration side, it's true he contributed to destroy the crumbly exiles' front but instead of a trigger he was a magnifying glass which brought to light all the unresolved problems. Speaking of Italian Freemasonry, in this case too, his support to the democratic cause wasn't the key factor for Frapolli and De Luca's success, but having on their side a long-standing freemason was surely helpful in their fight against the moderates.

However, beyond the moral and political judgements about him, Crouy-Chanel's legacy towards Italian Freemasonry was unquestionably important: in 1875 the Supreme Council of Turin he co-founded and guided during its first years would be recognised by the Supreme Councils gathered in Lausanne as the only regular one in Italy (Vatri).

REFERENCES

Andreu, Francesco. "Lettere Inedite Del P. Ventura." *Regnum Dei* n. 20 (1964). Print.

Banque Commerciale et Foncière, Sous La Raison Delacodre et Compagnie. Prospectus et Statuts. Paris: Boucher, 1824. Print.

Cassa mobiliare credito provinciale e comunale. *Società Anonima Stabilita Con Atti Pubblici Rogati Ghilia Notaio in Torino in Data 6 Novembre 1863 E 12 Maggio 1864 Ed Autorizzata Con Decreti Reali Dei 31 Gennaio E 10 Luglio 1864: Statuti.* Torino: Tip. Botta, 1865. Print.

Chélard, Raoul. *L'Autriche-Hongrie. La Hongrie Millénaire.* II. Paris: Chailley, 1896. Print.

Correspondance politique, Portugal. Archives du Ministère des Affaires étrangères. t. 145.

"Crouy-Chanel." *Dictionnaire de La Conversation et de La Lecture. Supplement.* t. III. Paris: Firmin Didot, 1872. Print.

Crouy-Chanel, François Claude Auguste de. "Letter to L'Indipendance Belge sub-editor." 18 Oct. 1861. Centro di Ricerche Storiche sulla Libera-Muratoria Archive (Turin).

"Empire Français." *Journal de l'Empire* 30 Apr. 1806. Print.

Furlani, Silvio. "La Crisi Dell'emigrazione Ungherese Dopo Il 1860." *Archivio trimestrale* n. 4. Ottobre-Dicembre (1984). Print.

Frapolli, Lodovico, Letter to Albert Goodall. 1871. Luigi Polo Friz Private Archive.

Gerothwohl de Croÿ-Chanel, Henry. *Biographie Du Prince Auguste de Crouy-Chanel de Hongrie (1793-1873).* Paris: Derenne, 1882. Print.

Glikman, Juliette. *Louis-Napoléon Prisonnier. Du Fort de Ham Aux Ors Des Tuileries.* Paris: Aubier, 2011. Print.

Gran Bolla di fondazione del G ∴ Concistoro. Luigi Polo Friz Private Archive.

Hidalgo y Esnaurrízar, José Manuel. *Apuntes Para Escribir La Historia de Los Proyectos de Monarquía En México Desde El Reinado de Carlos III Hasta La Instalación Del Emperador Maximiliano.* Paris: Hermanos, 1868. Print.

Il Diritto. 26 Mar. 1862.

Il Diritto. 28 Nov. 1863.

Journal des Débats. 5 Sept. 1832.

Kovalovszky, Nicolas. "Un Prétendant Au Trône de Hongrie. Le Prince Auguste Crouy-Chanel." *Nouvelle Revue de Hongrie* Avril (1941). Print.

L'Alba. 14 Jan. 1848.

L'Alleanza. 18 Jun. 1862.

L'Impartial Dauphinois. 5 Sept. 1873.

L'Unità Cattolica. 19 Apr. 1864.

Le National. 5 Sept. 1832.

Martignac, Jean-Baptiste de, Letters to Villèle. 4 and 7 July 1823. *Mémoires et Correspondance Du Comte de Villèle. 1823-1824.* IV. Paris: Perrin, 1904. Print.

Ministero degli affari Esteri. Commissione per la pubblicazione dei documenti diplomatici. *I Documenti Diplomatici Italiani. Prima Serie: 1861-1870.* IV. Roma: Istituto poligrafico dello Stato, 1974. Print.

Moral Roncal, Antonio Manuel. "El Infante Don Francisco de Paula Borbón: Masonería Y Progresismo a La Sombra Del Trono." *Investigaciones históricas. Época moderna y contemporánea* n. 20 (2000). Print.

Novarino, Marco. *All'Oriente Di Torino. La Rinascita Della Massoneria Italiana Tra Moderatismo Cavouriano E Rivoluzionarismo Garibaldino.* Firenze: Chiari, 2003. Print.

—. *Grande Oriente d'Italia. Due Secoli Di Presenza Liberomuratoria.* Roma: Erasmo, 2006. Print.

Nyáry, Albert. *Les Droits Des Arpad (Crouy-Chanel de Hongrie)*. Paris: Impr. Dupray de la Mahérie, 1862. Print.

Oliveira Marques, António Henrique de. "Manuel Bernardo Perreira de Chabi." *Dicionário de Maçonaria Portuguesa*. Vol. 1. Lisboa: Delta, 1986. Print.

Ouvrard, Gabriel J. *Mémoires de G.-J. Ouvrard, Sur Sa Vie et Ses Diverses Opérations Financiéres*. Paris: Moutardier, 1827. Print.

Patrucco, Carlo E. "Documenti Su Garibaldi E La Massoneria Nell'ultimo Periodo Del Risorgimento Italiano." *Bollettino storico-bibliografico subalpino* n. III (1914). Print.

Poinsett, Joel, Letter to Henry Clay. 22 Sept. 1825. *Diplomatic Correspondence of the United States Concerning the Independence of Latin-American Nations*. Ed. William R. Manning. III. New York: Oxford University Press, 1925. Print.

Polo Friz, Luigi. *1866. Una Missione Segreta Di Lodovico Frapolli a Berlino. L'emigrazione Ungherese*. Roma: Gangemi, 2007. Print.

—. "Lodovico Frapolli, La Loggia Massonica Dante Alighieri E L'emigrazione Ungherese." *«Rivista di Studi Ungheresi»* n. 13 (1998). Print.

—. "Ludovico Frapolli E L'emigrazione Ungherese Nel Risorgimento Italiano." *«Rassegna storica toscana»* n. 2.luglio-dicembre (1993). Print.

Polsi, Alessandro. *Alle Origini Del Capitalismo Italiano: Stato, Banche E Banchieri Dopo L'unità*. Torino: Einaudi, 1993. Print.

Rousseau, François. "Charlotte-Joaquin de Bourbon. Reine de Portugal (1775-1830)." *«Revue des questions historiques»* n.s. t. LI (1914). Print.

Saint-Edme, and Germain Sarrut, eds. "Biographie de M. A. De Crouy-Chanel." *Biographie Des Hommes Du Jour*. t. V p. I. Paris: Impr. Pierre Badouin, 1840. Print.

—, eds. "Crouy-Chanel de Hongrie." *Biographie Des Hommes Du Jour*. t.III p.II. Paris: Krabbe, 1837. Print.

Sarrut, Germain. *Les Fils d'Arpad*. Paris: Dentu, 1861. Print.

Supplemento al Giornale di Padova. 10 May 1867.

Vatri, Giuseppe M. *Il Rito Scozzese Da Nazionale a Universale (1802-1907). Documenti, Costituzioni E Guida Rituale.* Torino: L'Età dell'Acquario, 2008. Print.

Villeneuve, Jean Esprit Marie Pierre Lemoine de, and Antoine-Auguste Carette, eds. *Recueil Général Des Lois et Des Arrêts. 1828-1830.* Vol. 9 1° série. Paris: Sirey, 1842. Print.

www.ingramcontent.com/pod-product-compliance
Lightning Source LLC
Chambersburg PA
CBHW070801280326
41934CB00012B/3010